confirmation basics

Updated and Expanded

CONCORDIA PUBLISHING HOUSE · SAINT LOUIS

3558 S. Jefferson Avenue, St. Louis, MO 63118-3968
1-800-325-3040 • www.cph.org

Edited by Mark S. Sengele

This publication may be available in braille, in large print, or on cassette tape for the visually impaired. Please allow 8 to 12 weeks for delivery. Write to Lutheran Braille Workers, P.O. Box 5000, Yucaipa, CA 92399; call toll-free 1-800-925-6092; or visit the Web site: www.LBWinc.org.

Manufactured in the United States of America

Your comments and suggestions concerning the material are appreciated. Please write to Concordia Publishing House, 3558 S. Jefferson Avenue, St. Louis, MO 63118-3968.

4 5 6 7 8 9 10 30 29 28 27 26

Section 1: This Thing Called Confirmation

Section 2: Models for Confirmation

Section 3: Beyond Confirmation Instruction

Section 1

This Thing Called Confirmation

If you spend any amount of time in a Lutheran congregation, you will eventually hear about or experience confirmation. Each church seems to have its own set of traditions when it comes to Confirmation Sunday. Most folks in the pew take confirmation entirely for granted: "It's something we've always done." But what exactly is confirmation? In this section, we will explore the answer to that question as we take a look at the history and practice of confirmation in the Lutheran Church, as well as the development of Luther's Small Catechism.

1

What Is Confirmation? A Brief History

by Marvin Bergman

In churches that practice confirmation, there are paradoxes. Pastors of Presbyterian churches invest much time and effort in confirmation, and yet, the commitments of young people made in their confirmation seem to be as lasting as the spring flowers on the altar. In the Episcopal Church, in which confirmation is a sacrament, the rite is seen as a practice in search of a rationale. In discussing the history of confirmation in the Roman Catholic Church, a scholar observed that no other sacrament has had such a checkered history or has been so subject to a search for meaning as confirmation.

That there are paradoxes in the history of confirmation in Lutheran churches is no surprise. While confirmation is fundamental to the identity of millions of Lutherans, confirmation is described as an unsolved problem in Lutheran congregations that will remain unsolved. Though confirmation is one of the strongest customs of Lutheran congregations, there is a lack of agreement on the meaning and purpose of confirmation. Even though confirmation is seen by some members as being more important than Baptism, there is an absence of consensus in the popular mind-set as to what confirmation is. While a history of confirmation of itself will not solve all of these issues nor create consensus, it does establish a common understanding and foundation for discerning what confirmation was and what role it should play now and in the future.

"Confirmation" in the Early Church

Though confirmation as we know it today does not appear in the New Testament or the Early Church, the practice of confirmation is rooted in the New Testament. Christ's command to "Go therefore and make disciples of all nations, baptizing them in the name of the Father and of the Son and of the Holy Spirit, teaching them to observe all that I have commanded you" (Matthew 28:19–20) serves as the foundation of confirmation. In the Great Commission, there is one mission with two sides: outreaching and teaching. Confirmation, in the Early Church and today, is the Church's response to Christ's command to go and disciple.

This happened throughout the New Testament. Beginning with the witness of the women at the tomb and the apostles, the message of the risen Lord spread rapidly. One example is the account of events caused by Saul's persecution of the Church in Jerusalem. While the apostles remained in Jerusalem, "those who were scattered went about preaching the word" (Acts 8:4). The persecuted traveled to Phoenicia, Cyprus, and Antioch (Acts 11:19–20), where they told Jews and Gentiles what had happened on Good Friday and Easter. From the beginning, the Christian faith was a traveling faith, moving from rural Palestine eastward to the Indus Valley and westward to Roman Britain in less than two centuries.

Romans 6 gives a hint of how one became a Christian. There, Paul portrayed Baptism as uniting one to the death and resurrection of Christ. That Baptism, since the earliest days of the Church, was connected with instruction is seen in the work of scholars who suggest that all of the New Testament documents had a catechetical purpose. Matthew, for example, can be seen as a catechism that prepared one for Baptism and Holy Communion. Paul, in his Letter to the Colossians, built on the tradition of instruction in the synagogues to teach new converts who were encountering trouble caused by semi-Gnostic teachings.

The New Testament reveals that families played important roles in the expansion of the Church. Paul, for example, spoke of the faith handed down from generation to generation in the families of grandmother Lois, mother Eunice, and Timothy (2 Timothy 1:5).

Christians witnessed spontaneously in their daily lives in their relationships with relatives, friends, and co-workers. Conversations of Christians and pagans, the witness of martyrs, and events in Christian communities provided opportunities for witness. The awakening of faith occurred in homes, at work, in meetings, or in gatherings rather than in a formal way or in a class. The chief content of their witness was the number-one issue in life: "Who is your God? An idol, or the living God?" Laity played more of the role of a sponsor rather than a formal teacher in this part of the Christian journey sometimes called a "precatechumenate."

Origen described one way in which the precatechumenate occurred. A Christian would begin by conversing and testing those who would listen to his witness. He would then take aside those who displayed interest for additional conversation and instruction. When they made a confession of faith in Jesus as Lord, marked by a change in lifestyle, this was seen as readiness for entering the catechumenate.

Though the number of new Christians increased rapidly, there is no clear evidence of a structured plan of instruction for converts in the first and second centuries. However, Justin Martyr, in his *Apology* (around AD 150), described the rite and doctrine of Baptism and added that that instruction occurred prior to Baptism. The *Didache* presupposed instruction prior to Baptism. The works of Clement revealed the existence of a catechumenate in Alexandria around the year 200, where pagans, neophytes, and catechumens gathered in one group to listen and to receive instruction.

What is clear is that the development of a process, the catechumenate, served as entry into the Christian community. Its focus was the transformation of pagan adults. Though the catechumenate took many forms, the content was an initial confession of faith in Jesus, entrance into the catechumenate, instruction in the Word of God and the Creed, Baptism, chrismation (anointing of consecrated oil), laying on of hands, and reception of Holy Communion. This was followed by additional instruction named "mystagogy" (instruction in the "mysteries" of the faith). Instruction was provided by teachers, clerical or lay.

In the early part of the third century, the practice of a priest giving one who was baptized an anointing at the font began. The one baptized then was brought to the bishop for the laying on of hands and another anointing. In the same century, the bishop of Rome insisted that one who is baptized receive the anointing of oil from a bishop, though presbyters (pastors) were the ones who chiefly administered this rite in Gaul and in Spain.

"Confirmation" was thus part of Baptism in the sense that a candidate, after being baptized, was "confirmed" with the anointing of oil, prayers, the sign of the cross, and the laying on of hands. The candidate then participated in Holy Communion. One view suggests that confirmation in the West probably originated as a dismissal that marked the end of the catechumenate in the service of Baptism. By the end of the third century, the entry of converts to the Christian faith was a single rite with three parts: a water bath; chrism, which marked dismissal; and reception of the Eucharist.

In AD 324, the Roman Emperor Constantine gave the impression of being the champion of the Christian faith by ordering all soldiers to worship the supreme God on the first day of the week. This resulted in a large number of converts seeking entrance to the Christian Church, which led to reducing the time of one's involvement in the catechumenate. The Church then established seven weeks of Lent as a time of intense formation. By minimizing instruction and supervision, some candidates never connected with the Liturgy of the Word and were not supervised by leaders in structured groups. Some were accepted as candidates for Baptism very quickly. By the end of the fourth century, the catechumenate was not what it was one hundred years earlier. At the close of the fifth century, the catechumenate became more of a period of retreat and reflection rather than instruction and formation, resulting in a catechumenate that existed more in theory than in practice.

One exception to these generalizations was the outstanding work of Augustine, a bishop and catechist in North Africa in the fourth and fifth centuries. In his published works, one learns from a master teacher in his discussion of the "who," "what," "how," "why," and "where" (the social context) of catechesis. He, for example, noted that what is important in the life of a teacher is the joy of catechizing.

Historical evidence indicates that a large number of the children of Christians were enrolled in the catechumenate with their parents, who then provided Christian instruction for their children. Sources say little about how parents translated this intent into practice. With Christians often meeting in homes, parents most likely took their children along to worship and perhaps to catechetical instruction. There was no specific catechumenate for children, whether baptized or not.

In the fifth century, leaders of Western churches began to use the term "confirmation," since the bishop "confirmed" the priest's Baptism through chrismation and the laying on of hands. *Confirmation* as a term was first used in the Council of Orange in AD 441 and then again by Pope Leon I in a letter in AD 458. Later in the fifth century, a French bishop delivered a homily in which he noted that confirmation provides an increase in the grace given in Baptism, which strengthened one for spiritual struggles. Thus, anointing by the bishop became the forerunner of confirmation as practiced in the Middle Ages.

Confirmation in the Middle Ages

In churches in the East, the initiation rite involving adults and children was unified in one rite consisting of Baptism, Holy Communion, chrism, laying on of hands, and prayer. Begun in the Early Church, this rite continued in Eastern churches through the Middle Ages and up to today.

However, the initiation rite of churches of the West came to be divided into three separate rites: Baptism, confirmation, and first Communion. One factor that led to the decline of the unified initiation was the success of the Church in the late Roman Empire, when large numbers of people were attracted to the Church and became members. In a churched society, the focus shifted from the Baptism of adults to infant Baptism, which in turn led to a near disappearance of the catechumenate and with it catechetical instruction.

When the practice of baptizing infants shortly after birth became even more widespread, chrism was separated from Baptism, with the former being reserved for a bishop. By the ninth century, a theology of anointing developed, stating that chrismation confers more of the Holy Spirit, who strengthens the gifts given in Baptism. The Sacrament of Baptism was seen as being "confirmed" by a special outpouring of the Holy Spirit through anointing, which strengthened one to confront the challenges of living as a Christian. In confirmation, the distinctive grace of the gift of the Holy Spirit for strength was received through the laying on of hands and chrism, while the Spirit was given in Baptism for the remission of sin. By 1150, "confirmation" was numbered as one of the seven sacraments.

During the Middle Ages, confirmation was not a burning issue. Instead, the theological meaning of confirmation continued to be developed. In the thirteenth century, Thomas Aquinas, described as the most important Scholastic theologian who discussed confirmation, spoke of bodily and spiritual growth through confirmation. The grace given in confirmation is an increase of the grace already present in Baptism, with the special grace of the sacrament of confirmation being that of enabling one to grow in holiness and ability to battle the enemies of faith.

During these centuries, the Church did not sponsor any formal institutions for the education of adults and children. Instead, catechesis was viewed as the responsibility of parents and godparents. Their catechetical instruction centered largely in handing on the teachings of the Nicene Creed and the Lord's Prayer through oral learning.

Catechetical instruction of adults occurred in the homilies delivered by priests. The teaching roles of bishops and priests were seen to be very important, with catechetical instruction being the focus of preaching at least every other week. The liturgies of the Church served to provide continuity in the faith.

There were medieval catechisms for the laity, consisting of the Creed, the Lord's Prayer, the Decalogue, a Double Command to Love, Seven Works of Mercy, Seven Cardinal Virtues, Seven Mortal Sins, and the Seven Sacraments. The method of instruction was dictation by an instructor and recitation by students. The first person to focus on the instruction of children by the Church was Gerson, who in the early 1400s defended his practice of teaching children in the face of opposition to this practice.

During the late Middle Ages, some critics of rampant apathy in the Church became reformers who initiated their work by restructuring confirmation. The Waldensians, in the latter part of the twelfth century, withheld the laying on of hands until instruction in the fundamentals of the faith had occurred through a catechetical approach to teaching and learning. In the fifteenth century, the

Bohemian Brethren insisted that Baptism was valid only when connected to a personal confession of faith, with confirmation serving as the rite that permitted full participation in a congregation and in the Eucharist.

Luther on Confirmation and Catechesis

The impact of the sixteenth-century reformers to reeducate and reorient large populations of baptized Christians to a personal, living faith inspired by the Gospel of Jesus Christ is described as among the greatest in two thousand years of Christian life and practice. Leading the way was Martin Luther, who through his preaching, catechisms, recognition of the role of parents in the formation of faith, and the enlistment of city leaders to establish schools for boys and girls, initiated major changes in the lives of people.

One target of Luther's reformation was the medieval practice of confirmation. In his *Babylonian Captivity of the Church*, Luther expressed amazement that the laying on of hands was turned into a sacrament. Perhaps, he added, bishops insist on the laying on of hands in order to have something to do! Though Jesus touched children with His hands, and the apostles imparted the Holy Spirit and cured the sick through the laying on of hands, Luther rejected confirmation as a sacrament on the basis of its absence in the Scriptures and the lack of a divine promise. For Luther, it was enough to regard confirmation as a churchly rite or ceremony similar to other ceremonies such as the blessing of water.

Instead of giving attention to confirmation as a rite, Luther placed emphasis on the instruction of congregations, parents, and children. Even before the posting of the Ninety-five Theses in 1517, Luther delivered a series of sermons on various parts of the catechism at St. Mary's Church in Wittenberg. These sermons were published as a collection in 1522 in his *Personal Prayer Book*. Appeals by theologians of Wittenberg and pastors for a resource led Luther to write the Small Catechism in 1529. It consisted of three parts on separate sheets, each addressed to the heads of households.

Within a short period of time, the large sheets appeared in a booklet form in which Luther wrote a preface for pastors and preachers. Describing the ordinary person as knowing absolutely nothing about the Christian faith and recognizing that many pastors were unskilled and incompetent teachers, Luther urged the pastors to preach and teach the basics of the faith by using the catechism.

Initially, Luther placed his greatest emphasis on the family as the God-ordained institution to nurture and teach faith. By the middle of the 1520s, however, Luther realized that many parents were unskilled, unwilling, or unable to take the time to carry out their calling of teaching their children. He then turned to others who could provide instruction, especially pastors, teachers, and secular authorities who could lead the way in establishing schools. The intent was that such leaders would supplement the instruction of parents, while each was to give special attention to one's own calling, such as a pastor providing instruction for a congregation. Luther made special pleas to parents to educate their sons and daughters in schools so that they could learn the catechism and lead their families in living as Christians.

With instruction based on a catechism being Luther's focus, another facet of the genius of the reformer is seen in his arrangement of the parts of the catechism. Perhaps Luther was the first theologian to begin instruction with the Ten Commandments, followed by the Creed and the Lord's Prayer. The messages of the order of the catechism are (1) the Ten Commandments, which tell us that we're sick, sick unto death, and that we need medicine; (2) the Creed, in which a gracious God shows us where we can find the medicine that we desperately need in the gifts of the Father, the Son, and the Holy Spirit; (3) the Lord's Prayer, which teaches us how we should desire and receive the gifts a gracious Lord wants us to have. These central messages of the Scriptures provide a worldview that is totally different from any other paradigm.

Lutheran Confirmation Models

Arthur Repp's study of confirmation in Lutheran churches, based on many primary sources, is described as the most extensive study of its kind (Concordia Publishing House 1964). Repp, for example, found that for a long time—centuries in some cases—the very word *confirmation* was an offense to a large number of Lutheran churches. However, a recognition of the necessity to strengthen faith created by Holy Baptism through instruction, to make confession of sins and to receive Absolution, and to prepare for participation in the Lord's Supper led to the present practice of confirmation.

The gradual development of confirmation in Lutheran churches, however, did not follow a uniform pattern. Through a complex number of personalities, influences, and cultural forces, six major types, or models, of confirmation developed in Lutheran churches. Their influence on confirmation understandings and practices today warrant a review of their characteristics.

The Catechetical Type

The first model developed by Lutherans was the catechetical, which gave special attention to instruction based on the Bible and the catechism as a way of preparing for Holy Communion.

There was no linkage to confirmation or a rite of any kind. Instead, through catechetical instruction, the preaching of catechetical sermons several times a year, a reading of the catechism from the pulpit, making confession in preparation for the Lord's Supper, instruction by parents, and schools that provided instruction in the catechism, a foundation for the faith lives of adults and children was laid. Following instruction, there was an examination of children by a pastor, either privately, in a home, or in the presence of the congregation.

The three important elements of the catechetical type were instruction, an examination for demonstrating preparation for the Lord's Supper, and a confession of faith accompanied by prayers of the congregation.

The Hierarchical Type

When one considers the Rite of Confirmation known today, the role of Martin Bucer becomes influential through his introduction of two additional elements: a surrender to Christ as a confession of faith and a vow of obedience to the Church. The origin of his hierarchical model is linked to Bucer's ministry in Strassburg in 1523, where he soon encountered the criticism of Anabaptists. Their charge was that his church baptized children who were too young to have a personal faith, which then led to a moral laxity. His response was to develop a church order that called for baptized children to be well instructed in the faith and to make a public confession of the faith accompanied by hand-laying and prayer. Bucer emphasized that what is required of children at the time of confirmation is a solemn and sincere profession of faith, as well as a faith that evidenced fruit in one's lifestyle. Those who produced the fruit of the Spirit and were willing to submit to the discipline of the Church were to be admitted to the Lord's Table. The vow of obedience to the Church also implied submission to discipline imposed by a pastor and the elders of the congregation.

Bucer, by adding two elements not present in the catechetical approach, gave confirmation an emphasis more congenial to Zwinglian than to Lutheran theology.

The Sacramental Type

A third type of confirmation that appeared in sixteenth-century Lutheran churches is the sacramental. This form of confirmation retained elements of the Roman Catholic tradition, such as a bestowing of the Holy Spirit through the laying on of hands as a completion of Holy Baptism and the conferral of a fuller membership in the Church not given in Baptism. This confirmation type was given impetus by Bucer, who described the first of three sacramental ceremonies as consisting of confirmation and laying on of hands. In this ceremony, a vow of surrender to Christ and obedience to the discipline of the Church was followed by a prayer invoking the presence of the Holy Spirit through the laying on of hands by the pastor. However, the role of Bucer in this model is controversial in that his definition and understanding of sacramental ceremony are not clear. For some, his intent was to state that the laying on of hands was necessary in order for Baptism to be valid. Others interpreted this rite to designate nothing more than a prayer over and for people.

The sacramental type continued to exert influence in Lutheran churches for centuries, seen especially in the importance given to the laying on of hands, interpreted by some as granting the Holy Spirit through this action.

The Traditional Type

In the sixteenth century, some Lutherans desired a confirmation based on traditions of the Church that did not violate confessional principles. This model did not develop a uniform pattern except for one feature, that confirmation was not connected with a first Communion. Instead, the focus was on Holy Baptism, followed by instruction and then one's presentation by parents and sponsors to pastors in the presence of a congregation to make a public confession of faith. Though instruction was required prior to admission to Holy Communion, the confession of faith was not associated with a first Communion.

A Luther colleague who encouraged a reformation of confirmation was Philip Melanchthon. He urged that each individual be examined in the essentials of the Christian faith and that a public prayer be offered for the person. In his Apology of the Augsburg Confession, Melanchthon pointed out that to promise the grace of God is not by human authority, and that any rite that lacks the command of God is not to be called a sacrament. Instead, confirmation is a rite received from the Fathers, which the Church does not require as necessary for salvation.

Melanchthon urged that catechetical instruction be provided on specific days in all churches and that when a child reached the age of discretion, he would make a public confession of faith. A prayer would then be offered, accompanied by the laying on of hands. In this way, confirmation could be seen as a valuable ceremony to serve the maintenance of doctrine, a proper understanding of the faith, and good discipline. Melanchthon and other Lutheran theologians who assembled at Celle in 1548 were ready to admit children to Holy Communion prior to confirmation.

During the seventeenth century, the practice of confirmation spread slowly, with a majority of churches in Germany and Scandinavia preparing young people for their first Communion through the catechetical approach without a rite. Then, the quality of catechetical instruction declined, and services that featured catechetical sermons were poorly attended. One factor was a failure to adjust to changing conditions such as higher levels of education. Parrotlike memorization became the subject of satire. In efforts made to inspire reform, greater attention was given to confirmation as a renewing of one's baptismal covenant.

The Pietistic Type

After a century-and-a-half struggle of reforming the Church, one result was that in some communities in Germany, nearly everyone was a baptized Lutheran. However, some began to react against their perceptions of a heavy, cognitive-centered faith that resulted in a lethargy that impacted daily life. One who responded to this perception was Philip Spener, who taught that religion is a matter of the heart and not of the head. For him, a living faith was one that led to a conversion of the heart expressed in conviction, fellowship, and service.

Spener saw confirmation as a glorious opportunity for this rite to be turned into one of conversion. Confirmation was a time for one to make a witness to a personal faith and a life that reflected commitment. The value of Baptism centered in its covenant, which needed to be renewed on a regular basis. He also added a solemn promise, or vow, to the renewal of the covenant, with the confession of faith expressing a personal faith. Catechists were expected to lead their catechumens through several stages on the way to salvation to demonstrate a personal conversion and a living faith. Only those who had demonstrated a genuine conversion were admitted to the Lord's Table. An added element in this confirmation model was the assignment of special verses selected for individuals. The influence of Pietism also led to confirmations at around age 15 or 16 instead of earlier confirmations at age 12.

The Rationalistic Type

When Rationalism became a motif of the culture in eighteenth-century Germany, the Church reflected this worldview by giving special attention to the question "How can religious truth be proven?" Religious truths were presented for the purpose of being grasped rationally, resulting in catechetical instruction being turned into an intellectual exercise. Instead of memorizing and then understanding, the order was reversed by emphasizing comprehension. Special attention was given to the subjects of God, virtue, and immortality, with the heart of the Christian faith, the Gospel, being ignored.

Under the influence of Rationalism, confirmation grew in importance, while Holy Baptism became less important. Confirmation became the second half of Baptism, the more important half. In confirmation, one assumed the duties of a responsible member of a congregation and received certain privileges. Confirmation also was turned into a youth festival that recognized one's "coming of age." In some communities, attending school for a certain number of years became a prerequisite for confirmation. Confirmation also became a graduation marking the end of schooling!

Civic and social responsibilities were attached to confirmation by making one eligible to get a job, to attend a state school, and to declare one's allegiance to the state. To impress on young people the significance of confirmation, the practice of selecting individual memory verses for confirmands and turning a confession of faith into a declaration of one's loyalty through a vow became more widespread. Confirmation thus became associated with church, civic, legal, and economic privileges.

When observers noticed that as many as 80% of the young people who participated in confirmation never again partook of Holy Communion, there were many proposals to reform confirmation. Some proposed that confirmation be seen as an ordination of the laity, while others called for a separation of communicant membership through confirmation and voting membership. Another proposal called for a "biblical confirmation" through a laying on of hands, which marks one as an active member of the Church. In spite of the many proposals, no major changes were made in the practice of confirmation in Germany. Confirmation had become so deeply entrenched in the society that little change was possible.

Confirmation in the Twentieth Century

When Lutheran immigrants arrived in the United States, they carried with them memories and experiences of their own confirmation. Ordinarily, their beliefs and practices reflected the type of confirmation they had experienced. For example, the influence of Pietism was evident in some churches where confirmation was seen as an awakening of one's heart and a renewal of the baptismal covenant.

There was one exception. Those who had lived through the years of German Rationalism rejected many of the assumptions and perspectives of this intellectual movement. C. F. W. Walther, for example, emphasized that the promise made by a confirmand was not the first time that such a promise was made. This was a reminder that a promise made by a catechumen was not as significant as interpreted by those influenced by Rationalism.

The most significant attempt to explain what confirmation is in the twentieth century, and perhaps in the history of Lutheran churches, was made by representatives of the three largest Lutheran bodies in the 1960s and 1970s: the American Lutheran Church, The Lutheran Church in America, and The Lutheran Church—Missouri Synod. In 1964, each president appointed five representatives, who formed the Joint Commission on the Theology and Practice of Confirmation. In its first meeting, the commission initiated studies of the theology, history, and practice of confirmation by focusing on these topics: History of Confirmation; The Current Situation; Theology of Confirmation; A Definition of Confirmation; The Practice of Confirmation; and Steps toward a Better Understanding by Clergy And Laity.

In 1966, the Joint Commission conducted a survey, "Current Concepts and Practices of Confirmation in Lutheran Churches." The questionnaire was sent to 538 pastors, 291 nonparish pastors, and 2,152 lay leaders. Based on an analysis of results, a study book for discussion, *Confirmation and First Communion,* was sent to every pastor of the three church bodies. After more than 192,000 copies of the study book were distributed, input from 86,000 participants representing nearly 25% of all congregations was summarized.

Highlights of the report published in 1970 include these discussions: "Confirmation and the Means of Grace; Confirmation and the Mission of the Church; Membership in the Church through Baptism; Confirmation as Involving All Educational Experiences from Baptism to Mid-Adolescence; Continuing Education and Caring Ministries throughout One's Life; The Privilege of Communion Given through Baptism; First Communion to Be Determined by Individual Readiness Rather Than the Rite of Confirmation; Grade Five as an Opportune Time for First Communion; The Small Catechism as a Way of Interpreting the Scriptures and Life; A Variety of Rites at Significant Times during One's Growth Being Implemented by Congregations."

The Report of the Joint Commission on the Theology and Practice of Confirmation was affirmed by the Board of Parish Education of The Lutheran Church—Missouri Synod in an overture to the 1971 convention of the Synod, held in Milwaukee. The resolution urged that the report and recommendations of the Joint Commission be adopted and that the Synod direct appropriate boards and departments to help congregations implement the recommendations.

Another overture concerning the Joint Commission was presented to the same convention by the Commission on Theology and Church Relations. This resolution thanked the Joint Commission and especially the Board of Parish Education for their work, called for the Commission on Worship to reexamine the Rite of Confirmation in the Agenda, and urged that the present emphasis on the values of combining confirmation and first Communion be retained.

The resolution adopted by the Milwaukee Convention thanked the Joint Commission on the Theology and Practice of Confirmation and urged congregations to evaluate their confirmation and first Communion practices, while also commending the recommendations of the Commission on Theology and Church Relations and the Joint Commission as guidelines in their study of confirmation.

Confirmation in the LCMS Today

As in previous centuries, commonality, diversity, and challenges in confirmation are seen in a study of confirmation in the LCMS conducted in 2006–8. For example, the importance of confirmation is seen in the perspectives of confirmation leaders, confirmands, and parents. When leaders assessed the importance of confirmation in the context of their entire ministries, 96% stated that confirmation was "very important" or "important"; 99% of the parents and 93% of the confirmands rated confirmation at the same levels.

There are other examples of a level of consensus. Grade 8 as the time for young people to confirm their faith in the Rite of Confirmation was reported by 79% of the leaders. It was reported that 76% of the leaders indicated that young people are invited for the first time to Holy Communion during or after the Rite of Confirmation. An "examination" of confirmands in some form as part of the Rite of Confirmation is practiced by 85% of the leaders. And 81% of the leaders agreed totally or to some extent that for most Lutherans, confirmation is the most important Christian education event in their lives.

There is diversity in views and practices of confirmation. When leaders were asked "Who does the confirming in the Rite of Confirmation?" 36% responded that "the pastor" did this; 16% replied "the congregation"; 35% responded that it was the "youth"; and 13% gave other responses. When the leaders were asked at what age young people were ready to receive Holy Communion, 15% said "nine to ten"; 26% said "eleven to twelve"; 32% said "thirteen to fourteen"; 3% said "fifteen to sixteen"; and 24% said "when one is ready."

Leaders reported their levels of satisfaction in confirmation ministry were "high," 29%; "moderate," 57%; "low," 13%; "not sure," 2%. Parents of confirmands described the levels of their satisfaction with the confirmation ministries of their congregations as "high," 57%; "moderate," 30%; "low," 11%; "no opinion," 2%. When high school youth reflected on their confirmation experiences, their satisfaction levels were "high," 36%; "moderate," 51%; "low," 6%; "no opinion," 7%.

A number of challenges in confirmation ministry were identified by leaders. The three leading challenges named in confirmation ministries anticipated five years from that time were the need for greater parent involvement and commitment, schedule conflicts and time pressures, and a post-confirmation lack of involvement by youth. The greatest frustrations in confirmation ministry reported by leaders were lack of commitment by parents and youth, schedule conflicts and time restraints, and youth dropping out of church. Of the leaders, 56% indicated that the view of confirmation as a graduation in their congregations is very visible or visible, while 34% indicated that this view is somewhat visible.

Other challenges include confirmands finding time in their schedules for confirmation activities. This was described as a challenge or as being difficult or very difficult by 67% of the leaders. The levels of leaders' satisfaction with parent participation in the confirmation ministry were "high," 8%; "moderate," 41%; low," 41%; "there is no parent participation," 11%.

Leaders reflected a number of views related to Luther's Small Catechism. The importance of a confirmand's clear grasp of the key content of the catechism was described as very important or important by 91% of the leaders. The level of interest expressed by confirmands in Luther's Small Catechism was described by leaders as "high," 8%; "moderate," 51%; "low," 36%; "no interest," 4%. When leaders responded to the statement "Most young people continue to use Luther's Small Catechism after the rite of confirmation," 87% disagreed. That the catechism is appropriate for youth to use as a prayer book was affirmed by 49% of the leaders, while 51% did not affirm this use of the catechism. Regarding the format of Luther's Small Catechism, 44% of the leaders recommended that the 1986 version be revised, while 55% affirmed this version.

Another challenge is the number of youth who do not continue to confess and practice their faith after confirmation. Only 8% of leaders reported that the number of youth still active in the congregation as seniors in high school were "80% or more"; 15% of leaders gave the number as "60–80%"; 36% said it was "40–60%"; 21% reported active youth as "20–40%"; and another 21% said "20% or less" were still active.

Opportunities for a confirmation ministry to reach youth not connected to Christ were assessed by 7% of the leaders as "many"; by 41% as "some"; by 43% as "limited"; and by 9% as "none." The number of nonconfirmed senior high school youth known by leaders to be candidates to begin confirmation were "5 youth or more," 10%; "3–4 youth," 14%; "1–2 youth," 31%; "no youth," 45%. Opportunities for youth confirmation to equip confirmands to share their faith were described by 18% of leaders as "many"; by 47% as "some"; by 32% as "limited"; and by 3% as "none."

When commonalities, diversities, and challenges related to the views and practices of confirmation are placed in the context of a single directive by the Lord of the Church consisting of four action words: "Go," "Make Disciples," "Baptize," and "Teach" (Matthew 28:19–20), one sees paradoxes that await being addressed.

Issues in Confirmation

Here are the issues in confirmation that demand the church's attention, grouped according to the following key issues: The Confirmation Rite and Ritual; The Practice of Confirmation: Rite and Catechesis; Confirmation and the Sacraments: Relationship to Baptism and Relationship to the Lord's Supper; Confirmation and the Church's Life.

The Confirmation Rite and Ritual

What is confirmation?

Is confirmation primarily a one-time festival event in the life of a young Lutheran? Is confirmation primarily a rite of passage? The most significant issue in Lutheran confirmation is identifying what confirmation is, since one's response will shape the mission, goals, strategies, and resources of this ministry.

Is confirmation primarily a rite of passage?

Many Lutherans remember the day of their confirmation and see this day as a rite of passage. While rites play an important role in the formation of identity, is offering a rite of passage part of the Church's mission? Is it possible that sponsoring such a rite leads to confusion, such as interpreting the Rite of Confirmation as a graduation?

Who is confirming?

Who does the confirming in confirmation? Does the pastor confirm? Does a young person confirm faith? Does a congregation do the confirming? Or is it the Word of God that confirms faith throughout the life span? What does "confirming" mean?

Does the laying on of hands in confirmation bestow the Holy Spirit?

Though the Lutheran Confessions do not recognize the laying on of hands as a Means of Grace, it is evident in the New Testament that the laying on of hands resulted in the gift of the Holy Spirit (Acts 8:17). Lutherans traditionally have rejected the notion that the Holy Spirit is given through the laying on of hands but have asserted that the Spirit is given in Baptism. Given this, how might we reassess the role of the laying on of hands in Baptism and confirmation? Can the gift of the Holy Spirit be attached in any way to the laying on of hands?

The Practice of Confirmation: Rite and Catechesis

Is confirmation to be shaped by culture?

As Repp's landmark study demonstrated, confirmation in Lutheran churches has served various purposes at different times. During the era of Pietism in Germany, confirmation was a time to demonstrate a faith that centered in the heart rather than in the head. In the twentieth century in the United States, greater attention was given to relationships and community. To what extent does culture deserve a role in shaping confirmation?

Why do so many Lutheran youth drop out after the Rite of Confirmation?

For years, some people have been disappointed with the results of confirmation. In 1953, a researcher reported that the Synod lost 28% of the communicant membership by defection in 1950. With confirmations making up a large proportion of gains in communicants, he wondered about the number of confirmands who dropped out of the church. In 2007, a research study of the state of education in LCMS congregations found pastors reporting that approximately 46% of those who confirmed their faith were active as seniors in high school.

Does basing confirmation ministry on a "schooling" model equip disciples of Christ?

When an educational model is based on grade levels, the goal is to graduate.

Confirmation and the Sacraments: Relationship to Baptism and Relationship to the Lord's Supper

What is the relationship of confirmation to Baptism and Holy Communion?

Though there is a common understanding of Holy Baptism among Lutherans, why has confirmation often overshadowed Baptism?

Is confirmation necessary for Holy Communion?

While the traditional order has been infant Baptism, confirmation, and the Lord's Supper, a report issued in 1970 by representatives of the three largest Lutheran bodies in the United States emphasized that the right to commune is given through Baptism and that confirmation is not a prerequisite for Holy Communion, an emphasis reflected in the provision of a rite for "First Communion prior to Confirmation" in the *Lutheran Service Book: Agenda.*

At which age can Holy Communion be received "worthily"?

"The Report of the Joint Commission on the Theology and Practice of Confirmation" (1970) recommended that first Communion and confirmation be separated as two distinct events. A second recommendation was that through proper preparation, young people during grade 5 be invited to the Sacrament. When is a young person ready for this Sacrament?

Confirmation and the Church's Life

How can confirmation become part of the revitalization of congregations?

What happens in confirmation is a mirror of what is happening in a congregation. Often, active youth are members of active families. Inactive youth probably belong to inactive families. How can confirmation ministry serve as a catalyst in revitalizing families and congregations?

How can confirmation ministry connect with unchurched youth and their families?

The most important study of the spirituality of American youth published in this decade found that while youth see themselves as deeply spiritual and as Christians, less than one-half have been baptized or have confirmed their faith. How can confirmation ministry seize opportunities for connecting with this large and very significant generation?

The history of confirmation has shown us how confirmation has lost its way, run aground on its own ambiguity. Yet the resources exist to right the ship and restore to confirmation a clearly delineated role in the church's catechetical and sacramental life. Chief amongst those resources is the confirmation rite in the *Lutheran Service Book: Agenda*. As the church attends to these questions, confirmation will take on a more circumscribed but vital role that will serve the life of faith of all God's people.

Rev. Dr. Marvin Bergman is professor emeritus at Concordia University Nebraska. He has conducted an extensive study of confirmation practices in The Lutheran Church—Missouri Synod.

Data cited in this chapter are based on a study conducted by the author, "What's Happening in Confirmation in The Lutheran Church—Missouri Synod?" Subjects of the study included a random sample of pastors and DCEs of the Synod as well as other leaders named by pastors as being engaged in confirmation ministry. Additional subjects of the study were confirmands, their parents, senior high school youth who had confirmed their faith, presidents and educational executives of districts of the Synod, and professors of the Concordia University System who specialize in congregational education. Chief financial support was provided by Thrivent Financial for Lutherans, with additional support being provided by the Departments of Youth Ministry and School Ministry of the Synod, the Board for District and Congregational Services, Concordia University Nebraska, and the Nebraska District of The Lutheran Church—Missouri Synod. Special thanks also to John O'Hara of the Department of Statistics, The Lutheran Church—Missouri Synod, and to Andy Dwyer of the Nebraska Education and Research Center, the University of Nebraska—Lincoln.

Resources for Further Study

Concordia Publishing House neither endorses nor disclaims any of the information available through the following sources. This resource list is provided simply for your information.

"A Report for Study," *Confirmation and First Communion: A Study Book*. St. Louis: Concordia Publishing House, 1968.

Arand, Charles. *That I May Be His Own: An Overview of Luther's Catechisms*. St. Louis: Concordia Publishing House, 2000.

Austin, Gerard. *The Rite of Confirmation: The Use of Oil and Chrism*. New York: Pueblo Publishing Company, 1985.

Bakke, O. M. *When Children Became People: The Birth of Childhood in Early Christianity*. Minneapolis: Fortress Press, 2005.

Blanke, Mark. "The Religious Education Crisis in the LCMS and a Call to Action," nonpublished report, 2007.

Bunge, Marcia. *The Child in Christian Thought*. Grand Rapids: William B. Eerdmans Publishing Company, 2001.

Carrington, Philip. *The Primitive Christian Catechism*. New York: Cambridge University Press, 1940.

Dix, Don. *The Theology of Confirmation in Relation to Baptism*. London: Dacre Press, 1947.

Dorn, Harold. "The Confirmation Instruction of Children, A Survey." *Concordia Theological Monthly* 24.3 (1953).

Dujarier, Michel. *A History of the Catechumenate*. New York: William H. Sadlier, Inc., 1979.

———. *The Rites of Christian Initiation*. New York: William H. Sadlier, Inc., 1979.

Finn, Thomas. *Early Christian Baptism and the Catechumenate*. Collegeville, MN: The Liturgical Press, 1992.

Fisher, J. D. C. *Christian Initiation: Baptism in the Medieval West.* London: S.P.C.K., 1965.

———. *Christian Initiation: The Reformation Period.* London: S.P.C.K., 1970.

Fisher, Robert H. "Confirmation Outside the Anglican Tradition," *Confirmation: History, Doctrine, Practice*. Edited by Kendig Brubaker Cully. Greenwich, CT: The Seabury Press, 1962.

Gilbert, W. Kent, ed. *Confirmation and Education*. Philadelphia: Fortress Press, 1969.

Gonzalez, Justo. *The Story of Christianity*, vol. 1. New York: HarperCollins, 1984.

Kavanagh, Aidan. *Confirmation: Origins and Reform*. New York: Pueblo Publishing Company, 1988.

Lindberg, Luther. "Lutheran Confirmation in Historical Perspective," *Confirmation: Engaging Lutheran Foundations and Practices*. Minneapolis: Fortress Press, 1999.

Made, Not Born: New Perspectives on Christian Initiation and the Catechumenate. Notre Dame: University of Notre Dame Press, 1976.

McGatch, Milton. "The Medieval Church," *A Faithful Church: Issues in the History of Catechesis.* Edited by John H. Westerhoff III. Wilton, CT: Morehouse-Barlow Co., 1981.

Mitchell, Leon. "Christian Initiation, Rites of Passage, and Confirmation," *Confirmation Re-Examined*. Edited by Kendig Brubaker Cully. Wilton, CT: Morehouse-Barlow Co., 1982.

Osmer, Richard. *Confirmation: Presbyterian Practices in Ecumenical Perspective*. Louisville: Geneva Press, 1996.

"Report of the Joint Commission on the Theology and Practice of Confirmation." St. Louis: Board of Parish Education, The Lutheran Church—Missouri Synod, n.d.

Repp, Arthur. *Confirmation in the Lutheran Church*. St. Louis: Concordia Publishing House, 1964.

Scaer, David. "Confirmation as a Sacramental Rite." *Logia* 15 (2006).

———. *Discourses in Matthew: Jesus Teaches the Church*. St. Louis: Concordia Publishing House, 2004.

Smith, Christian. *Soul Searching: The Religious and Spiritual Lives of American Teenagers*. New York: Oxford University Press, 2005.

Truscott, Jeffrey. *The Reform of Baptism and Confirmation in American Lutheranism*. Lanham, MD: The Scarecrow Press, Inc., 2003.

Turner, Paul. *Confirmation: The Baby in Solomon's Court*. New York: Paulist Press, 1993.

———. *Sources of Confirmation: From the Fathers through the Reformers*. Collegeville, MN: The Liturgical Press, 1993.

Whitaker, E. C. *Martin Bucer and The Book of Common Prayer*. The Alcuin Club, 1974.

Wiencke, Gustav. "Confirmation Instruction in Historical Perspective." *Lutheran Quarterly* 7.2 (1955).

2

What Is Confirmation? Shaping a Word-Filled, Sacramental Life

by Kent Burreson

The history of confirmation and the fundamental questions regarding confirmation's role and purpose demonstrate the difficulty pastors, congregations, catechists, and confirmands of The Lutheran Church—Missouri Synod have in answering the question "What is confirmation?" One receives nearly as many answers as there are catechized confirmands. Confirmation is the epitome of a rite and process in search of meaning, a rite desperately seeking a rationale reflective of Lutheran theology in the twenty-first century. Confirmation's ambiguity is rooted in its checkered liturgical history prior to the sixteenth century, the diverse responses of the Lutheran reformers to confirmation's catechetical and liturgical aspects, the changes in the practice of confirmation as a rite and a process from the seventeenth century through the Missouri Synod's existence, and challenges present in a postmodern and a post-church age. Since history cannot answer for us the question "What is confirmation?" we must turn, as we always should, to theology.

Confirmation, as a rite and a process of catechesis, must be defined by its place within the ministry of the Church: the Word-determined, sacramental mission of the Father in His Son, Jesus Christ, by the Spirit. As the General Notes for the rite in *Lutheran Service Book: Agenda* say, "Confirmation is a custom of the Church and not a sacrament. It links the catechumens to their Baptism, celebrates the reception of the Lord's Word among them and, in cases where the candidates have not yet communed, welcomes them to the Lord's Table" (p. 28). The Means of Grace/forgiveness provide the *raison d'être* for confirmation. Its purpose must always be to support and strengthen the Church's Word-filled, sacramental life of faith. Every aspect of confirmation, catechetically and liturgically, should serve this purpose. In emphasizing the proper place for confirmation, we will also find the resources to answer the questions posed in the last essay, which demonstrate how confirmation has gone off course. But ultimately, we must answer the fundamental question "What is confirmation?" Succinctly, it is the Church obeying the command of her Lord to "make disciples of all nations" (Matthew 28:19) by teaching them the baptismal life of Jesus, the Son of God, lived in the Word and fed by the heavenly Supper.

Obeying the command of Christ to make disciples is never done in a vacuum. As the Church seeks to position confirmation properly and circumscribe its role within the Church's sacramental life, it must accept the history of confirmation that has indelibly shaped current attitudes and practices. All of the historical types of confirmation discussed in the previous chapter contributed to our present practice. The catechetical type focuses attention on the priority of catechesis and the process for catechizing. The hierarchical type influences our belief that the confirmand's personal affirmation of faith in Christ and vow of fidelity to the Church and her teaching is critical to confirmation. Representing the sacramental type, the traditional ceremonies of the medieval-based Rite of Confirmation, especially the laying on of hands, contributes to the seriousness with which the Church conducts the rite. The traditional type stresses the priority of the Reformation-altered Rite of Confirmation itself; its connections back to Baptism integrate with post-baptismal instruction. The Pietistic type keynotes the desire for confirmation to be a *personal* confession of faith reflected in such practices as bestowing a confirmation verse on the confirmands and encouraging them to develop their own personal confession of faith. Even the Rationalist type contributes something positive, that membership in the Church should be active and that the life of faith should be intellectually rigorous. It is not necessary to eradicate all of these influences in order for confirmation to find its proper place in the Church's life. However, some of the practices and attitudes have a priority over others within a practice that serves the sacramental life of faith. How can we prioritize the various aspects of confirmation rightly? The Rite of Confirmation paves the path for us.

The Confirmation Rite and Ritual and Its Relationship to Baptism

The introduction to the Rites of Baptism, Confirmation, and Membership in the *LSB Agenda* is clear about the purpose of confirmation:

> **The rite of Confirmation, though not commanded by Christ in Holy Scripture, is, nevertheless, a salutary custom that marks the catechumen's confession of faith after a period of thorough and extensive catechesis in the Small Catechism. It is also a celebration of the gifts that God gave the catechumen in Baptism and affords the confirmand the opportunity to confess his or her faith publicly before the Church. (*LSB Agenda*, p. 3)**

Here, priorities are apparent. The Rite of Confirmation is not commanded by Christ, unlike Baptism and the Lord's Supper, and so it derives its significance from the life of faith, a faith begun in the waters of Baptism and nourished in the Supper of Christ. Training in the Word (extensive catechesis) is critical for sustaining this life of faith. It is a faith that must be confessed in the Body of Christ and before the world as the great commission of Luke 24:45–49.

All of this means that confirmation cannot be understood solely as a one-time event. Confirmation is first a *process* begun at Baptism and continued throughout life. Immersion in the Word of God, verbal and sacramental, is the primary food for the confirmation journey. Catechesis, or instruction in the Word, fills much of the process of confirmation. The foundation for this instructional process is the baptismal mandate of Christ in Matthew 28:18–20:

And Jesus came and said to them, "All authority in heaven and on earth has been given to Me. Go therefore and make disciples of all nations, baptizing them in the name of the Father and of the Son and of the Holy Spirit, teaching them to observe all that I have commanded you. And behold, I am with you always, to the end of the age."

Each Christian, at Baptism, is blessed with the gift of the Holy Spirit, the teacher par excellence in St. John's trinitarian theology (see John 14; 16; 1 John 2). Baptism immerses the Christian into the life of the Holy Spirit, who, in turn, continually immerses the Christian into the Word and Sacraments. St. Paul reflects this immersion by using a relatively rare Greek word to convey the uniqueness of Christian instruction in the content of the faith, the word from which we derive the term *catechesis*. This catechesis, instruction in the Word or immersion in Christ, is the constant way of life for the baptized people of God. A Lutheran understanding of confirmation will take this scriptural reality seriously. It will not allow confirmation to be viewed as a one-time educational ministry of the Church. It will affirm that confirmation is a lifelong process of instruction and immersion in the Word—in Christ—proceeding out of Baptism.

This runs counter to some current attitudes that confirmation is even more significant than Baptism itself. Such notions feed the perception that confirmation is a pinnacle rite, a rite of completion or graduation. Such notions focus on the human element in confirmation, what the confirmand and the Church are doing in the rite. How easily we can forget that what God, through His Word and Spirit, does in the rite is primary. The public act of confession and other significant human actions in the rite derive their significance from God's action through the Word and in Baptism and the Lord's Supper. Something has gone terribly awry when confirmation overshadows its own source—Baptism. When one sees confirmation as a lifelong process flowing from Baptism, then confirmation is set within a proper framework in relation to the Word and Means of Grace.

Conceiving of confirmation as a lifelong process might seem to prevent emphasizing a particular, festal celebration of confirmation and public confession of the faith by young adults. Certainly, when the Rite of Confirmation is celebrated at the end of eighth grade, it takes on the role of a spiritual "rite of passage." The Church should ritually mark significant spiritual transition points in people's lives, including the transition from child to teenager and from teenager to young adult. But the Church should mark ritually (confirm) transitions throughout all of life, beyond only the transition from childhood to adolescence. Through a more thorough practice of ritually marking transitions in human life, adolescent confirmation would take its place as one among many such transitions, and we would be less likely to see confirmation as spiritual graduation, an emphasis destructive of the very purpose of confirmation as a way of life. The Rite of Confirmation, slightly adapted, could be seen as something that could be repeated throughout the Christian life, especially to mark passages in human life, such as a return to the Church's sacramental life and as a conclusion to periods of intense catechization. This challenges Lutherans to consider additional times and ways of offering intense catechization beyond adolescence, particularly in the late teenage/early adult years. This would allow the sacramental life to play a formative role in shaping the individual at all times of personal self-realization and soul searching. Practicing the repetitive nature of confirmation in both its catechetical and liturgical aspects will only be possible, however, if confirmation is weaned from its one-time use as a preparation for first Communion and membership in a local Christian congregation. The mean to this end is to celebrate the confirmation of Baptism at the conclusion of all intense periods of catechization, including the traditional time in older childhood/adolescence.

What is the place of the Rite of Confirmation, then, at a more traditional age? It marks the confirmand's life as one lived out of Baptism, on the foundation of the Word of God, fed by the body and blood of Christ. Thus, fundamental to its purpose is the rite's orientation back toward Baptism. It reimmerses the catechumens in the significance of their Baptism and an ongoing baptismal life. Central, therefore, to a Lutheran understanding of confirmation is what one might call ritual or liturgical parallelism. The rite parallels as closely as possible the texts and potentially also the ceremonies of Baptism. Confirmation does not have an independent existence ritually. It functions, much like Confession and Absolution, as a return in trust to the promises made by the Lord at an individual's Baptism. The Lord speaks again the words of promise given in Baptism, proclaiming to the catechumen their continuing, lifelong benefit.

The structure of the rite makes this abundantly clear. It begins at the same point as the baptismal rite, with the words of the Lord that institute Baptism in Matthew 28, adding the Lord's promise to remain with His Church and these catechumens "to the end of the age," until He comes again. This leads into the confirmand's renunciation of the devil and his works and ways and confession of the triune God. This is the same renunciation and the same threefold confession of the Apostles' Creed as at Baptism. Through this, the confirmand once again confesses that he or she is named and embraced by the Father's story of salvation in the Lord Jesus through the Holy Spirit. The assumption throughout the rite is that the confirmand *is already* a member of the Church through Baptism. Confirmation does not bestow some additional form of membership that did not exist previously. (Compare this to the confirmation rite in *Lutheran Worship*, which indicated that confirmation was a rite that bestowed membership in the Church.) The words that conclude the confession of faith echo the welcome of the baptized into the Church in the baptismal rite and affirm an ongoing baptismal life in the Body of Christ:

> **We rejoice with thankful hearts that you have been baptized and have received the teaching of the Lord. You have confessed the faith and been absolved of your sins. As you continue to hear the Lord's Word and receive His blessed Sacrament, He who has begun a good work in you will bring it to completion at the day of Jesus Christ. (*LSB Agenda*, p. 30)**

No graduation here, but an unfinished and ongoing task that the *Lord* will complete on the blessed Last Day.

That confirmation is an affirmation of Baptism is most apparent in the confirmand's blessing/prayer. It echoes the post-baptismal blessing/prayer (whose source is the ancient post-baptismal pastoral anointing) by using the same text with the laying on of hands. The latter practice, present in many sixteenth-century rites of Baptism, follows the apostolic custom of intercessory prayer, identifying that the prayer is for that particular individual through the laying on of hands. This act consciously links confirmation to Baptism, its purpose being to immerse the catechumen once again in the Lord's promises made at Baptism. For the first time in a Missouri Synod agenda, the post-baptismal pastoral anointing, or sealing, is an option. This post-baptismal act is, as the history has shown, the source of the Western Rite of Confirmation. The post-baptismal anointing is the sealing, or confirmation, of the gift of the Holy Spirit in Baptism. Picking up on imagery such as that of 2 Corinthians 1:21–22, "And it is God who establishes us with you in Christ, and has anointed us, and who has also put His seal on us and given us His Spirit in our hearts as a guarantee," the anointing symbolically declares that in Baptism, both in the washing itself and in the broader context of the Word operating in the entire baptismal rite, the baptized have received the gift of the Holy Spirit. Anointing dramatically and concretely conveys that the Holy Spirit has been poured out on this human person in body and soul. The laying on of hands at confirmation then affirms the anointing and new birth of the Holy Spirit received in Baptism.

Does the laying on of hands in confirmation bestow the Holy Spirit? First, one must ask whether the laying on of hands and anointing in the baptismal rite bestows the Holy Spirit? In one very clear sense, absolutely not. The Lutheran Confessions do not recognize the laying on of hands as a Means of Grace; therefore, the promise of the Holy Spirit cannot be associated with the laying on of hands or anointing (regardless of the descriptive evidence in Acts 8:17). The Holy Spirit is found in Baptism itself. On the other hand, the entire rite is a ritual extension of the operation of the Word in the Baptism proper. The rite is intended to convey through Word and prayer no more and no less than what is conveyed in the Baptism itself. In that sense, one can say that the Holy Spirit is given in the laying on of hands and anointing, insofar as they are part of the baptismal rite. These ritual acts are no different than the text associated with them, which may be said to bestow the Holy Spirit insofar as it prays for the strength of the Holy Spirit. But one cannot say that the newly baptized has not received the Holy Spirit if the laying on of hands and anointing are not done. What then of the laying on of hands in confirmation? It does not bestow the Holy Spirit in some way apart from or in a fundamentally different way than the Spirit poured forth at Baptism. Yet, insofar as the Rite of Confirmation is an extension of Baptism itself, one can say that the Spirit's ongoing bestowal continues in the laying on of hands at confirmation. Otherwise, why would we bother with the confirmation rite at all, if we don't really believe that the Word and Spirit are active in it?

Added to the creedal, baptismal questions are questions that evoke vows from the confirmand. In these questions, there can be no doubt that confirmation is not a graduation, but the very shape of the Christian life, lived in striving to be faithful to the confession of God's name and life. The shape of that life is to continue "to hear the Word of God and receive the Lord's Supper faithfully" (*LSB Agenda,* p. 30). It is a life shaped by the cross, which means it is incomplete until the day of the Lord's coming. It is a life that proclaims "the Lord's death until He comes" (1 Corinthians 11:26). The life of discipleship reflects the call of Jesus: "And He said to all, 'If anyone would come after Me, let him deny himself and take up his cross daily and follow Me'" (Luke 9:23). The confirmation rite witnesses to the catechumen that from the moment of Baptism on, his or her life has been one lived under the sign of the cross.

Confirmation owes its existence to the desire to connect Baptism to the life of the Christian in the various stages of human life. The prayer at the end of the Rite of Confirmation, which is new to *Lutheran Service Book* (*LSB Agenda*, p. 31), makes this clear in its first few lines:

> **Almighty and most merciful Father, in the waters of Holy Baptism You have united Your children in the suffering and death of Your Son Jesus Christ, cleansing them by His blood. Renew in them the gift of Your Holy Spirit, that they may live in daily contrition and repentance with a faith that ever clings to their Savior.**

Confirmation is the confession of the confirmand's ongoing, baptismal life as part of the Father's story of salvation in His Son, Jesus, by the power of the Holy Spirit.

Who then does the confirming in the rite, the confirmand or God? In light of the early history of confirmation as the seal of the Holy Spirit and since the text for the laying on of hands in the rite is the text for the post-baptismal anointing in the medieval baptismal rite, confirmation is something done by the Word of God and therefore by the Father, Son, and Holy Spirit. What of the others involved? Does the pastor confirm? Does a young person confirm his or her faith? Does a congregation do the confirming? Or, is it the Word of God that confirms faith throughout the lifespan? The answer to all these would be *yes*. All participants in the rite are involved in confirming faith because what is being confirmed is the relationship between the triune God and His child through God's Word, the means of forgiveness, and faith in those words and means. Obviously, the child is involved insofar as it is his or her faith. The pastor represents God and the Church through his proclamation of the Word and the prayers offered in the Church's name. The Church intercedes for the faith life of the confirmand. Confirmation is an act of God *and* of the entire Body of Christ.

Confirmation and the Lord's Supper

While the fundamental relationship that shapes confirmation is its relationship to Baptism, it also cannot be understood apart from its relationship to the reception of the Word of God and the Lord's Supper. While its relationship to the Lord's Supper is the most disputed, the relationship to the Word ought not to be ignored. Confirmation, and the process of catechesis associated with it, is a process by which faith receives the Word of God as the living Word that shapes the attitudes of the heart, the thoughts of the mind, the orientations and uses of the body, and the desires of the soul. We will consider the implications of this in the next section.

As Repp's catechetical models of confirmation show, there has always been a strong connection between confirmation as a catechetical process and the reception of the Lord's Supper for the first time. Lutherans have always taken seriously the words of Paul in 1 Corinthians 11:28, "Let a person examine himself, then, and so eat of the bread and drink of the cup," as expressed through means for preparing for the Lord's Supper such as Martin Luther's Christian Questions with Their Answers (*LSB,* pp. 329–30). Confirmation, both as a rite and as a catechetical process, should instill a continual life of preparation for receiving the Lord's body and blood.

But is confirmation necessary before the first reception of the Lord's Supper? If confirmation is understood as a catechetical process that prepares one to receive the Lord's Supper rightly—that is, with true faith discerning the Lord's presence both in the bread and wine and in the corporate Body of Christ—then confirmation is necessary before first Communion. On the other hand, if confirmation is understood as a rite affirming the baptismal life, then it cannot be understood as a prerequisite for receiving the Holy Supper. In fact, making the Rite of Confirmation a prerequisite, as de facto happens in the practice of many congregations, is a strong denial of Luther's own description of what constitutes proper preparation for receiving the Lord's Supper in the Large Catechism: "Whoever believes the words has what they declare and bring. . . . This is the entire Christian preparation for receiving this Sacrament worthily" (LC V 33, 36). Faith as proper preparation must not be replaced by knowledge of doctrine.

Given the emphasis on confirmation as both catechesis and rite, confirmation has traditionally followed Baptism and preceded the first reception of the Lord's Supper. However, a report issued in 1970 by representatives of the three largest Lutheran bodies in the United States emphasized that the right to commune is given through Baptism and that neither the thorough catechetical instruction of the traditional confirmation process nor the Rite of Confirmation is a prerequisite for Holy Communion. Finally, over thirty years later, this understanding is reflected in the LCMS with the provision of a rite for "First Communion prior to Confirmation" in *Lutheran Service Book: Agenda.* As the notes for this rite indicate, it is

> **intended to be used to admit to the Lord's Supper baptized children who have not yet been confirmed. Candidates for admission to the Lord's Supper have learned the Ten Commandments, the Creed, and the Lord's Prayer. They have received careful instruction in the Gospel and Sacraments. Confessing their sin and trusting in their Savior, they desire to receive the Lord's Supper for the forgiveness of sins and the strengthening of their faith in Christ and their love toward others. (p. 25)**

Faith and the life of faith through Baptism and the Word of God is the proper preparation for receiving the Lord's Supper, as this first Communion prior to Confirmation rite celebrates. The Rite of Confirmation ought never be a prerequisite for the Supper, but should be an immersion in the life of faith, which includes the food of the Supper, a life already bestowed in Baptism.

Of course, this raises the question of which age one can receive the Lord's Supper "worthily." When is a young person ready for this sacrament? With this question now separated from the Rite of Confirmation, we can address it in relation to Christ's mandate and institution of the Lord's Supper. The reformers (as witnessed by the Lutheran church orders) engaged this question not in terms of age, but in terms of individual readiness. Thus, children might be introduced to the Lord's Supper at various ages. The concern of the reformers was that children participate in the Sacrament in a worthy manner, partaking of the body and blood of Christ to their benefit, using it in faith. On the basis of the four records of the institution narrative, as well as Mark 10:13–16 and 1 Corinthians 11:17–32, the reformers clearly express that faith, with regard to the Lord's Supper, includes a cognitive, intellectual component. This entails the ability to understand and take to heart the words of promise given in the institution narrative with regard to the signs of the Sacrament, Christ's body and blood.

Yet, most of the church orders indicate that individual readiness to participate in the Supper will be apparent prior to age twelve and usually around ages seven or eight. In most cases, this would be prior to the age of abstract reasoning, which includes the ability to comprehend, verbally enunciate, and distinguish the bodily presence of Christ in the Supper in the bread and wine and the benefits offered in the Supper. What type of cognitive ability is entailed in a worthy reception of the Sacrament? Does it mean simply the ability to recite by heart the chief parts of the catechism, including the Words of Institution? Or does it imply the ability to explain intelligibly the use and benefits of the Lord's Supper?

The ambiguity of this issue encourages a continued examination of the institution narrative, first of all, as the interpretive foundation for the Lord's Supper, in order to determine when a person may participate in the Supper. The passages from Mark 10:13–16; 1 Corinthians 11:27–32; and John 6:32–59 would also help to formulate an answer to the question. Might it be possible that the institution narrative indicates that worthy participation is determined relative to the cognitive abilities particular to each of the various stages of human life? Thus, the mandate of Christ to "do this in remembrance of Me"—that is, to partake and receive the benefits of the Supper in faith—requires that one do so with whatever cognitive abilities are appropriate to one's stage of human development. Thus, young children, even though incapable of abstract reasoning, nevertheless would be able to participate worthily in the Lord's Supper according to their own stage of cognitive development.

In the end, the practice of confirmation today should include movement toward separating the Rite of Confirmation from first Communion. Confirmation should be seen as an ongoing immersion in the baptismal life, which includes regular reception of the Holy Supper beginning at an earlier age appropriate to each individual child. Confirmation as a rite should affirm that life, not seek to establish a life of faith in the Supper at a stage of human life when establishing the rhythm of participating in the Supper may be difficult to accomplish.

The Practice of Confirmation: Rite and Catechesis

The connection between confirmation and the Lord's Supper reflects the purpose of confirmation as a rite and as catechesis: to strengthen and nourish a life of discipleship in faith through the Word and the Means of Grace. Yet it doesn't seem to be working. For many Lutheran youth, the life of active discipleship ceases after the Rite of Confirmation has ended. In 2007, a research study of the state of education in LCMS congregations found pastors reporting that approximately 46% of those who confirmed their faith were active as seniors in high school. That means that 54% were no longer active. Why is this the case, and how might it be corrected?

The Confirmation rite and catechetical instruction should work hand-in-glove to promote a life of discipleship in the Word and Means of Grace within the Body of Christ. Two key issues arise that work against this faith formation: challenges in the predominant age-based educational model for formation in confirmation and inadequate efforts at addressing the cultural context of today's youth. Addressing these issues will facilitate a practice of confirmation in which catechesis and rite work in coordination to shape a life of faithful discipleship.

Basing confirmation catechesis on an educational model that is structured on grade levels (as opposed to faith maturity levels) reinforces the perception that the goal is to achieve certain performance levels and to graduate from confirmation. The rite then serves as the passage from discipleship, rather than formation for it. If catechesis is intended to immerse a child in the life of faith, then the texts and experiences of catechesis should engage that life. The primary texts should be those that give shape to the life of faith and can be internalized (committed to memory and reflected upon): Word of God (Scriptures), catechism, and hymnal (in order of priority). Catechesis should shape the child to live a life of repentance and regeneration (Law and Gospel) out of the primary words or narratives of the Word of God that center on God's story of salvation in Christ Jesus. The catechism (the Six Chief Parts of the Word), which serves as a summary of the Word and its primary language and story, should mold the basic ways of thinking and acting as a disciple in this world. The hymnal, in liturgies and hymns or songs, develops that basic language and story in biblically and sacramentally rich ways for the Christian to pray and sing. Through these primary texts of catechesis, Christian disciples are forged to live in right relationship to God, the Body of Christ, fellow humans, and the creation. Other resources, such as movies, songs, and so forth, enable a dialogue between these primary texts and the realities of life in a particular cultural context.

If confirmation as rite and catechesis are intended to form disciples, then the multiple agents involved in confirmation should work as one body instead of at cross purposes to one another. As a rite that extends out of Baptism, confirmation's sacramental overtones entail that the called representative of God, the pastor, serves as the primary catechist. In addition, as the shepherd of the life of Christ's Body and of the maturity of discipleship of each individual Christian within it, the pastor serves as the primary model and evangelist of a mature life of faith. Confirmation is a spiritual matter, and the pastor is the spiritual overseer of the church. Since catechesis occurs on a daily basis, parents also serve as primary models of faith for their children. One of the problems that furthers a confirmand dropout approach is that parents neglect the catechesis of their children and turn the effort over to the church's catechetical program, especially to the pastor. What this tells children is that catechesis and confirmation really are not all that important. Discipleship can be worn on the sleeve and discarded at will. Instead, parents should prioritize and reinforce the shape of catechesis within the church with teaching and modeling at home. Finally, the Body of Christ should stand alongside the pastor and the home. One way to accomplish this is to give mentors or local sponsors to the newly baptized to walk with them through the Rite of Confirmation and their lifelong catechesis.

The other primary factor working against confirmation is the failure to attend adequately to the cultural context of today's youth. The models for confirmation and essays at the end of this book provide engaging ways for responding to this failure. Confirmation, both catechesis and rite, must be shaped by culture, or it will fail to form disciples of today's youth. In terms of catechesis, it means that formation must immerse confirmands fully in the life of faith in relation to the totality of their person: their souls, minds, emotions, and bodies. The pastor and other catechists of the congregation should make use of the three primary texts of catechesis and all resources from within the cultural context that help form the confirmand in a discipleship of faith. These would include such things as other texts, music, art, theatre, movies, food, tactile resources, hands-on exercises, and mentoring.

One particular resource central to the life of faith within the life of the Body of the Church is ritual. Because ritual involves all the senses, it catechizes in holistic ways in relation to Word and Sacraments. Ritual also expresses the life of faith in terms of receiving God's merciful activity and responding with prayer, praise, and thanksgiving—the rhythm of worship. The churches of the LCMS have failed to adequately tap into the catechetical riches of ritual. Roman Catholics have provided resources for ritual-based catechesis of adults with the Rite of Christian Initiation of Adults (RCIA). More recently, German Roman Catholics have developed a post-baptismal catechumenate modeled on the RCIA, but in this case intended for forming the faith of those baptized as infants. The benefit of this approach is that it organizes the catechumens' formation around the Word, the Means of Grace, and the Church's corporate life in worship and in service to the world. It ritually structures the reception of the Word, Baptism, the forgiveness of sins, and the Lord's Supper in the catechumen's life and shapes a way of life in love for God and service to the neighbor centered in forgiveness and love. Since it engages all of the senses, it works against abstract and intellectualizing understandings of catechesis and confirmation. Finally, by its ritual nature, the catechumenal process keeps catechesis and the Rite of Confirmation intimately wedded for the sake of a life of discipleship. The LCMS would be well-advised to develop a Rite of Christian Initiation for Adults and a corresponding post-baptismal catechumenal process for children.

Confirmation and the Church's Life

Ultimately, clarity about what confirmation is and its role in the life of faith will allow it to serve the Church's life. As a humanly derived rite, if it does not serve the Church's life, and cannot be reformulated to do so, then it ought to be cast on the ritual trash heap of history. Let us remind ourselves again what confirmation is: It is the Church obeying the command of her Lord to "make disciples of all nations, baptizing them in the name of the Father and of the Son and of the Holy Spirit, teaching them to observe all that [He] has commanded [us]." Confirmation should serve the formation of disciples from Baptism to death as living members with one another within the one Body of Christ. This formation focuses on the discipling of the whole person—body, heart, mind, and soul—through hearing the Word, sacramental participation, catechetical instruction, and immersion in ritual throughout the stages of human life, including adolescence.

Through such a holistic and comprehensive approach, confirmation can become part of the revitalization of congregations. Such an approach requires a commitment on the part of the pastoral staff, the congregation, and parents and confirmands. The entire congregation must see confirmation not as something the families of confirmands do, but as a vital part of the ministry of the Word in the congregation's entire life together. This means many should be involved in confirmation, from young couples without children to the senior members of the congregation, as catechists, sponsors, mentors, prayer partners, and others. The parents of confirmands must be committed to the rigors of holistic formation for faith, formation that begins and ends in the home. Confirmation and catechesis are expressions of active righteousness, shaped by the Law's operation in the institutional life of the Church on earth. Research has clearly shown that parents who are not active in the Church's life will mold children who are not active. Parents whose children are in confirmation instruction should be expected to commit themselves to an active life of faith, including regular participation in worship, in adult instruction in the faith, and in the confirmation program itself. In doing so, confirmation will be valued across the congregation's life and will energize the life of the entire congregation.

Central to the holistic formation of confirmands is their identity as witnesses. Being a disciple means being a witness of what one has seen and heard, Christ crucified and risen in the Word proclaimed and the Means of Grace experienced. Disciples are witnesses of the crucified and risen Lord. Confirmation should orient confirmands (and the entire congregation) toward a life of perpetual witness in word and deed. They must see their formation in the faith as formation for the sake of the world, especially their relatives and friends who have not received the witness of Jesus Christ. Confirmation formation should structure opportunities for the confirmands concretely to witness to their confession of faith in family contexts, at school, and at leisure. The youth ministry of the congregation should be integrated with confirmation to provide opportunities for witness and service for the confirmands. Confirmands should be able to witness out of the holistic, ritualized nature of their formation—out of their bodies, hearts, minds, and spirits—to those who have not seen Jesus.

Conclusion

The first of the two concluding collects in the Rite of Confirmation summarizes well the intentions of confirmation:

> **Lord God, heavenly Father, we thank and praise You for Your great goodness in bringing these Your sons and daughters to the knowledge of Your Son, our Savior, Jesus Christ, and enabling them both with the heart to believe and with the mouth to confess His saving name. Grant that, bringing forth the fruits of faith, they may continue steadfast and victorious to the day when all who have fought the good fight of faith shall receive the crown of righteousness. (*LSB Agenda*, p. 30)**

Through the instruction and modeling of catechesis and the Rite of Confirmation itself, confirmands, at whatever age, are shaped to live a life of faith immersed in the Word and the means of forgiveness. It is a life confirmands are formed to live steadfast, in the face of the sin, evils, and death of this earthly life, to the day when the crown of Christ's life is placed on them forever. To that end, we teach and confirm disciples—shaping a Word-filled, sacramental life.

Rev. Dr. Kent Burreson serves as associate professor of systematic theology and dean of chapel at Concordia Seminary in St. Louis, Missouri.

3

Catechism Foundations

by John T. Pless

Introduction

Church historian Mark Noll has observed that the expansion of Lutheranism as a worldwide church is due in large part to the success of Luther's Small Catechism. Compact and concise, the Small Catechism embodies the essential components of the faith in a form that is at once both memorable and accessible to mind and heart. The Small Catechism represents a classical form of catechesis that is evangelical at its core. It has served as a confession of the Church, a missionary tract, and a handbook for Christian teaching, prayer, and life.

The Catechism before the Small Catechism

Luther worked with a catechetical tradition that stretched back to the fledgling Church. Yet he formulated his catechism using defining texts such as the Ten Commandments, the Apostles' Creed, and the Lord's Prayer so that they would be opened up through the proper distinction of the Law from the Gospel.

From the third and fourth centuries onward, the Creed and the Our Father played a foundational role in catechesis. The Early Church saw the Creed as a compendium of Scripture that would guide the Christian through the biblical terrain. The Our Father was seen as a companion to the Creed. Examples of catechetical preaching are found in Church Fathers such as Ambrose,

Augustine, and Cyril. In fact, Early Church catechesis was more at home in the liturgy than in the classroom. Homilies were catechetical in nature.

In the Early Church, instruction regarding the sacraments took place just prior to the Easter Vigil (e.g., Chrysostom and Theodore of Mopsuestia), so that the catechumen might anticipate Baptism and the Lord's Supper, or following the Vigil in Easter Week (e.g., Cyril of Jerusalem and Ambrose), so that the newly baptized might reflect on what they had received.

In the Middle Ages, the chief components of the catechism were the Creed, Our Father, and Ten Commandments. However, the Decalogue (Ten Commandments) played a modest role in catechesis. Instead, catalogues of virtues and vices (e.g., seven virtues and seven deadly sins) were used for self-examination and moral direction. Only in the thirteenth century did synodical decrees mandate instruction in the Ten Commandments. In the Medieval Church, the sacraments were rarely topics for catechesis until the Fourth Lateran Council (1215) required annual Confession and Communion. By the end of the Middle Ages, other materials such as prayers, catalogues of sins, listings of good works, the Hail Mary, and other prayers to the saints had accumulated around the catechism. The "catechism" learned by Luther as a child would have been this configuration of teaching and devotional texts.

The Path to the Formulation of the Catechisms

As early as July 1516, Luther preached on the catechism. By 1522, the practice had been established in Wittenberg of preaching on the catechism four times per year. Luther's catechisms, both the small and the large, were born in the pulpit. Heinrich Bornkamm describes the birth:

> **_The Large Catechism_ is one of Luther's greatest artistic achievements. From this initial work a second sprang forth, _The Small Catechism._ While the mastery of the larger work lies in the wealth and liveliness of its articulating the faith, the beauty of the smaller work lies in the precision with which it made matters of faith luminous and memorable. Without the preparatory condensation of the catechetical sermons into _The Large Catechism_, there would have been no crystallization of the entire substance into _The Small Catechism._ (_Luther in Mid-Career_, p. 601)**

Not only were the catechisms derived from preaching, but they would also serve the hearers in providing a hermeneutical framework to understand the sermon.

In addition to his catechetical sermons, another source that would flow into the catechisms would be tracts designed to replace the "confessional manuals" of the Medieval Church. These short pieces were intended to teach the laity how to make an evangelical use of confession. Included in this category would be such pieces as *Instructions on Confessions,* 1518 (WA 1:257–65); *A Short Explanation of the Ten Commandments, Their Fulfillment and Transgressions,* 1518 (WA 1:247–56); *The Sacrament of Penance,* 1519 (AE 35:3–22); *A Discussion on How Confession Should Be Made,* 1519 (AE 39:27–47); *A Short Form of the Ten Commandments, A Short Form of the Faith, A Short Form of the Our Father,* 1520 (WA 7:204–29). Composed for lay use, these tracts were aimed at assisting evangelical Christians in making a salutary confession of their sins in repentance wrought by the Law and then in laying hold of the promise by faith in the words of the Absolution. These early pastoral texts would be building blocks as Luther moved to provide a concise form of Christian teaching geared toward repentance, faith, and holy living.

Luther's devotional literature was also a source of influence in his preparation of the catechisms. In particular, we might note *Personal Prayer Book,* 1522 (AE 43:3–45) and *A Booklet for the Laity and Children,* 1525. Several of Luther's "catechism hymns" actually predate the publication of the catechisms: "These Are the Holy Ten Commands," 1524 (*LSB* 581); "We All Believe in One True God," 1524 (*LSB* 953/954); "From Depths of Woe I Cry to Thee," 1523 (*LSB* 607); "O Lord, We Praise Thee," 1524 (*LSB* 617). From both a literary and theological perspective, it may be observed that concepts expressed in these hymns will find their way into the Small Catechism.

Luther's own catechisms may be seen as a response to three events: (1) the request of Pastor Nicholas Hausmann for a catechism to use in the instruction of the "common folk" in 1524; (2) controversy between Agricola and Melanchthon on the place of the Law in the Christian life; and (3) a remedy to the maladies diagnosed in the Visitations of 1528. The impact of the Saxon Visitations is seen in Luther's preface to the Small Catechism:

> **The deplorable, miserable condition that I discovered recently when I, too, was a visitor, has forced and urged me to prepare this catechism, or Christian doctrine, in this small, plain, simple form. Mercy! Dear God, what great misery I beheld! The common person, especially in the villages, has no knowledge whatever of Christian doctrine. And unfortunately, many pastors are completely unable and unqualified to teach. <This is so much so, that one is ashamed to speak of it.> Yet, everyone says that they are Christians, have been baptized, and receive the holy Sacraments, even though they cannot even recite the Lord's Prayer or the Creed or the Ten Commandments. They live like dumb brutes and irrational hogs. Now that the Gospel has come, they have nicely learned to abuse all freedom like experts. (*Concordia,* SC Preface 1–3)**

Luther's Design and Intentions for the Catechisms

Luther saw the catechism as a book to be used in home and congregation. While Luther prepared the catechisms for pastors, he clearly intended the Small Catechism to be used by fathers in providing Christian instruction within the household. The careful literary craftsmanship evidenced in Luther's nuanced phrases and his repetition of key words would make the catechism a useful tool for reinforcing the evangelical message that the laity were hearing from Saxon pulpits as God's Word echoed in ordinary households.

The catechism provided a basic summary of Christian doctrine, along with a template for teaching. Luther's pattern for catechesis is outlined in the Preface to the Small Catechism: (a) avoid changes or variations in the text; (b) after people have learned the text, teach them to understand it; (c) once people have been taught the shorter catechism, take up the longer catechism (*Concordia,* SC Preface 7–9, 14, 17). Luther intended the Small Catechism to be a handbook for Christian doctrine, a prayer book, and a book for the ongoing Christian life.

The theological structure of the Small Catechism is geared to the proper distinction of Law and Gospel. Luther departs from the traditional medieval ordering of the Chief Parts as Lord's Prayer, Creed, and Ten Commandments. He explains his rationale for the sequencing of the Ten Commandments, Creed, and Our Father:

> **Thus the commandments teach man to recognize his sickness, enabling him to perceive what he must do or refrain from doing, consent to or refuse, and so he will rec-**

ognize himself to be a sinful and wicked person. The Creed will teach and show him where to find the medicine—grace—which will help him to become devout and keep the commandments. The Creed points him to God and his mercy, given and made plain to him in Christ. Finally, the Lord's Prayer teaches all this, namely, through the fulfilment of God's commandments everything will be given him. In these three are the essentials of the entire Bible. (AE 43:14)

The Ten Commandments

Luther placed the Ten Commandments at the beginning of the Small Catechism, as the Law precedes the Gospel. In the First Commandment, God asserts Himself: "You shall have no other gods." Luther begins not with the prologue from Exodus 20:2, "I am the LORD your God, who brought you out of the land of Egypt, out of the house of slavery," but with the bare fact of God's lordship. Thus in his 1525 treatise *How Christians Should Regard Moses*, Luther writes, "This text makes it clear that even the Ten Commandments do not pertain to us. For God never led us out of Egypt, but only the Jews. The sectarian spirits want to saddle us with Moses and all the commandments. We will just skip that. We will regard Moses as a teacher, but we will not regard him as our lawgiver—unless he agrees with both the New Testament and the natural law" (AE 35:165). Luther understands the Ten Commandments as reflecting the Law written into creation. As such, it demands that man recognize himself as dependent on and accountable to the Creator. God is the one who is to be feared, loved, and trusted above all things. "Nature also has these laws. Nature provides that we should call upon God. The Gentiles attest to this fact. For there never was a Gentile who did not call upon his idols, even though these were not the true God" (AE 35:168). Thus in the Large Catechism, Luther defines what it means to have a god:

A god means that from which we are to expect all good and in which we are to take refuge in all distress. So, to have a God is nothing other than trusting and believing Him with the heart. I have often said that the confidence and faith of the heart alone make both God and an idol. If your faith and trust is right, then your god is also true. On the other hand, if your trust is false and wrong, then you do not have the true God. For these two belong together, faith and God [Hebrews 11:6]. Now, I say that whatever you set your heart on and put your trust in is truly your god. (*Concordia*, LC I 2–3)

Many a person thinks that he has God and everything in abundance when he has money and possessions. (*Concordia,* LC I 5)

Therefore, I repeat that the chief explanation of this point is that to "have a god" is to have something in which the heart entirely trusts. (*Concordia,* LC I 10)

The relationship between the First Commandment and the remaining nine needs to be demonstrated in such a way as to demonstrate that the First Commandment is the source of all of God's Commandments and that the First Commandment is embedded in each of the others. Luther demonstrated this by placing the epilogue (see Exodus 20:5–6; Deuteronomy 5:9b–10) to the First Commandment as the conclusion to the Decalogue itself. Each commandment is taught in light of the First Commandment. "Everything is to flow from the First Commandment's power. . . . Now you see how the First Commandment is the chief source and fountainhead that flows into all the rest. . . . So beginning and end are fastened and bound to each other" (*Concordia*, LC I 327–29).

The remaining nine commandments are dependent on the first. The prohibitions and requirements of Commandments 2 through 10 confiscate every dimension of human life for the true God.

Apostles' Creed

As the Gospel follows the Law, Luther moves from the Decalogue to the baptismal creed. The threefold division of the Creed is reflective of the doctrine of the Trinity. Faith is defined both as knowing and trusting in the one true God. Living faith is connected with the First Commandment. "Only a faith that ventures everything in life and in death on what is said (in Scripture) of God makes a person a Christian and obtains all he desires from God. No corrupt or hypocritical heart can have such a faith; this is a living faith as the First Commandment demands: I am your God; you shall have no other gods" (AE 43:24–25).

The First Article renounces every idolatry and false belief. Trust is located only in God. "I take the risk of placing my confidence only in the one, invisible, inscrutable, and only God, who created heaven and earth and who alone is superior to all creation. Again, I am not terrified by all the wickedness of the devil and his cohorts because God is superior to them all" (AE 43:25). This trust is steadfast in spite of everything that contradicts it. "I trust in him steadfastly, no matter how long he may delay, prescribing neither a goal, nor a time, nor a measure, nor a way (for God to respond to me), but leaving all to his divine will in a free, honest, and genuine faith. If he is almighty, what could I lack that God could not give or do for me?" (AE 43:25).

Faith is confessed in God, the Father Almighty, maker of heaven and earth. Luther's exposition of the First Article personalizes creation: "God has made *me* and all creatures . . . given *me* my body and soul, eyes, ears, and all my members, my reason and all my senses." The God who gives also provides as He uses clothing, food and drink, shelter, spouse and children, land and animals to support the body and life He has created. His care extends over His creation as He defends, guards, and protects. The First Article is inclusive. All that the Creator does, He does out of "fatherly, divine goodness and mercy, without any merit and worthiness in me." In his explanation, Luther brings justification by faith alone into the First Article. Calling God "Father" presupposes the Second Article. God's Fatherhood is known only from the Son. Only in this way is God's fatherly goodness evident in creation.

The Second Article unfolds the confession that Jesus is Lord by bringing the intricacies of Nicene Christology into a concise statement: "Jesus Christ [is] true God, begotten of the Father from eternity, and also true man, born of the virgin Mary." In the Large Catechism, Luther notes that the whole Second Article hinges on the word *Lord*. Jesus is this Lord who redeems me, a lost and condemned person. Without elaborating a theory of the atonement, Luther confesses that redemption entails both purchase and victory. Jesus has "purchased and won me from all sins, from death, and from the power of the devil"; not with gold or silver but with His blood, suffering, and death. The outcome of Jesus' redeeming work is seen in terms of ownership. The one redeemed is no longer under condemnation; that is, under the ownership of sin, death, and the devil. Instead, he or she belongs to Christ, is relocated in His kingdom to "serve Him in everlasting righteousness, innocence, and blessedness," grounded in His resurrection from the dead.

The Third Article sets forth the work of the Holy Spirit. Here, Luther confesses faith by first saying what faith is not. It is not belief generated by "my own reason or strength." Positively, faith is worked by the Holy Spirit, who "has called me by the Gospel, enlightened me with His gifts, sanctified and kept me in the true faith." When Luther confesses the Third Article, he is not only confessing how we are brought to faith but also how we are kept in faith. It is within the Church that the Spirit daily and richly forgives all sins. The outcome of the forgiveness of sins is the resurrection of the body and eternal life.

The Lord's Prayer

The exposition of each article of the Creed concludes with "This is most certainly true." The certainty of the Creed is the platform that gives boldness and confidence to prayer.

If the Creed is the summation of God's Word to us in the trinitarian Gospel, then the Lord's Prayer gives voice to the faith created by that Word. There is a certain parallelism between the catechism's explanation of the first three commandments, the Creed, and the petitions of the Lord's Prayer. Luther utilizes the Lord's Prayer both to teach what prayer is and to teach Christians how to pray. The Lord's Prayer is seen first as God's Word to us and then as our words to God based on His command and promise. Luther's exposition of each petition of the Lord's Prayer uncovers human need and God's gracious provisions in His Son for sinners.

Holy Baptism

In the Medieval Church, Baptism had become an isolated item on the sacramental spectrum, overshadowed by penance and the Mass. Baptism was seen as a rite of initiation associated mainly with the removal of the guilt of original sin. The significance of Baptism was largely confined to the beginning of the Christian life. In the Small Catechism, Luther embraces a more inclusive view of Baptism as embracing the whole of the Christian life, while addressing several doctrinal themes essential for an evangelical understanding of Baptism.

In the Small Catechism, Luther deals with four aspects of Baptism: foundation (Part I); content (Part II); efficacy (Part III); and significance (Part IV).

Luther answers the foundational question "What is Baptism?" with Matthew 28:19. Baptism is not just water but water joined to the command and Word of God. The certainty of Baptism is anchored in the Lord's Word. It is not a ritual of cultic initiation established by human beings but it is the very work of God.

Luther moves quickly to Baptism's benefits. Baptism works the forgiveness of sins, rescues from death and the devil, and bestows eternal salvation (Mark 16:16). These promises of God are received by faith. Here, we see Luther's creativity in equating the redemption won by Christ with the redemption bestowed in Baptism as he draws the language of the Second Article into Baptism. The Christ who has "purchased and won me from all sins, from death, and from the power of the devil" by His death on the cross now delivers these goods as Baptism "works forgiveness of sins, rescues from death and the devil, and gives eternal salvation to all who believe this."

Baptism receives its efficacy not from natural characteristics of the water as an agent of cleansing but from the creative Word of God joined to the water. It is this Word of God that makes Baptism the washing of regeneration described in Titus 3:5–8. As in the second part of the catechism's treatment of Baptism, the gift of the Sacrament is linked with faith: "faith which trusts this word of God in the water." Faith does not constitute Baptism but receives the promise made in the Sacrament.

Perhaps the most significant aspect of Luther's treatment is found in the fourth part, where he answers the question of Baptism's significance. No longer simply a rite of initiation, Baptism is the rhythm of Christian life: dying and rising (Romans 6). Luther enlarges this theme in the Large Catechism:

> **So a truly Christian life is nothing other than a daily Baptism, once begun and ever to be continued. For this must be done without ceasing, that we always keep purging away whatever belongs to the old Adam. Then what belongs to the new man may come forth. But what is the old man? It is what is born in human beings from Adam: anger, hate, envy, unchastity, stinginess, laziness, arrogance—yes, unbelief. The old man is infected with all vices and has by nature nothing good in him [Romans 7:18]. Now, when we have come into Christ's kingdom [John 3:5], these things must daily decrease. The longer we live the more we become gentle, patient, meek, and ever turn away from unbelief, greed, hatred, envy, and arrogance. (*Concordia*, LC IV 65–67)**

The aim of catechesis is aptly summarized in the Large Catechism:

> **Therefore, every Christian has enough in Baptism to learn and to do all his life. For he has always enough to do by believing firmly what Baptism promises and brings: victory over death and the devil [Romans 6:3–6], forgiveness of sin [Acts 2:38], God's grace [Titus 3:5–6], the entire Christ, and the Holy Spirit with His gifts [1 Corinthians 6:11]. In short, Baptism is so far beyond us that if timid nature could realize this, it might well doubt whether it could be true. (*Concordia*, LC IV 41–42)**

Confession and Absolution

The insertion of a short order of Confession between Holy Baptism and the Sacrament of the Altar was intended by Luther to catechize people in the evangelical use of Confession and Absolution. The original formulation of the catechism did not contain material on Confession or the Office of the Keys. The brief order for Confession was added in June 1529. The questions were added to the brief order in 1531. The Office of the Keys was derived from Andreas Osiander and included in editions of the catechism already in Luther's lifetime.

The practice of Confession and Absolution is anchored in the preceding portions of the Small Catechism:

Third Article: "In this Christian Church He daily and richly forgives all my sins and the sins of all believers."

Fifth Petition: "We are neither worthy of the things for which we pray, nor have we deserved them, but we ask that He would give them all to us by grace, for we daily sin much and surely deserve nothing but punishment."

Fourth Part of Holy Baptism: "It [Baptism] indicates that the Old Adam in us should by daily contrition and repentance be drowned and die with all sins and evil desires, and that a new man should daily emerge and arise to live before God in righteousness and purity forever."

Confession is made on the basis of the Ten Commandments.

"Luther's discussion of confession, along with the shape of his liturgical rite, shows how he redefines its essence and practice so that it ceases to be a burden and instead becomes an instrument by which the Gospel is conveyed personally to an individual" (*That I May Be His Own*, p. 169). Luther provides basic pastoral instruction by providing answers to three questions:

- What is confession?
- Which sins is a person to confess?
- Which sins are these?

These three questions with their answers are followed by a brief form of Confession and Absolution intended as an evangelical alternative to the Roman practice.

Luther included "A Brief Exhortation to Confession" in a 1529 revised version of the Large Catechism. In this exhortation, he lays out several key points to undergird the teaching and practice of Confession and Absolution:

- Confession should be voluntary and free of papal tyranny.
- The practice of Confession ought to be free of the unreasonable and tortuous demand that the penitent be able to enumerate his sins.
- People should be taught how to use Confession evangelically for the comfort of terrified consciences.
- Christian liberty ought not be used as an excuse for setting private Confession aside. Evangelical freedom is not freedom from the Gospel!
- Private Confession stands with other forms of Confession in the Church (see the Fifth Petition of the Lord's Prayer, where we confess to God and the neighbor).

The Sacrament of the Altar

Luther's work of catechizing his people on the Lord's Supper was conducted on two fronts. On the one hand, his teaching was directed against the Roman Catholic doctrine of the Mass. On the other hand, it was aimed at the followers of Zwingli (the Sacramentarians), who denied that Christ's body and blood were truly present under the bread and wine. "In four brief questions, Luther provides a single, yet full summary of these debates. Questions 1 and 3 appear to have in view the Sacramentarians. Questions 2 and 4 appear to be aimed more at the Roman Catholic Church inasmuch as these questions deal with the benefits of the Lord's Supper and the worthiness of those who receive it" (*That I May Be His Own*, p. 171).

Luther's pastoral goal was that Christians know what the Sacrament is, what its benefits are, and how it is to be used in faith. The Large Catechism lays out Luther's approach to evangelical catechesis regarding the Sacrament:

- The Sacrament is established by the Word of Christ and is to be used according to His Word: "Everyone who desires to be a Christian and go to this Sacrament should know [about it]. For it is not our intention to let people come to the Sacrament and administer it to them if they do not know what they seek or why they come" (*Concordia*, LC V 2).

- The Sacrament of the Altar is "the true body and blood of our Lord Jesus Christ, in and under the bread and wine, which we Christians are commanded by Christ's Word to eat and to drink" (*Concordia*, LC V 8).

- The Word makes the Sacrament. "The Word must make a Sacrament out of the element, or else it remains a mere element" (*Concordia*, LC V 10).

- The Lord's Supper refreshes and strengthens the Christian. "On this account it is indeed called a food of souls, which nourishes and strengthens the new man. For by Baptism we are first born anew [John 3:5]. . . . Therefore, the Sacrament is given as a daily pasture and sustenance, that faith may refresh and strengthen itself [Psalm 23:1–3] so that it will not fall back in such a battle, but become ever stronger and stronger" (*Concordia*, LC V 23, 24).

- The forgiveness won on the cross is delivered in the Supper. "Therefore also, it is useless talk when they say that Christ's body and blood are not given and shed for us in the Lord's Supper, so we could not have forgiveness of sins in the Sacrament. Although the work is done and the forgiveness of sins is secured by the cross [John 19:30], it cannot come to us in any other way than through the Word" (*Concordia*, LC V 31).

- Faith receives what the Sacrament gives. Luther accents the "*for you*."

- The Sacrament ought to be received frequently. "So those who want to be Christians may prepare to receive this praiseworthy Sacrament often. For we see that people seem weary and lazy about receiving the Sacrament" (*Concordia*, LC V 39–40).

- Christ's command and promise, and our need, ought to compel us to the Sacrament frequently. "We must never think of the Sacrament as something harmful from which we had better flee, but as a pure, wholesome, comforting remedy that grants salvation and comfort. It will cure you and give you life both in soul and body. For where the soul has recovered, the body also is relieved" (*Concordia*, LC V 68).

Daily Prayer

The words "for all this it is my duty to thank and praise, serve and obey Him" at the conclusion of the explanation of the First Article of the Creed serve as the anchor point for the Daily Prayers and the Table of Duties in the catechism.

The fact that the Small Catechism is a prayer book is made evident in the fact that Luther includes an order for prayer at mealtime as well as orders for Morning and Evening Prayer. Luther's life as a monk had been shaped by the rhythm of the sevenfold daily office. The monastic pattern of the prayer offices served as a pattern for the laity, even though they were unable to participate in these services. For example, the ringing of the bell would make the laity aware that the office was being prayed, and it invited them to mark the hour by reciting the Lord's Prayer. "Confessional manuals and prayer books likewise promoted a laicized monastic routine. . . . In other words, in the late Middle Ages, the ideal piety, even for the lay person, was a 'clericalized' piety that promoted an introspective conscience" (*That I May Be His Own*, p. 173).

Luther keyed daily prayer to the rhythm of everyday life: morning, evening, and meals. On these daily occasions, when our lack of autonomy is most evident, we praise and thank God for gifts of daily bread that sustain us, gifts absolutely necessary for life in this world. These are times for praying the catechism, as Luther instructs us to pray the Creed and the Our Father morning and evening, to sing a the hymn on the Ten Commandments as we go to our labor, and to pray the Lord's Prayer as a table prayer. Luther's use of the Creed and the Lord's Prayer, texts associated with the baptismal liturgy, grounds daily prayer in God's name, which is put on us in Baptism.

Morning and Evening Prayer reflect a baptismal foundation in (1) the sign of the holy cross, along with the name into which we are baptized; (2) the Creed, which is the confession of the Church into which we were baptized; and (3) the Lord's Prayer, prayed over us at the font. The morning and evening collects were modeled after prayers already in existence. They reflect the themes of thanksgiving, supplication, and commendation.

In the mealtime prayers, Luther incorporates elements of the Church's liturgy, such as psalm texts, the Lord's Prayer, reverence, and folded hands. The prayers at table are reflective of the gifts confessed in the catechism's exposition of the First Article and the Fourth Petition.

Table of Duties

The Table of Duties was Luther's "evangelical alternative to medieval piety that was based on ascribing holiness to certain structures and not to others" (*That I May Be His Own*, p. 176). These are the true "holy orders" where God is served. In calling these stations in worldly life "holy orders," Luther engages in a deliberate polemic against the Roman view of priestly/monastic holiness. Rather, there is a God-given holiness to ordinary places of life and work where faith is active in love.

We confess under the First Petition that God's name is hallowed when "we, as the children of God, also lead holy lives according to it [God's Word]." The Table of Duties shows us where holy lives are lived—in our vocations in this world. It is in this world that God is to be served and obeyed. Luther places the three estates (or hierarchies) of ministry, marriage, and state in the conceptual framework of the "two governments," using New Testament passages to define the believer's responsibilities in the world.

Conclusion

The Formula of Concord would come to call the catechisms "'the layman's Bible' because everything necessary for a Christian to know for salvation is included in them, which is handled more extensively in the Holy Scriptures" (*Concordia*, FC Ep Introduction 5). Condensing the teaching of the Holy Scriptures into a concise handbook, the Small Catechism would function as something of a map to orient the user to the Bible in order to be drawn to Christ in repentance and faith, living within one's vocation in love toward the neighbor. In the nearly five hundred years since its composition, the Small Catechism has proven itself a durable tool for transmitting the faith and a reliable template for Christian prayer and life.

Rev. John T. Pless serves as professor in the Department of Pastoral Ministry and Missions at Concordia Theological Seminary in Fort Wayne, Indiana.

Resources for Further Study

Concordia Publishing House neither endorses nor disclaims any of the information available through the following sources. This resource list is provided simply for your information.

Arand, Charles. *That I May Be His Own: An Overview of Luther's Catechisms.* St. Louis: Concordia Academic Press, 2000.

Bender, Peter. *Lutheran Catechesis.* Sussex, WI: Concordia Catechetical Academy, 2008.

Bornkamm, Heinrich. *Luther in Mid-Career.* Philadelphia: Fortress Press, 1983.

Kolb, Robert. *Teaching God's Children His Teaching: A Guide for the Study of Luther's Catechism.* St. Louis: Concordia Seminary Publications, 2004.

Nestingen, James. "Luther's Cultural Translation of the Catechism." *Lutheran Quarterly* (Winter 2001): 440–52.

Pless, John T. "Catechesis for Life in the Royal Priesthood" in *A Reader in Pastoral Theology.* Edited by John T. Pless, 63–70. Fort Wayne: Concordia Theological Seminary Press, 2001.

———. "The Catechism as Handbook for the Vocation of the Laity in Worship and Prayer" in *The Pieper Lectures 2006: The Lutheran Doctrine of Vocation.* Edited by John A. Maxfield, 81–97. St. Louis: Luther Academy, 2008.

Section 2

Models for Confirmation

If you grew up in the Lutheran Church, you probably have distinct memories of your confirmation instruction. The pastor probably did most of the talking, while you sat in the classroom taking notes or doodling in the margins of your blue *Luther's Small Catechism with Explanation*. You worried about the memory work that you forgot to study until just before class. The thoughts of your public questioning can still cause cold chills to run down your spine. Depending on your congregation's tradition, you were confirmed on either Palm Sunday or sometime in May.

In this section of *Confirmation Basics*, we will examine six models for confirmation instruction, each with unique characteristics and benefits. We pray that these samples will spark an idea or serve as a starting point for your own unique model of confirmation instruction.

4

A Traditional Approach

by Paul Hemenway

Tradition That Works

The year 2014 marked the fifty-fifth anniversary of Good Shepherd Lutheran Church and the thirtieth anniversary of our Christian day school. During these years, the congregation has outgrown its facility more than once. With sixteen hundred baptized members and nearly four hundred students in the day school, the dedicated pastoral and teaching staff stays very busy.

Yet in many ways, Good Shepherd defies what some "experts" claim congregations must do to grow. The sanctuary, built fewer than sixteen years ago to alleviate overcrowding, has no big screens. The organ leads congregational singing from *Lutheran Service Book*, which replaced the red-covered *The Lutheran Hymnal* just a few years ago. The predominant features of worship are Word and Sacrament, and you're more apt to find a Bible study group meeting in the building than any other type of support group.

If you haven't guessed by now, Good Shepherd is a very traditional congregation. That tradition extends to their approach to confirmation instruction for both adults and youth. They use two books to teach confirmation—the Word of God and *Luther's Small Catechism with Explanation*.

Building a Foundation

Committing Scripture to memory has always been a significant part of Christian education. Jesus wants us to be as familiar with the Word of God as we are with the food we eat: "It is written, 'Man shall not live by bread alone, but by every word that comes from the mouth of God'" (Matthew 4:4). We learn the Word of God in different ways. We read it, talk about, picture it with art and music, and especially, we commit it into our hearts.

Some years ago, Good Shepherd's senior pastor established the "Learning by Heart" program for students in the day school. "Learning by Heart" provides a framework for learning many of the foundational Scriptures as well as Martin Luther's Small Catechism. Each level is graded and builds successively until the students are familiar with approximately 150 Bible passages and the Small Catechism by the sixth grade.

Selected Scripture verses have been designated as Key Passages. Each grade level has three Key Passages, which are studied repeatedly and reviewed each year until all twenty-one passages are firmly committed to memory. The Key Passages include the following:

- **Kindergarten:** Psalm 119:105; Psalm 50:15; Matthew 5:48
- **First Grade:** Romans 8:28; Romans 1:16; Romans 1:17
- **Second Grade:** Matthew 6:33; John 8:31; 1 John 1:7
- **Third Grade:** John 3:16; Acts 4:12; Matthew 5:16
- **Fourth Grade:** Romans 13:10; 1 John 3:15; Psalm 51:5
- **Fifth Grade:** John 11:25; Ephesians 2:8–9; 1 John 1:8
- **Sixth Grade:** Isaiah 55:11; Acts 2:42; 1 Peter 4:8

By the time students enter formal confirmation instruction in seventh grade, they have already memorized the Six Chief Parts with their explanations and have a working knowledge of the Scripture passages used throughout the catechism. This foundation built over the past seven years not only serves to enrich the formal confirmation instruction, but it also becomes a treasure these students can call upon for the rest of their lives.

Two Programs

The majority of confirmands receive their instruction as part of their regular schedule in the day school. All students attending the school receive the same religious instruction, even if they are not members of the congregation. It requires a team effort to cover the instruction in four classrooms each morning. On Monday, homeroom teachers focus on "Learning by Heart" recitations and a Bible overview seminar. Thursday morning begins with an all-school chapel service. On Tuesday, Wednesday, and Friday, the senior pastor, associate pastor, vicar, and director of Christian education lead the sessions in each of the junior high homerooms. Each quarter, the class leaders switch classrooms.

Students who do not attend school at Good Shepherd attend ninety-minute sessions on Tuesday evenings. Seventh and eighth grades are combined for these sessions, which are led on a rotating basis by one of the pastors or the vicar. We also offer an optional but strongly encouraged session for fifth and sixth graders on Tuesday evening. The fifth and sixth graders use the book *100 Bible Stories* from Concordia Publishing House to review some of the key accounts in Scripture.

Actual instruction for seventh and eighth graders in Day School and Midweek comes directly from the Bible and Small Catechism. Class leaders engage students in lively discussions based on the text in the catechism, while helping students relate the principals of the faith to their everyday lives. Because of their experience with the "Learning by Heart" program, day school students are at a distinct advantage. Their pre-existing knowledge of the catechism allows the pastors to explore the students' understanding and deal with questions they have about the content of the Six Chief Parts.

To assist review of the catechism, the senior pastor developed a series of worksheets for students to complete and submit. The worksheets help leaders gauge the students' level of understanding concerning specific sections of the catechism. If leaders observe a shortfall in any one area, they can adjust the instruction to meet these needs.

Beyond the Classroom

Good confirmation instruction reaches beyond memorization, worksheets, and classroom discussion. Leaders want young people to be able to evaluate what they hear and apply it to their daily living. One tool used to help students grow in their understanding of the Word is the Sermon Summary page. As you enter the church narthex, you notice a rack mounted at a kid-friendly height on the wall. The pockets in this rack hold various children's bulletins and Sermon Summary pages. Confirmation students simply pick up the form they need on the way into church, complete it, and drop the completed form off in the box provided. Sermon Summaries are optional, but students earn extra credit for each one completed.

The Sermon Summary forms ask students to outline the main points of the sermon as well as to identify the Law and Gospel points. Leaders review how to identify these elements of the sermon in class. As they review Sermon Summaries, they look for patterns of growth and understanding.

If you would ask students about the most difficult part of their confirmation process, they would likely have something to say about their personal faith presentations. Starting at the beginning of eighth grade, pastors work with students to develop a brief oral presentation concerning their personal faith. Students learn their Baptism date and trace the work of God in their lives from before their birth to the present. Many students include information concerning family members, teachers, or others who serve as faith mentors. During the season of Lent, three to four students are scheduled to present their statements of faith at each Wednesday service.

On two consecutive Sunday evenings during Lent, students and parents are invited to come to church and prepare a personalized confirmation banner. These banners incorporate symbols of the Church along with the confirmand's name and selected Bible verse. Church leaders provide the instructions, materials, and pattern ideas. Families work together to execute the chosen design and complete the banner. The finished banners line the walls of the sanctuary during the week leading up to the Rite of Confirmation.

In the final weeks before the Rite of Confirmation, leaders spend the majority of their class time reviewing the eighty questions used for public questioning. Pastors provide students with a list of the questions and review the answers, pointing out specific passages of Scripture and sections of the catechism used to answer each question. Public questioning takes place on the Friday evening before Palm Sunday. Students, parents, and family friends gather for this special evening. The congregational elders attend to show their support for these young people who are about to confirm their faith in Christ. The pastors address questions to the whole group, calling only on those who volunteer. The pastors carefully monitor responses because each student is required to answer at least one question. Public questioning is not designed to intimidate students; rather, it is to help them to celebrate all they have learned and committed to memory for these past nine years.

As in many traditional congregations, the celebration of the Rite of Confirmation occurs on Palm Sunday. To accommodate the number of people who desire to attend the service, congregational leaders adjust the normal Sunday schedule to add a third worship service, at which they celebrate the rite.

Opportunities for Growth

We realize that no one confirmation program or model meets the needs of every church. The traditional model works well for this congregation. Each year, we evaluate the process and look for ways to strengthen the program to serve the needs of young people without compromising our core values concerning the Scriptures and the Confessions. The addition of a full-time DCE dedicated to working with youth and families allows the congregation to consider how they might incorporate a confirmation retreat into the existing program. As they look to the future, they want to involve the elders in a study concerning the "when" of confirmation. This ongoing process of observation and evaluation allows church leaders to communicate clearly the Word of God to the young people for their personal and spiritual growth.

Rev. Paul Hemenway completed his vicarage and served as associate pastor at Good Shepherd Lutheran Church, Collinsville, Illinois. He now serves as senior pastor at Trinity Lutheran Church in Springfield, Illinois.

5

Family-Based Confirmation Model

by R. J. Grunewald

Outsourcing

According to a *New York Magazine* article, any essential parental task can be outsourced. If, for example, you were open to handing over the tasks related to the first year of your child's life—because we all know how exhausting the infant years can be—you could hire a professional to come in and handle it for you. For a mere $170,000, you could outsource the thousands of diapers, the sleepless nights figuring out if your kid's sick or just teething, the puzzling times of trying to understand why the child is crying, the burping, the cuddling, the swaddling.

Now maybe this seems a bit extreme. So let's take it down a notch. Maybe childproofing your house overwhelms you: the idea of crawling around, going into every nook and cranny, trying to figure out which areas of your house are actually the most unsafe. For $1,000, you could hire a child-proofing consultant to come in and let you know which electrical outlets really need to be covered and to teach you how the Drano should be out of reach in an upper cabinet.

Perhaps your child struggles with thumb sucking—for a while it was cute, but now it's time for it to stop. You could hire a thumb-sucking guru from Chicago to fly in and provide a consultation. For $40,000, the guru would let you know how to correct the problem and would even throw in two follow-up phone consultations at no extra charge.

There is even a service called Bootie Camp, which boasts a 97 percent success rate at potty-training—for a fee, of course.

Spiritual Outsourcing

While it may be disturbing to consider handing over these key parenting milestones to someone else, many of us see this exact practice occurring in our congregations. The essential spiritual development of children has been outsourced to church professionals.

Now don't misunderstand me; I believe what pastors and Christian educators do is important. But it is nothing compared to the lifetime a parent spends with his or her child, teaching, shepherding, and influencing the child's spiritual development. There is no greater spiritual influence in the lives of young people than their parents.

The preacher Jonathan Edwards once said, "Every Christian family ought to be, as it were, a little church." How are the little churches in your congregation doing? How are the "pastors" of these little churches doing at shepherding their children?

Martin Luther understood the significance of parents as spiritual leaders in the household. We can see this in his statement at the beginning of the Small Catechism, "As the head of the family should teach them in a simple way to his household." If catechesis is never more than a classroom activity, we have failed in our understanding of what it means to be disciples of Christ and what it means to be a parent who helps raise young disciples of Christ.

A Family-Based Approach to Confirmation

At Faith Lutheran Church, we have been using a family-based approach to confirmation for about ten years. Confirmation has not only become a means to catechize students as they learn the Lutheran faith but it has also become a tool to help parents fulfill their vocations as mother and father.

We have found that taking a more family-oriented approach to confirmation encourages three important developments:

Parents Have Opportunities for Regular Conversations

In Deuteronomy 6:4–9, we read the words from Moses that are foundational to our understanding of teaching the faith:

> **Hear, O Israel: The Lord our God, the Lord is one. You shall love the Lord your God with all your heart and with all your soul and with all your might. And these words that I command you today shall be on your heart. You shall teach them diligently to your children, and shall talk of them when you sit in your house, and when you walk by the way, and when you lie down, and when you rise. You shall bind them as a sign on your hand, and they shall be as frontlets between your eyes. You shall write them on the doorposts of your house and on your gates.**

There is a sense in this Scripture passage that the conversations are regular and repeated. Unfortunately, far too many of our families have not figured out how to have regular conversations, especially about things of a spiritual nature. If we are not careful, our confirmation programs can encourage parents to outsource these conversations instead of leading them. By using a family-based approach to confirmation, we help parents learn to have conversations along the way. We have structured conversations around a particular subject, but while structuring conversations, we are also forming our parents so that they are learning how to talk and ask questions about the unplanned spiritual topics that might come up throughout any given day.

What would it look like if we taught our parents to have conversations around the dinner table, at the foot of the bed, in the mornings before sending the kids off to school, and during the drive to the next sporting event? I have a feeling our families and our churches would look significantly different than they do now.

Parents Are Equipped with the Tools

If you are a parent, you've likely realized that you are in way over your head. The moment I became a parent, I realized I had absolutely no idea what I was doing. I immediately learned the value of Google, where I could learn what was normal and what I should be doing in order to make sure I don't mess up my kids too much.

As church leaders, we can't forget that many of our parents feel this same way in the realm of spiritual conversations. They want to be the kind of parents who talk to their kids about the Bible; they want to pray with their kids. But they don't know how. Because they don't know how, they default to relying on the professionals to take on the discipleship role. The problem with this is that while a pastor or DCE might have a significant role in the life of a child, it pales in comparison to the role of a parent. The handful of hours a youth leader has with a student is nothing compared to the lifetime a parent spends with his or her kids.

By integrating confirmation into the life of a family, you can give families the tools to have conversations that they didn't know they could have. As a pastor, you can equip parents to be the teachers by giving them the tools, the training, and the resources to teach their children what matters the most. And when we equip parents to fulfill their vocation as parent, we also set up pastors, DCEs, and youth directors for success.

Parents Are Spiritual Shepherds

Carrying out Jesus' command to "go . . . and make disciples" starts in the living room, around the dinner table, and at the side of the bed. Parents shepherd their children and play an unrivaled role in the formation of the kids' spiritual lives.

By handing over confirmation instruction to parents, we can help re-elevate the parents' vocation and help them understand just exactly how important they are. A father can begin to see his role not only as a provider but also as the spiritual shepherd who cares for the souls of his family. While a parent is certainly not a pastor in the traditional sense of the word, a parent is the spiritual shepherd of his family. A father plays a pastoral role as he cares for, teaches, hears confession, and even offers forgiveness to his children.

In a very important way, we need to help parents understand that they are the primary spiritual shepherds in the lives of their kids.

In a single-parent home where the mother is the only parent, she can rely on the pastor for spiritual help in shepherding her family.

Basics of Family-Based Confirmation

Because we want to equip parents in their role as the primary disciple makers in the home, we decided to develop our confirmation program into one of the primary tools we give parents to help them use their role as a parent to shape their kids' spiritual lives. What we have learned in our years of doing family ministry is that parents often have a desire to have spiritual conversations and a devotional time with their kids, but do not necessarily have the tools to understand how to make that desire a reality.

In order to help our parents be the primary confirmation teachers, we've created a program and resources to help set them up for success.

Over the course of two years, we take parents through material to teach their child the Apostles' Creed, the Lord's Prayer, the Ten Commandments, Baptism, Communion, the Office of the Keys, and key accounts from both the Old and New Testaments. We divide the material into two years, although each year works independently of the other.

Sample Lesson Scope for Family-Based Confirmation

The following is a sample of our lesson scope for Years 1 and 2 of confirmation. We have all students work on the same year of material regardless of grade in order to keep everyone doing the same lessons. This means that a student may begin the confirmation program with either Year 1 or Year 2, depending on which cycle we are on.

Year 1

1. Apostles' Creed 1
2. Proverbs
3. Apostles' Creed 2
4. David
5. Apostles' Creed 3
6. Daniel
7. Lord's Prayer Intro
8. Lord's Prayer 1
9. Jonah
10. Lord's Prayer 2
11. Lord's Prayer 3
12. Ecclesiastes
13. Lord's Prayer 4
14. Abraham
15. Lord's Prayer 5
16. Moses
17. Lord's Prayer 6
18. Stewardship
19. Lord's Prayer 7
20. Worship

Year 2

1. Baptism
2. Communion
3. 1st Commandment
4. Acts
5. 2nd Commandment
6. Timothy
7. 3rd Commandment
8 Ephesians
9. 4th Commandment
10. Philippians
11. 5th Commandment
12. The Gospels
13. 6th Commandment
14. Romans
15. 7th Commandment
16. James
17. 8th Commandment
18. Vocation
19. 9th & 10th Commandment
20. Office of the Keys

NOTE: *We spend additional time studying the Lord's Supper in a retreat format during our students' seventh-grade year.*

How Do Lessons Work?

Once we give parents the material, the lessons are relatively simple. We ask all of our parents to commit to designating a regular time each week for confirmation. We suggest parents set aside about forty-five minutes to do the lessons, and we encourage families that it may take a few lessons to get the hang of the rhythm of the lessons and conversations.

Families will study twenty lessons together in a given year, using a short DVD video, student and parent workbooks, the Bible, and *Luther's Small Catechism with Explanation.*

The Basics of a Lesson

Every lesson consists of five sections. As we teach our parents to use the material, one of the important things we stress is that the lesson is just a guide. As parents get more comfortable with the material and a particular topic, parents have the freedom to go "off script" in order to encourage the conversation that happens. The goal is not to complete the lessons perfectly but to have significant conversations about these subjects.

Each lesson is composed of five main sections:

1. **Parent's Prayer:** We want to encourage parents to pray with their children. Sadly, far too many families do not take the time to pray together, and because of that, many families do not have any idea how to pray together. We supply a guided prayer in every lesson, while also encouraging parents to make up their own prayers to begin the lesson.
2. **The Teaching:** The teaching portion of each lesson happens through video. We provide a five- to seven-minute video lesson meant to begin the conversation. The video is hardly exhaustive of all the information that can be discussed on a particular doctrine, but it sets the tone and communicates an idea that will carry into the family conversations.
3. **Scripture and Catechism Reading:** For every lesson, we have students and parents open up to a particular portion of Scripture in order to spend time reading what the Word says about a particular subject. In addition to a portion of Scripture, if the lesson is one of the chief parts, we also have families read from the Small Catechism together. This is a great opportunity for parents to have their children do some of the reading.
4. **Discussion Questions:** This is the primary focus of the lesson; it is the main opportunity for parents and students to talk together about what is learned in the teaching, the Scriptures, and the Small Catechism. We provide four or five questions with a parent workbook that also guides parents with discussion points and answers along the way. We want to emphasize the importance of the conversation, not simply filling in all the right answers. We want to encourage parents to hear and listen to their kids, and we want kids to have the opportunity to hear the story of their parents.
5. **Student's Prayer:** We end every lesson in a similar way to how we begin—with prayer. Like the opening prayer, we also have a guided prayer that is written out; but unlike the opening prayer, we have students lead it.

Student Expectations

As students and families complete confirmation instruction, there are a few items we track throughout the year:

- Testing
- Attendance
- Volunteer Service

Tests: We have six tests covering all twenty lessons throughout the year, each one designed with the purpose of making sure families are completing the lessons. These tests are not to measure comprehension; they are more to have some accountability for completion. If students do not pass a test, we have individual conversations to determine why they were unable to pass, and then we arrange an opportunity for them to retake the test when they are ready.

Attendance: We expect students to attend worship at least three times a month and junior high activities two times a month. In our context, we have a very active student ministry; given that confirmation does not programmatically include time with other students, we require attendance in our youth activities to help confirmands get to know other students.

Volunteer Service: Students are expected to volunteer at least ten hours within our congregation. The hope with this volunteer service is that they will begin to understand how their gifts and passions can serve the greater Body of Christ and their particular congregation.

Parent Expectations

Because confirmation is primarily led by the parents, parent involvement is the primary way students get confirmed. We can set exceptions, but only in rare cases are students confirmed without parents actually being the primary confirmation teachers.

The expectations for parents are relatively simple: we expect that parents are doing the lessons with their children. In order to encourage and equip parents to do this, we do everything we can to make it as easy as possible. We provide the tools and training for those tools so that they feel well prepared. We provide parents with the information they need for the lessons, and we try to be available to talk as needs arise within the various lessons.

We also offer the following tips:

1. Be prepared. Read through the lesson before discussing it with your child.
2. Set a specific time and place to do the lessons each week.
3. Remember that you are the primary spiritual role model for your student.
4. Share from your life. Be honest, and share your thoughts and struggles.
5. Prioritize this time in your life and your child's life.
6. If you don't know how to answer a tough question, tell your students "I don't know."

Sample Lesson from Parent Guide

The following is a sample of a lesson found in the parent guide workbook that all of our parents use for confirmation. The student guide is similar, except the answers and suggested talking points are all removed. The student guide acts as a workbook for students to take notes and record their answers to the questions.

Lesson 5: Apostles' Creed 3

1. Parent's Prayer

Feel free to pray your own prayer, or use the following as an outline:

Dear God,

Please be with us in our time together; bless the discussions that we have, and help us understand the things we talk about today. Help us to learn new things and to be reminded of things that we have already learned. In Your name we pray. Amen.

2. The Teaching

Watch: Lesson 5: Apostles' Creed—Holy Spirit

To view a sample of this lesson, you can find one online at http://vimeo.com/12141331.

3. Scripture Search

Read through the following section of Scripture:

Acts 2:1–41

Read through the following sections of the Small Catechism:

In the Explanation of the Small Catechism, read the meaning of the Third Article and Questions 154–59.

4. Question Time

When was a time you felt guilty about something you had done? Why do people feel guilty when they do things that are wrong?

Share times that you've felt guilty as well. Talk about how the Holy Spirit helps show us our sin in our lives so that He can change our hearts.

What would be some ways you would describe how the Holy Spirit works in people's lives?

Reflect on some of the things pointed out in the lesson, such as changing our hearts and helping make the right decisions. Jesus uses the description of a Helper in John 14:16, 26 to describe the Holy Spirit.

Read Romans 12:4–8. As Christians, the Holy Spirit gives us special gifts. What do you think some of your gifts are?

Share some of your gifts, and help your student by pointing out gifts you see in him or her.

What are some ways the Holy Spirit works to bring people to faith? How does He lead people to live a godly life?

The Holy Spirit brings people to faith and empowers believers as they live out their faith. The main way this happens is through God's Word. This can happen as we hear God's Word at church, through conversations, in our homes, or as they are applied in Baptism and Communion.

When you look at your own faith and choices, what are some ways that you can see the Holy Spirit working?

Encourage your student to think back to how he or she became a Christian, whether recently or throughout his or her entire life. How has the Holy Spirit helped create and grow that faith in his or her life? Were there certain people, places, or events that the Holy Spirit used? Be sure to share your own experiences as well.

Work together to define the following words.

Sanctification—*to make holy*

Holy Spirit—*the Third Person of the Trinity*

Empower—*to help us do something we don't have the power to do ourselves*

5. Student's Prayer

Feel free to use this prayer or to create your own.

> Dear God,
>
> Thank You so much for giving us the gift of the Holy Spirit. There are so many ways He works in my life, and I am thankful for that. Continue to guide and empower me and help me make the right decisions; help me change my heart when I make the wrong decisions. Amen.

R. J. Grunewald is a pastor at Faith Lutheran Church in Troy, Michigan. His writing can be found at rjgrune.com.

6

Home/Family-Based Model

by Carolyn Bira

As I do this day; the father makes known to the children Your faithfulness. (Isaiah 38:19)

Give ear, O my people, to my teaching; incline your ears to the words of my mouth! I will open my mouth in a parable; I will utter dark sayings from of old, things that we have heard and known, that our fathers have told us. We will not hide them from their children, but tell to the coming generation the glorious deeds of the Lord, and His might, and the wonders that He has done. (Psalm 78:1–4)

In the opening words of his Small Catechism, Martin Luther stated the ideal model for Christian education, "As the head of the family should teach them in a simple way to his household." If only Christian education were that simple—fathers faithfully instructing their children in the truths of the Christian faith. Almost all of us who work in the church have become painfully aware of the fact that this is just not the way it works. In the vast majority of cases, parents drop their children off at church each week in the hopes that we can somehow create faith in them.

Instead of throwing up their hands while trying to do the job of the parents, our congregational leaders decided it was time to try something different. Our church needed to train the *parents* for their most important job—teaching their children to know the Lord Jesus Christ as their personal Savior.

Many parents operate without a clue concerning the basic teachings of the Christian faith. Even for those parents who know Jesus as their Savior, the rudiments of Luther's Small Catechism are frequently not a part of their general knowledge. Admittedly, these are broad generalizations. There are parents who were raised in the church with a solid basis of catechetical training who are more than able to share their faith with their own children. But these "wonder parents" are not the norm.

While we know that parents serve as the most effective faith educators, we know with equal certainty that most parents are ill-equipped to handle the task.

Experience has taught us that in families where faith is just a part of life and not a lifestyle, the children stand a slim chance of developing a working, life-impacting faith. Since the habits and disciplines of the faith are not modeled at home, they have no perceived value. Shortly after confirmation, these children disappear, never to be seen again—except for the occasional holiday or wedding. Life with God is quickly tossed aside for other pastimes, exactly what these young people see their parents doing. It is unfair and unrealistic to expect a child to surpass the ways of his or her parents in regard to mature faith.

So what can you do about this troubling situation? The answer seems like an oxymoron after reading the preceding paragraphs. Yet the reality remains—parents are the greatest influencers of a child's faith. We need to hold parents responsible for the outcome with their own children. This is where we as faith educators come along. It is *our* job to equip and empower parents to fulfill the role assigned to them by God. In our congregation, this translates to family-based faith instruction. Martin Luther noted the same problems in his day and addressed them by developing the Small Catechism. The catechism still provides a perfect model of what a child needs to know for faith development.

Legacy

In response to months' worth of research and interviews with parents and children, followed by hours of brainstorming and praying, our congregation leaders developed Legacy to address the issues discussed earlier. Legacy combines the creative talents of several pastors, DCEs, seminary students, and laymen over the course of five years. The basic curriculum was hammered out, tried, and refined. Thus far, the material has met the goal we desired most—young people remaining in the faith (and in the church) beyond eighth grade.

Our first task involved helping parents, children, and even church leaders see that when children reach the end of the eighth grade, they don't suddenly "arrive" at a mature faith. As a church, we had compounded the problem by establishing a ritual that felt like a graduation ceremony. Confirmation took place in May at the end of the eighth-grade year, complete with robes.

When you graduate from something, what do you do? You move on. Far too many of our children were moving on and out of the church permanently. Somewhere along the way, we lost the connection between these children's heart of faith and their everyday life. They viewed the end of the confirmation program as "time served" and moved on to the joy of high school minus involvement in their church. This was unacceptable. In response to this problem, our congregation chose to separate participation in Holy Communion and the end of the eighth grade. We also eliminated the confirmation ceremony—no more white robes, red carnations, and the feeling of graduation.

The Greenhouse—A Place Where the Faith Grows

The goal of Legacy involves creating a safe, nurturing environment where parents and their children can begin to talk about the faith. We unabashedly accept the fact that parents need to learn and grow along with their children. Classes and learning experiences provide for the parents as well as for the children—sometimes together and sometimes separately. Children benefit greatly from seeing their parents engaged in Bible-based learning experiences. One of Legacy's greatest strengths results from parents modeling the behavior we desire for the students. Children maintain what they have been shown via lifestyle far more frequently than what they have been told or lectured about when it comes to faith-based living.

So, what is taught at Legacy? The Bible serves as the primary text for the class, followed closely by the Six Chief Parts of Luther's Small Catechism. Lutherans have used this same curriculum for almost five hundred years. Legacy spans three years (grades 6–8), with all grades focusing on the same material at each session.

There are sixteen Legacy sessions during the school year. This number was chosen since it allows us to fully cover all of the material without adding further stress to the schedules of the participants.

Years ago, public schools recognized the church's role in assisting with the education of the children. Sadly, this is no longer the case. Instead, churches constantly compete for the time and loyalties of the children and their parents. Instead of battling the schools and students for more time, the number of "at church" sessions was reduced to sixteen to accommodate school events and calendars. Even while reducing the number of formal class sessions, we managed to increase the number of faith-based conversations between parents and children by supplying parents with resources to accomplish this goal at home.

Major Components of Legacy

Hands-On Learning Situations

When we began designing Legacy, we knew that we wanted to keep traditional classroom style instruction to a minimum. Our goal was to provide active, hands-on, practical learning experiences for all of our participants.

Dinner

Each Legacy session starts with dinner. With today's busy, informal lifestyles, few families gather around the dinner table. The content of the meal remains secondary to actually having families sit down together for a meal. We direct parents and students to sit together (no gathering of junior high girls in the corner, please) so they may begin their conversations over the meal. Dinner closes with guided family prayer time. These dinners are hosted by various groups in the congregation, providing service opportunities for members of the congregation (stewardship) and good modeling for the young people.

Family Prayer Time

Before families arrive for Legacy, we place cards with guided prayer directions at each place. At the close of the meal, families use the Scripture reading and directions on the card to wrap up their dinner conversations and conclude in prayer.

List **three things** in your life that cause you to want to rejoice twice! Read the verse on the other side of this card aloud, and thank God for those three things.

1.

2.

3.

Make copies of these note cards to cut and paste on cardstock.

Philippians 4:4–7

Rejoice in the Lord always; again I will say, rejoice. Let your reasonableness be known to everyone. The Lord is at hand; do not be anxious about anything, but in everything by prayer and supplication with thanksgiving let your requests be made known to God. And the peace of God, which surpasses all understanding, will guard your hearts and your minds in Christ Jesus.

Prayer/Learning Journal

We issue a Legacy Journal to every student and parent at the first session of the year. During the sessions, we allow time for participants to write in their journal regarding what they learned or discussed that day. Responses are solicited from stickers placed in the journal at each session. These stickers relate information shared in the lesson. Each participant also receives a sticker containing the catechism Chief Part discussed during that session. By the end of the year, participants will have a complete "catechism," including their thoughts and prayers concerning what they learned during the year. Journaling serves as a key part of each lesson.

Take-Home Devotional Guide

We provide a take-home sheet that parents use for family devotions/discussion. For a lesson on the Fourth and Fifth Petitions of the Lord's Prayer, we provide the following:

Legacy Take-Home Devotional

Give us this day our daily bread. And forgive us our trespasses as we forgive those who trespass against us. (Fourth and Fifth Petitions of the Lord's Prayer)

1. As a parent, prepare yourself spiritually for this family devotional time. Just a few moments spent in prayer before you meet with your children will make all the difference in the effectiveness and value of this experience for them. Gather a Bible and this devotional sheet before you meet.

2. You will need to prepare the following before you meet for your family devotion this week. Make five slips of paper and write the following words on them:

   forgive repent confess sin sorrow

   Fold each slip of paper so you can't read the word on it, and bring it to the devotion.

3. After you have gathered your family (and turned off all electronic distractions), read the opening prayer below aloud, make up your own prayer, or do both.

   Dear Father in heaven, You have given us the perfect model of forgiveness. You reached out to us and offered forgiveness and salvation without our even knowing that we needed You. Teach us to be people who forgive as freely as You do, with all sincerity and honesty. When we struggle to love another and offer others forgiveness, help us remember how You forgive us. In Jesus' name we pray. Amen.

4. Drop the folded slips of paper on the table, and let each person take one. Have family members open their slip of paper and read the word to themselves. Tell them *not* to show their word to anyone else. Now, using the concordance in the back of their Bibles, have each person find a verse that he or she believes uses the word well—in a way that is meaningful for him or her.

5. After all have found a verse, have them read the verse, leaving a "blank" (don't say the word) in the spot that uses their word. Have the rest of the family guess what the word is, based on the context of the passage. The family member who guesses correctly gets a point for that round. Play until all have had a turn.

6. Discuss these questions:

   a. What does it mean to forgive someone?

   b. Is it easy or hard to forgive? Why?

   c. How can you become a better "forgiver"?

7. Close with the Lord's Prayer.

Special Events

The sixteen-session Legacy schedule includes several special events. The majority of these special events surround worship opportunities. However, we also include servant events, a closing dinner, and holiday celebrations. Each special event offers families structured activities for sharing spiritual experiences, guided faith conversations, and opportunities for parents to influence their child's faith formation.

Content Breakdown

Sixth Grade

During the first year of Legacy, students are exposed to the Six Chief Parts of the Small Catechism with an emphasis on the facts. These are the types of questions answered during this year:

- What is a creed?
- What are the roles of the Father (emphasis on His role as Creator), Son (emphasis on His role as Savior), and Holy Spirit (emphasis on the fact that He is with us now)?
- What are the Ten Commandments? (This includes explaining words such as *covet, adultery*, and *idolatry*)
- Where did we get the Lord's Prayer?
- How do I pray?
- What is a sacrament?
- What is Baptism?
- What is Communion? What does it mean to me?

During the first year of Legacy, we instruct students in the fundamentals of the Lord's Supper. We present this instruction using information and vocabulary designed with sixth graders in mind. Following the presentations, parents and students meet with the pastor. Together, they discern if the child understands what he or she has been taught about Communion. If all parties agree that the student truly understands the basic teachings concerning the Lord's Supper, that student is then invited to partake in the Sacrament with his or her family. If at any time the student drops out of Legacy, his or her continued presence at the Lord's Table is reexamined. Completion of the Legacy program is part of the expectation for our young people.

Sample Lesson for Sixth Grade
Introduction to Baptism

Lesson Objective

Baptism is the work of God through the power of the Holy Spirit. In Baptism, God comes to us and brings us into His kingdom. The main point to get across is that Baptism is a present reality. Your Baptism is not a past event, but a daily renewal. The key concept is not "I *was* baptized," but "I *am* baptized."

Open with prayer.

Sacrament Review

Take a few minutes to review what students know so far:

1. *How many sacraments are there?* Answer: Two. *What are they?* Answer: Baptism and the Lord's Supper.
2. *What is a sacrament?* Answer: A sacrament is a Means of Grace that involves earthly elements and God's Word.
3. *What is grace?* Answer: Grace is God's riches at Christ's expense. In grace, the Lord has provided a way of salvation, not because we earned it, but because He loves us. God displays His grace in Baptism and Communion as He forgives our sins through them.
4. Read Matthew 28:18–20. Say: *Tonight, we explore the Sacrament of Baptism and what it means to us every day of our lives.*

H_2O Investigation Station

You will notice that there is a jar of water on the table. Ask the students: *Is there anything special about this water? This is not a trick question.* Answer: *No. It is just regular tap water.*

Next ask them: *What are some of the different ways we could use this water?* Let the students come up with as many answers as they can. Say: *Tonight, as you already know, we are going to be looking further at Baptism. Baptism uses regular water, but it does much more for us and to us than regular water can.*

Hand out the night's all-school Baptism journal stickers.

Now hand out the first journal sticker for the evening, and give students time to journal about it.

The Significance of Baptism

Our Baptism means that our old Adam with his evil deeds and desires should be drowned by daily regret for sin and repentance and die, and that day by day a new man should arise, as from the dead, to live in the presence of God in righteousness and purity now and forever.

What is the difference between "I was baptized" and "I am baptized"?

How does that understanding of your Baptism affect how you live each day?

The Power of Baptism

It is certainly not the water that does such things, but God's Word in and with the water, and faith, which trusts this Word used with the water. God's Word makes it a washing through which God graciously forgives our sins and grants us rebirth and a new life through the Holy Spirit.

The power of Baptism is in the ________________.

Do you believe God's Word has power?

Why?

The Blessings of Baptism

Baptism works forgiveness of sins, rescues from death and the devil, and gives eternal salvation to all who believe this, as the words and promises of God declare.

What are the three blessings of Baptism?

-
-
-

If someone who had been baptized and who believed in the promises of Baptism died, what would you know about where that person went?

Why do you believe this?

A Baptism Brainstorm

Post on the wall a sheet of newsprint with the following written on it: *Why am I baptized?*

Give the students markers, and allow them a few minutes to write down everything they can think of to answer this question. Don't spend too much time analyzing the answers. Just have the students write them down.

Next, hand out journal sticker 2, which speaks of the blessings of Baptism. Read it aloud, and help the students complete it (hint: answers to the three blanks are found on the sticker itself).

Bible Study Time

Have students open their Bibles to Romans 6:1–5. Have one of the group members read the passage aloud.

Say: *This passage is hugely important in helping us understand the power, blessings, and actions that are found in Baptism.* At this point, you will need to instruct the group members about the concept of original sin. *We need Baptism because we are all born as sinners. Because Adam brought sin into the world, every single one of us is born to sin. We cannot escape that fact.*

Now, in Baptism, that old sinful person within us (sometimes called the old Adam) dies with Jesus Christ on the cross, is buried with Jesus Christ in the tomb, and then is raised with Jesus Christ as a new man (a new Adam) to live with Him forever—all of this He does for us in Baptism. This is a picture of what has happened to us with Jesus on the cross, what will happen to us on the Last Day at the resurrection of the dead, and what is ours now to live in as we live daily in our Baptism.

Candle Project

Head to the kitchen, where you will be led in a Baptism candle project.

Closing journal and prayer time.

Hand out the journal sticker, and give students time to answer its questions. Offer help if needed.

Baptism Candle Project

This learning activity immediately follows the lesson on Baptism found above. In this activity, parents are invited to engage with their child in order to put together a candle that will be used during their home devotional. During the first part of the Legacy session, parents meet with their group leader to discuss the project and what each element symbolizes. Group leaders coach parents concerning appropriate discussions to have with their child as they make their candle.

Each component of the candle serves as a reminder of some element of the Sacrament of Baptism. While parents and students assemble the candle, they discuss each element and what it symbolizes as each recalls his or her Baptism.

Supply List

- ❑ Small glass container (one per student)
- ❑ Shells to place around the inside/outside of the containers (the shell is a general symbol used for Baptism)
- ❑ Wax
- ❑ Blue wax dye (represents water, the earthly element used in Baptism)
- ❑ Wax-melting containers
- ❑ Wicks for the candles (fire is used as a symbol of the presence and power of the Holy Spirit)
- ❑ Luther's Morning Prayer and Evening Prayers printed on clear labels to decorate the outside of the candle holder
- ❑ Hot glue gun (to affix shells to the candle container)
- ❑ Hot glue sticks
- ❑ Newspapers
- ❑ Small black rocks (our original and actual sin, buried with Christ in Baptism)
- ❑ Sand for the bottom of the candle (again, we are buried with Christ in Baptism)

Seventh Grade

The second year of Legacy exposes students to the Six Chief Parts of the Small Catechism with an emphasis on how our faith compares to other world religions and to the culture in which they live. During this year, we focus on the following questions:

- How is the Apostles' Creed unique?
- How is Christianity different from other world religions?
- How do I respond when my faith is challenged?
- Why is Baptism important to the faith?

Sample Lesson for Seventh Grade
The Threefold Purpose of the Law

Lesson Objective

To see how the Ten Commandments act in three ways (as a curb, a mirror, and a guide) among God's people and among those who do not believe in Him.

You might notice that there is no parental involvement in the actual lesson time for this session. Parents would be instructed concerning what the children were learning and given cues concerning appropriate questions and discussion points following this lesson.

Lead your class to the Balcony Room.

Open with prayer.

CURB

Say to the class: *Tonight, you will have three tasks to complete. Each of these tasks will point to one of the three purposes of God's Law.*

Your first task is to walk the "street" provided between the folding chairs behind the curtain.

Blindfold all of your students, and then have them hold hands. Lead them back behind the curtain to the maze created out of chairs. Their task will be to find their way through the maze, using the border of chairs as their guide. Start them off one at a time, but allow them to go through the maze together, in about thirty-second intervals. If they can complete the maze, they receive a prize (candy bar).

After everyone has completed the maze, take your students to a nearby table and give them their first "Three Purposes of the Law" sticker.

Read the sticker and 1 Timothy 1:9–10.

Say to the class: *The first purpose of the Ten Commandments is to show everyone in the world how to live so that we do not descend into chaos. Just as the chairs acted to keep you on the path to complete the maze, so God's Word keeps all people (because the Law is written on our hearts) in order. Without it, the world would descend into total chaos.*

MIRROR

Now on to the next task. This time, pair up your students. Each student will need a set of face paints and a brush (provided). Say to the class: Your assignment is to paint the face of your partner. You may *not* paint on your partner's clothes, below your partner's chin, or in your partner's hair.

They now have five minutes to take turns painting the face of their partner. When time is up, have each student draw on a piece of paper what they think their new face looks like. After students have a chance to do this, have them look in the mirror to see what they *really* look like.

(If students wish to wash off the face paint, provide wet wipes.) Next, give them the second "Three Purposes of the Law" sticker.

Read the sticker and Romans 3:19–20; 7:7.

Say to the class: *The second purpose of the Ten Commandments is to show us that we are sinners and that we need a Savior, Jesus Christ. Just as without a mirror you didn't know what your painted face looked like, so we don't know that we are sinners without the Law showing us where we have sinned.*

The Three Purposes of the Law

CURB

The Ten Commandments act as a curb because they help preserve order in the world by keeping the wicked actions of all people within bounds.

Read 1 Timothy 1:9–10.

MIRROR

The Ten Commandments act as a mirror because they show all people their sin and their need for a Savior.

Read Romans 3:19–20 and 7:7.

GUIDE

The Ten Commandments act as a guide because they tell Christians surrounded by a sinful world the way of life that is pleasing to God.

Read Romans 12:1–2 and Psalm 119:105.

GUIDE

Last task: Take your students (and all their stuff) to the kitchen. There, you will find a recipe and the ingredients for no-bake cookies.

Have the students make the cookies (which they may eat while they are writing in their journals).

Before they start eating, hand out the third "Three Purposes of the Law" sticker:

Read the sticker and Romans 12:1–2 and Psalm 119:105.

Say to the class: *The third purpose of the Ten Commandments is to serve as a guide for Christians, so that we will know how to live a life obedient to the ways and will of God. Just as the recipe shows you how to get the cookies right, so the Law shows us what pleases God and how to live a life that brings blessing and is a blessing to others.*

Discussion Plus

What seems like a bummer about keeping the Ten Words (Ten Commandments)?

What seems like the upside of keeping the Ten Words (Ten Commandments)?

Journal Time

Hand out the journal sticker.

Allow time for your students to think and write about these questions. If there is time, you may want to discuss their answers. Make sure they get to eat their cookies while they are writing!

Close with prayer.

Head home.

Eighth Grade

The final year of Legacy deals with young people in the midst of a normal, albeit difficult, point of development. Much, if not all, of their focus turns inward: What should I wear? How do I look? Does anyone like me? What about that girl/guy I like? The list of questions goes on endlessly for these young teens.

The eighth-grade Legacy materials are geared toward answering some of these questions. Parents are encouraged to allow the faith conversations to focus on the child. Most of the material deals with how faith directly affects children at this stage in life and equips them to deal with challenges and questions concerning their walk with the Lord.

During this year, we seek to answer questions such as these:

- What do the words of the Apostles' Creed mean to me in my everyday life?
- What does an active worship life look like?
- How do I pray and communicate with God?
- Why is my Baptism important?
- Why should I continue taking the Lord's Supper?

Sample Lesson for Eighth Grade My Personal Prayer Life

Lesson Objective

To experience several different approaches to prayer, with the goal of expanding the students' understanding of how diverse prayer can be for the believer.

For this lesson, we encourage parents to join their children for the entire lesson, participating in the stations that they may model what praying in these different ways might look like. The goal here is to create a shared experience parents and students can process later as a family. The children learn their greatest lesson by seeing their parents actively engaged in prayer!

The Blessing of Intercession

At this station, you will find postcards for you to write prayers for some new moms at Holy Cross. You will be writing three prayers, one per card. You can write the same prayer three times if you want, or make up a new prayer each time. These cards will be mailed tomorrow. They have already been addressed, so you know to whom they are going. Ask God to bless the mom and the baby. You can pray for good health and a safe delivery. Help these new moms know that they are loved and prayed for by the people at Holy Cross.

Praying the Psalms

Dear Lord, I ask You to be with me during this time of devotion and prayer. Please instruct my heart and grant me insight into Your Word today. In Jesus' name I pray. Amen.

Light the three candles.

Choose one (or two if you have the time) of the following: Psalm 1; 8; 88; 121; 148.

Read three times through the psalm you have chosen.

Read the psalm again. This time, place yourself into the psalm. Use "I" where it fits. If you want to expand on what one of the verses is saying and make it personal to your own situation, take the time to do that.

Journal about this experience. Write about any new thoughts or ideas you had while praying this psalm.

Lead your class to the Balcony Room.

Open with prayer. This time, everyone prays something out loud using Psalm 27. Divide the verses in the psalm by the number of people in the group. Give each of them a set of the verses. As the leader, begin the prayer with the first group of verses, personalizing the psalm as you pray. Then go around the group with each person following your lead. Students may need time to write something out first.

Let's Begin

Say to your class: *We will begin by watching a video called* Bad Home Environment. *It is about a teenage boy's difficult upbringing and the impact prayer has had on his life.*

After the video, discuss these questions:

- **What turned this boy's life around?**
  (Here you can stress that the prayers of just one teacher changed everything for this person.)

- **What made this teacher's prayers so effective? Do you think the teacher prayed anything "special"?**
  (No. The prayers weren't special; they were prayers like yours.)

- **Has anyone ever prayed for you that you know about?**
  (Allow students to share their experiences.)

- **Have you ever prayed for someone else? Do you know what happened because of your prayers?**

Moving On

Explain that the rest of this evening's session will be like last week. Say to the class: You *will now have the opportunity to experience two different types of prayer. During the next forty minutes, you will stop at two of the five stations provided in this room. There is a small poster at each station that will tell you what to do during the twenty minutes you have at that station. If you need more time at a station or if someone else wants to try that spot, you can come out to the center table and complete your work. If no one is waiting to try that station, you may stay there.*

"You Are There" Meditations

At this station, you will do what has through the centuries been called "discursive meditation." In this type of prayer activity, you will allow your imagination to place you at the scene of a biblical event. Then you will pray about what you have learned in reading the Bible this way. Follow these instructions:

Read Luke 22:47–53.

Watch the video provided.

Write in your journal, answering the following questions:

- Which of the people do you respond to the most? Which one seems most like you?
- How would you feel in this situation? What would you do?
- What questions would you like to ask the characters? As you ask those questions, what answers do you receive?
- What did you learn about this event in the life of Jesus?

The guidelines are as follows:

Only *one* person may be at any station at a time (except for meditation in the prayer chapel).

If you need more time at a station, take your material and move to one of the center tables to continue working so that another person can start that station.

If you have a question or need to talk with someone about your station, ask your leader—*not another student.*

Let's Start

Dismiss the students to whatever station they want to work at first. If two students want to work at the same station, one of them must make another choice. As the leader, watch the time. After twenty minutes, quietly alert the students that they are to move to another station.

Repeat this pattern.

Gather and Debrief

Discuss the following questions:

- What did you think about the two stations you visited? Were you surprised that any of these stations could be called "prayer"?
- What was your favorite activity?
- What was your least favorite activity?
- Are there any stations you would like to try again?

- Are there any stations you didn't get to try that you would really like to?
- What did you learn about yourself or about prayer?

Finally, give the students the all-school journal sticker and have them place it in their journals.

Closing prayer.

Together, as a group, pray the Lord's Prayer.

Head home.

Meditation in the Prayer Chapel

Take your Bible and journal to the chapel. Spend ten minutes in the chapel. Shut the door and find a comfortable seat. Please leave the candles alone. On the lamp stand, you will find a Bible and an instruction sheet regarding the practice of prayerful meditation. Read through the sheet, and try out some of the exercises. You may spend the time in any way you want. You may write in your journal, read and meditate on a verse from your Bible, or pray. You may want to write about your experience in your journal when you are finished, if you did not do so while you were there.

Parents

The Legacy program was never designed to be used at home; rather, we designed it for teaching both children and parents together. Shared spiritual experiences, with discussion and instruction, form the core of the Legacy program. In the end, the parents become the faith-teachers for their children.

Sometimes, the lessons are better served if the parents stay with their children for the lesson. At other times, we find it more appropriate for parents to be separate from their children, learning something meaningful for them as parents. We cannot overstate the importance of the students seeing their parents participate in this program. The "drop you off at the door" mentality speaks loudly to the child about the importance of life in the church and in the faith. When parents become part of the learning experience, the child learns that religious instruction is a core family value, something to be cherished, not something to be tolerated until it is over.

Parents-only sessions provide golden opportunities for teaching parenting skills. These classes become a type of parenting support group, where parents work with one another as they struggle with the challenges of raising young teenagers. Just remember to keep parents informed as to what their children are learning, and cue them in as to what kind of things to talk about after class is over.

Lord's Prayer

Give us this day our daily bread; and forgive us our trespasses as we forgive those who trespass against us.

You have seen the phrase "shared experience" used often in this chapter. This concept cannot be overemphasized. Much of the time, parents lack a common foundation for discussions concerning faith with their children. Thanks to Legacy, parents have built-in conversations waiting to happen.

If parents are not committed to the faith life of their children, no program will produce results. It takes time to shift the paradigm from "catechism for children" to "catechism for the family." Parents require training and instruction to understand the importance of their role in this process. Parents need to understand that Legacy cannot succeed without their participation. Most parents quickly see the benefits of their participation and renewed connection with their child.

Additional Elements of Family-Based Catechism Instruction

Worship

Several times during the year, we spend part of the Legacy hour in interactive worship. During these experiences, families sit together and are provided opportunities to gather around the Word and share prayer times. These worship experiences generally occur at the opening and closing of the Legacy program, for holidays, or for the Legacy Celebration (when the eighth graders are moved into the high school youth group and attend youth Bible study).

Legacy Celebration

We replaced the traditional Rite of Confirmation with a time of special recognition for the eighth-grade students. We invite these students forward as a group during a regular worship service and offer a special prayer for them. Parents are invited up to stand with their children during this prayer and be a part of the experience. Generally, we host a joint dinner with all Legacy families, celebrating this new phase of faith development for these new senior youth group members. Legacy becomes merely a step along the path, not an end unto itself.

Exceptions and Special Circumstances

As with any congregation, we have children who become part of our faith community without their parents. They attend with friends, grandparents, or other relatives. We do not exclude these students from participation in Legacy because their parents are unwilling or unable to participate. These situations provide opportunities for solid mentoring from other caring adults. We invite these willing adults to come alongside the students and share their faith.

While not as ideal as parent involvement, these mentoring arrangements can be very effective. We ask the mentoring adult to make a commitment to the child, ideally for the full three-year Legacy cycle. Basically, the mentoring adult comes to all of the Legacy sessions with that child and acts in the stead of the parents. Our mentors often find these experiences extremely rewarding and a time of great blessing for themselves and the young person.

When we succeed in fostering a lifelong faith-learning attitude, we have achieved one of our highest goals. Ideally, this faith instruction occurs within the context of the family, with parents modeling the faith for their child. As educational leaders in the church, we must enable and equip parents to teach the faith, thus allowing parents to fulfill their God-given vocation.

DCE Carolyn Bira created and directs the Legacy program at Holy Cross Lutheran Church in Flushing, Michigan.

7

A Classroom Model (with a Twist)

by Audrey Duensing-Werner

Confirmation with a Twist

Research has shown that the traditional classroom learning environment is not always the best way for students to learn. We also know that the greater number of ways you can have students look at a subject, the greater their understanding and retention of that information. A few years ago, we added a new twist to our otherwise traditional confirmation instruction. When we say "twist," we mean that the Six Chief Parts of Luther's Small Catechism are used together with some type of art form to help the young people better understand the material by using a visual learning process.

At the beginning of the year, we provide each student with a Small Catechism and a Bible. The church also provides a three-ring notebook with a supply of worksheets for the youth to fill out each week. (I usually copy enough worksheets to last the entire year—see below for sample worksheet.) Each week, we place a box of markers and a drawing pad on every table in the classroom.

Classes are broken into four-week sections, with each month focusing on a different section of the catechism. For example: September—Lord's Prayer; October—Holy Communion; November—Baptism; December—Apostles' Creed; January—Office of the Keys; February—Ten Commandments. In March, we prepare for a youth-designed worship service based on the Six Chief Parts, which is held the night before Confirmation Sunday.

We divide students into small groups, with a parent leader at each table. The parent leaders conduct small-group discussion based on each week's theme. The weekly worksheet provided in the notebooks looks like this:

Name ______________________________

Topic ______________________________

As you read about the topic (Ten Commandments, Apostles' Creed, Baptism, Lord's Prayer, Holy Communion, Office of the Keys), write a paragraph, in your own words, that would help others understand it.

What part in the meaning and definition strikes a chord in you?

What do you wonder about as you read it?

Tell of a story you've heard or a moment you can think of that would help you and others relate to the topic today.

At the end of class session 4, answer the following questions:

After reading, hearing, and studying this month's topic, name one thing that helped you see God differently.

How do you see God differently now?

The sequence of lessons for each month is similar. Following are examples of the monthly structure.

Apostles' Creed—Stained Glass Window

This month's signature craft is a stained glass window based on a section of the Creed. Depending on the skill level of your students and volunteers available, your stained glass could take many forms. The simplest form would be creating windows using construction paper to create the frame, with colored tissue paper for the glass. You could also use permanent colors on acrylic sheets, or if you are feeling brave, real stained glass. The finished stained glass windows should be about the size of an 8½ × 11-inch piece of paper. The class can hang their artwork around the building throughout the year.

Week 1

At the beginning of week 1, the first twenty minutes are devoted to opening the catechism, looking at the topic for the month, reading the meaning and definition, and then giving the class time to write out the answers to the four questions on the weekly worksheet. After individuals have written out their thoughts, they turn to their small group and spend some time going around the circle talking about the answers to the four questions. This takes another twenty minutes. Everyone has to speak about at least one of the questions; no one gets to pass. The table leaders help guide this discussion. After groups are finished talking, they are directed to take a piece of legal-sized paper and draw a picture representing the topic. Each group gets to share their picture in front of the room. The pastor/DCE or teacher/guest leader then takes a few minutes and gives the history and a deeper definition of the topic.

Week 2

At the beginning of week 2, the first twenty minutes are devoted to reviewing the worksheets students filled out last week. Small groups go around their tables to touch base on another one of their thoughts from the past week. Everyone has to speak about at least one of the questions; no one gets to pass. Then a guest glass artist is introduced to the class and shares a little bit about the craft and his or her faith. The artist can explain how the craft is used to share faith with others. The artist also shares simple step-by-step directions for the young people to create an art piece, either individually or in table groups. This activity takes most of the class time for week 2.

Week 3

The Small Catechism divides the Apostles' Creed into three articles. For this week, each table group draws a number out of a hat to determine about which article their group will design. Each group then further breaks down their assigned article into smaller segments. For example, the First Article might be divided into three sections: "I believe," "In God the Father Almighty," "Maker of heaven and earth." The leaders assign selected members of their group to design a symbol representing their assigned phrase.

After the young people have chosen their article and phrase out of a hat, they are to reread the explanation of the article and look up the passages listed in their Small Catechism. As students allow the Word of God to direct their thoughts, they take the sketch pad and begin thinking of or drawing simple symbols to represent their assigned phrase from the Creed. It also helps to have a banner book with simple symbols available to help trigger student creativity. Once students have selected their symbols and sketched the window, they can then begin assembling their stained glass window.

Week 4

At the beginning of week 4, the first twenty minutes are devoted to reviewing once again the worksheets students filled out a few weeks earlier. Groups go around their tables, touching base on one more of their thoughts. Everyone has to speak about one of the questions; no one gets to pass. The rest of the period is dedicated to finishing the stained glass project and handing in the worksheets.

The Lord's Prayer—Prayer Stations

This month, students create a prayer station for all of their classmates to experience. Their prayer station will help others spend time at the foot of the cross. Each station includes a candle, a cross, and a small table. The rest of the station elements are completely up to the creative minds in each table group.

Week 1

At the beginning of week 1, the first twenty minutes are devoted to opening the catechism, looking at the topic for the month, reading the meaning and definition, and then giving the class time to write out the answers to the four questions on the weekly worksheet. After individuals have written out their thoughts, they turn to their small group and spend some time going around the circle talking about the answers to the four questions. This takes another twenty minutes. Everyone has to speak about at least one of the questions; no one gets to pass. The table leaders help guide this discussion. After groups are finished talking, they are directed to take a piece of legal-sized paper and draw a picture representing the topic. Each group gets to share their picture in front of the room. The pastor/DCE or teacher/guest leader then takes a few minutes and gives the history and a deeper definition of the topic.

Week 2

The first twenty minutes of week 2 are devoted to reviewing the worksheets students filled out the previous week. Groups go around their tables and touch base on another one of their thoughts. Everyone has to speak about one of the questions. Unlike the other topics, each table group will get to design their own prayer station that relates to one of the petitions of the Lord's Prayer. Each table draws out of a hat a slip of paper with a petition number written on it. After groups have chosen their slip, they reread the explanation of their assigned petition and look up passages listed in the Small Catechism. As students study God's Word, they take their sketch pad and begin designing a prayer station through which the entire class will rotate.

Week 3

During week 3, table groups continue designing their prayer stations.

Each prayer station needs to have the following:

Written Element: An effective prayer station has a short piece written out and displayed at the station to help the participant focus on the petition. For the phrase "Our Father who art in heaven," you might write a statement something like this:

Spend a moment and talk to God the Father, Creator and Maker of all things.

As you sit in the presence of God the Father, share with Him how your day went. What were the highs and the lows you experienced?

Visual Element: Besides the candle and the cross provided for each station, is there a visual piece(s) that can be added to your station? Perhaps a picture of something or someone to look at while you are praying? or PowerPoint slides?

Hands-On Element: Is there a hands-on piece to add? Examples: a bowl of water to dip hands into, a nail to hold, a piece of clay to squish in hands.

Sensory Element: Are there items you can add to give smell, flavor, or hearing to your station? Examples: mint to taste, fragrance to smell, song to listen to.

Week 4

Devote the first twenty minutes of week 4 to reviewing again the worksheets students filled out a few weeks earlier. Table groups then set up their prayer stations in order. The class takes the rest of the period rotating from station to station. Allow two to three minutes per station before shifting the rotation. This should take about twenty minutes. Then clean up.

Baptism—Batik Pillow Cover

This month's project is an individual activity rather than a group project. Students create a personalized batik pillow cover using 100% cotton pillowcases. These covers remind students of their Baptism when they wake up in the morning and go to sleep at night. This project takes a bit longer than most—it might be best to plan this during a five-week month. Complete step-by-step batik instructions are available online.

Week 1

At the beginning of week 1, the first twenty minutes are devoted to opening the catechism, looking at the topic for the month, reading the meaning and definition, and then giving the class time to write out the answers to the four questions on the weekly worksheet. After individuals have written out their thoughts, they turn to their small group and spend some time going around the circle talking about the answers to the four questions. This takes another twenty minutes. Everyone has to speak about at least one of the questions; no one gets to pass. The table leaders help guide this discussion. After groups are finished talking, they are directed to take a piece of legal-sized paper and draw a picture representing the topic. Each group gets to share their picture in front of the room. The pastor/DCE or teacher/guest leader then takes a few minutes and gives the history and a deeper definition of the topic.

Week 2

Students spend the first twenty minutes of week 2 reviewing the worksheets they filled out last week and going around their tables. They are to touch base on another one of their thoughts. A guest artist shares a little bit about the craft and about how the craft is used to share his or her faith with others. The artist also shares simple step-by-step directions for the young people to make the pillow cover individually. This will take most of the class time for week 2.

Week 3

Instruct students to reread the explanation of Baptism in their Small Catechism and look up passages listed there. As students contemplate the Word of God, they take their sketch pad and begin thinking of or drawing out a simple symbol that could represent their Baptism. We also ask students to find their baptismal date. Once students have sketched out their symbol, they can pencil it onto their pillowcase and begin the batik process. After the batik is dry, students should use fabric paint pens to print their baptismal date on their pillowcase.

Week 4

At the beginning of week 4, the first fifteen to twenty minutes are devoted to reviewing the worksheets students filled out a few weeks earlier. Groups should go around their tables as individuals touch base on one more of their thoughts. The young people then will finish their batik project.

Ten Commandments—Mosaic Stepping-Stone

During this month, students create a mosaic stepping-stone. Many craft and garden stores sell forms to pour your own stepping-stones. Students use bits of colorful tile, glass gems, and other found objects to make a design in the form and then pour in the concrete mix. After the concrete sets, completed stepping-stones may be placed around the church property to form a walking trail that grows as the years go by.

Week 1

At the beginning of week 1, the first twenty minutes are devoted to opening the catechism, looking at the topic for the month, reading the meaning and definition, and then giving the class time to write out the answers to the four questions on the weekly worksheet. After individuals have written out their thoughts, they turn to their small group and spend some time going around the circle talking about the answers to the four questions. This takes another twenty minutes. Everyone has to speak about at least one of the questions; no one gets to pass. The table leaders help guide this discussion.

Each table group has to think of a simple way to teach all Ten Commandments to the entire class. They can use a song, a rap, a cheer, an acronym, or another format. Once each group has developed a way to remember the Ten Commandments, each individual table group teaches their idea to the entire group so that they will learn the rap, song, or cheer the group has developed. The pastor/DCE or teacher/guest leader then takes a few minutes and gives the history and a deeper definition of the topic to end the session.

Week 2

At the beginning of week 2, the first twenty minutes are devoted to reviewing the worksheets students filled out last week. All members of a table group share their answers to another one of the questions. A guest artist shares a little bit about his or her faith and how the craft expresses that faith to others. The artist then shares a simple step-by-step process for the young people to make the art piece, either individually or in table groups. This takes most of the class time for week 2.

Week 3

Divide each table group in half, and assign each small group one of the Ten Commandments. The table groups should reread the explanation of their assigned commandment from the Small Catechism and look up the related Scripture passages listed there. In addition, all groups should study the words of Deuteronomy 6:4–9. After contemplating these words of Scripture, students take out their sketch pads and begin thinking about or drawing a simple symbol that represents the commandment. Once they have sketched out their symbol, they can begin to select the tiles and other objects to make their mosaic stepping-stone.

Week 4

Use the first fifteen to twenty minutes of week 4 to review once again the student worksheets. Participants speak to any questions they have not yet answered. The young people finish their stepping-stone project.

Holy Communion—Coil Pots

The craft for this month involves making a simple pot with coils of clay. Directions and supplies are available online and in local craft stores. By using specialized clay, it is possible to finish the pots in a regular oven. You may also use standard clay, but this will require additional time for drying, glazing, and firing the pots in a kiln.

Week 1

At the beginning of week 1, the first twenty minutes are devoted to opening the catechism, looking at the topic for the month, reading the meaning and definition, and then giving the class time to write out the answers to the four questions on the weekly worksheet. After individuals have written out their thoughts, they turn to their small group and spend some time going around the circle talking about the answers to the four questions. This takes another twenty minutes. Everyone has to speak about at least one of the questions; no one gets to pass. The table leaders help guide this discussion. After groups are finished talking, they are directed to take a piece of legal-sized paper and draw a picture representing the topic. Each group gets to share their picture in front of the room. The pastor/DCE or teacher/guest leader then takes a few minutes and gives the history and a deeper definition of the topic.

Week 2

At the beginning of week 2, devote the first twenty minutes to reviewing the worksheets students filled out last week. As you go around the tables, students touch base on another one of their answers. Everyone has to speak about one of the questions; no one gets to pass. Introduce your guest ceramic artist, who shares how to use the craft to share one's faith. The artist guides students, using simple step-by-step directions to create the coil pot that each student will design next week.

Week 3

As class begins this week, share the words of Jeremiah 18:1–6 with the students.

The word that came to Jeremiah from the Lord: "Arise, and go down to the potter's house, and there I will let you hear My words." So I went down to the potter's house, and there he was working at his wheel. And the vessel he was making of clay was spoiled in the pot-

ter's hand, and he reworked it into another vessel, as it seemed good to the potter to do. Then the word of the LORD came to me: "O house of Israel, can I not do with you as this potter has done? declares the LORD. Behold, like the clay in the potter's hand, so are you in My hand, O house of Israel."

In Holy Communion, Christ meets us at His Table. We come to the Table knowing we are broken, like pottery at times, and in need of a Savior. He meets us there, and through His body and blood in, with, and under the bread and wine, He offers us His love and forgiveness. He re-creates us—reshapes us—like a potter does a pot.

The young people are to reread the explanation of Holy Communion in their Small Catechism and look up the Scripture passages listed there. As they meditate on the Word of God, students should take their sketch pad and begin thinking of or drawing a simple symbol that would help them remember Holy Communion. Examples might be a loaf of bread and a chalice or a cross and a heart representing Christ's death. Once students have sketched their symbol, they can begin forming their coil pot. Once the pot is partially dried, students can take a pencil or pointed object and trace their symbol onto their pot.

Week 4

Spend the first fifteen to twenty minutes of week 4 reviewing once again the worksheets students filled out a few weeks earlier. Everyone has to speak about one of the questions; no one gets to pass. The young people then finish their coil pot project.

Office of the Keys and Confession—Prayer Cloth

This month, students create a personal prayer cloth. We use white cloth table napkins, which can usually be purchased in bulk at discount stores and warehouse clubs. You will also need fabric paints or markers for students to create their designs. You may want to add beads or other embellishments to the edging after the paint is dry.

Week 1

At the beginning of week 1, the first twenty minutes are devoted to opening the catechism, looking at the topic for the month, reading the meaning and definition, and then giving the class time to write out the answers to the four questions on the weekly worksheet. After individuals have written out their thoughts, they turn to their small group and spend some time going around the circle talking about the answers to the four questions. This takes another twenty minutes. Everyone has to speak about at least one of the questions; no one gets to pass. The table leaders help guide this discussion. After groups are finished talking, they are directed to take a piece of legal-sized paper and draw a picture representing the topic. Each group gets to share their picture in front of the room. The pastor/DCE or teacher/guest leader then takes a few minutes and gives the history and a deeper definition of the topic.

Week 2

At the beginning of week 2, devote the first twenty minutes to reviewing the worksheets students filled out last week. Going around the tables, they are to touch base on another one of their thoughts. Everyone has to speak about one of the questions. After the discussion time, the table groups will head to different corners of the room, where there are bowls of water and strips of white cloth (1 × 2–3 inches) and washable markers. Direct the young people to write out things they need to confess. As soon as they have filled their cloths with their confessional words, they can dip their cloths in the bowl of water and watch them disappear. Help students understand how this is like our confession and God's forgiveness.

Week 3

Since this month's project is an individual effort, students will work on their own this week. Each person should look up the catechism section on Confession and the Office of the Keys. Direct students to spend time reviewing the Scripture verses found in this section.

Have students look up Philippians 4:6–7 and James 5:13–16 as you review the PARTS (Praise, Ask, Repent, Thanks, and Share) or ACTS (Adoration, Confession, Thanksgiving, and Supplication) of prayer.

PRAISE—Praising God simply means telling God things that are true about Him. Praising brings God pleasure and helps us keep our focus on the truth about God's nature and love for us.

ASK—Asking means letting God know about your needs and desires, as well as the needs and desires of those you care about. It's important to remember that God's answers to any request may be "yes," "no," or "wait."

REPENT—This section, admitting when we've done wrong, is difficult for most of us. God already knows our sins. He wants us to recognize and admit our sins so that He can cleanse us through Christ's death and resurrection. Repenting means telling God whenever there's sin in your life and asking Him to help you turn away from it with no intention of doing it again.

THANKS—Prayers of thanks tell God about all the things you're grateful for in life.

SHARE—Sharing means talking with God like you would talk with a close friend. Some people have the opinion that God is distant and uninterested, but the true God is loving and all-powerful. God wants to hear about what happens to you each day. God's power can give you strength for the little struggles and the big challenges that you face each day.

Instruct students to sketch symbols representing the Office of the Keys. Once students complete their design, they can transfer the drawing to the cloth napkin, using fabric markers or paints.

Week 4

For this final week, spend the first fifteen to twenty minutes reviewing one more question from the worksheet. All students should share in their small group. The rest of the session can be used to finish the prayer cloths. You may want to provide beads or other embellishments for students to use in decorating the edges of the prayer cloth. Students can use the prayer cloth during their personal prayer time as a reminder of Christ's forgiveness granted by grace through faith.

Not every student responds well to each craft/art project. Some students may struggle with the creative expression. Encourage these students as you work alongside them. We have found the guest artists extremely helpful in encouraging all of our students to express their thoughts and faith through the arts.

DCE Audrey Duensing-Werner was serving Faith Lutheran Church in Topeka, Kansas, at the time this article was written. Audrey presently serves as minister to families with young children at Concordia Lutheran Church in Kirkwood, Missouri.

8

Small-Group/ Mentor Model

by Derek Broten

Surmounting the Obstacles in Confirmation Ministry

Identifying the Obstacles

Not long ago, the leadership team of Woodbury Lutheran Church observed, with growing concern, patterns of behavior in our confirmation ministry. For many years, we had a traditional confirmation model of weekly classes, utilizing large-group teaching and small-group processing. However, we started to observe very busy families struggling to keep their schedules straight. We noticed that several of our students were missing almost half of the confirmation nights. We saw a distinct difference between the students who attended consistently and those who were simply fitting it in at their convenience.

At the start of each new school year, we were also frustrated by a lack of teachers and small-group leaders willing to commit a year of their time to mentor and create relationships with our students. We were seeing some of the same tensions in our leaders as we saw in our families—hectic and erratic schedules. Many of our leaders wanted to be on the substitute list because they could no longer make a yearlong commitment.

We also observed that our leaders were excited about certain topics during the year but not about others. On the nights when the leaders were engaged with the topic, their small-group discussions went well. On the nights the topic did not interest them personally, the leaders often guided the conversations toward topics of greater interest to themselves. This was one area of our program that was inconsistent.

Toward the end of the children's ninth-grade year, we did exit interviews before they were confirmed. Our concern increased each year, as students were unable to answer basic confirmation questions. Several students were able to articulate answers that were rather scripted, but they were not able to apply them in a personal way to their lives. Each year, the interviewers got together after the interviews and discussed their increased concern about the lack of understanding and faith application apparent in our ninth grade confirmands.

During those interviews, we also determined that students were relieved to complete their confirmation instruction because they saw it more as a burden than an opportunity. These students were less likely to stay involved in the life of the congregation because they found the process similar to a school experience. There was little excitement about continuing their faith journey; many of our students approached confirmation much like a graduation ceremony. We wanted them to be excited about the process and connected to a lifelong journey of faith. We were hearing from more parents that they were tired of forcing their kids to go to confirmation. Once their children were confirmed, these parents left the decision about continued involvement in the congregation solely up to their children.

Addressing the Obstacles

Several of us felt we needed to make some adjustments in our program. We started by addressing the obstacles earlier. We also realized that we needed to come up with a system of accountability that clearly communicated expectations for those entering the program. While some expectations were stated, consistent follow-through was missing. This led to grumbling among some parents.

We started our program makeover by taking a full year to pull together key leaders and parents. From there, we developed a program that we thought would be more effective. We wanted our youth to grow in their faith and get excited about what they believed. We did not want students to feel like they were participating against their will. We sought to partner with parents and involve them in the process by equipping them for a significant role in their child's faith development, just as Scripture intended. We committed to find a system that would be more teacher-friendly, capitalizing on individual areas of passion. We also wanted to develop a system that would address the numerous conflicts between family and church schedules while providing some flexibility. After a year of research and development, we implemented our Foundations program.

Basics of Our Program

In order to accomplish the changes we felt were necessary, we made a major shift in the structure of our program. Instead of having seventh, eighth, and ninth grade confirmation classes, we decided to organize the program around class offerings rather than student ages. We took the Six Chief Parts of Luther's Small Catechism and divided them into a series of five-week sessions, requirements, and retreats. The overall course structure would be divided between required courses (thirteen courses everyone must complete) and elective courses (focused on different topics, contemporary culture, or interests—students must complete two). We also offered some sessions as independent-study classes, where students could complete a packet at home with their parent(s).

Selected classes require family participation. (For the complete course listings, see the chart at the end of this chapter.)

Here is a list of some of the classes we designed:

- **God's Relationship with Us** (Commandments 1–3)—Required
- **Our Relationship with Others** (Commandments 4 and 8)—Required, Family
- **Marriage and Sexuality** (Commandment 6)—Required
- **Celebration of Life** (Commandment 5)—Required
- **Lord's Supper** —Required, Family
- **Biblical Themes** (Bible Themes)—Required
- **Prayer** (Lord's Prayer)—Required
- **Stewardship** (Commandments 3, 9, and 10)—Required, Family
- **Creation** (First Article)—Required
- **Holy Spirit** (Third Article)—Required
- **Alpha and Testimony** (14-week class)—Required, final year course

We created a list of desired outcomes for each course, designed to guide the lead teachers as they organized their courses. We provide outlines of outcomes and lesson plans for each night but allow teachers the freedom to make the class their own.

Most classes were open to students of different ages, but we reserved certain classes for those in their final year of confirmation instruction. Each person in the confirmation program registers at the beginning of the school year for the courses that they have not yet completed. We allowed those with the most courses completed to register first. Once class registration reaches a predetermined number, that session is closed in order to keep the classes small and relational. Our goal is to have one large-group teacher and four small-group facilitators, with no more than six students in each group. We thought it was important to keep the size small in order to allow students an opportunity to open up and participate in the discussion.

On a typical Wednesday night, we offer six or seven courses during each five-week session. We also have three or four courses offered during the summer for students who either want to work ahead or catch up. Once in a while, we will offer a Saturday afternoon course to give students additional options. We try to offer a lot of flexibility. For example, if one of our students takes the first fall session off because of fall sports, we provide ways for the student to catch up.

Students can take these courses in almost any order they would like. We do ask parents to be involved in those choices, because they know best what their child may or may not be ready for. Since some classes contain content requiring greater maturity, we provide parents, upon request, a list of desired outcomes to help them guide their child toward appropriate course selections. One course—Alpha and Testimony— is a fourteen-week course that goes over the basics of Christianity. This class can be taken only by those in their last year of confirmation.

Another change in our program requires our students to attend retreats and conferences. We observed that when our students attend these types of events, relationships are formed with their peers in ways we could not emulate in our classes. Some retreats are required (Life of Christ Retreat—Second Article; Alpha Holy Spirit Retreat—Third Article). Our youth ministry offers five or six additional retreat and conference options every year. We provide a list of these retreats, trips, and conferences along with specific dates. Students must select two of these optional retreats each year.

In addition to instruction and relationship development, our leadership team felt it was important to teach and develop spiritual discipline. We wanted to challenge our students and families to live in ways that are pleasing to Jesus. Therefore, we designed a Spiritual Discipline section to encourage students to live a disciple's life. Requirements include worship attendance (students complete ten sermon summaries a year), Bible Study (attend Sunday School a minimum of thirty-nine times), life of service (complete a total of thirty service hours or one mission trip), and evangelism (bring a friend to church).

A key emphasis in the redesign of our program was to get teachers and students into God's Word and to use it. We challenged our teachers to use the stories in Scripture—not just verses—related to each topic. There was a heavy emphasis on practicality, using stories and problems that students could relate to and that would challenge them in their daily walk. We wanted to use this program to challenge them, to help them think more deeply. This changed the way we taught the material, encouraging the use of different materials on each topic, including video, Internet, music, and other forms of expression in their culture to help students connect Christ's story to their story.

In studying current research on the key role parents have in the development of their child's faith walk, we made some changes to encourage and equip parents in that role. We wanted to challenge the whole family system, not just one piece of it, so we developed three different family classes, which at least one parent per child had to attend. We designed independent study courses to be completed as a family. These packets require students to sit down and work through the material with a parent. Initially, this met with some resistance from parents who were not excited about giving up their evenings to attend classes. Because we intentionally made these sessions highly interactive and encouraged family communication, parents were grateful that we "forced" them to go through these courses. This continues to be one of the key parts of our program.

Adult Leader Shift

One of the obstacles in our old program was an increasing difficulty in finding leaders willing to give a full year to this ministry. By cutting the sessions down to five weeks, we were able to open up more opportunities for leaders to serve shorter time frames. Previously, we had some leaders who, because of business trips, would be gone for two to three weeks at a time, so they were not able to serve. We were thrilled at the willingness and availability of people to serve for five weeks in a specific class.

This shift also gave us a chance to talk to our leaders about the topics and areas for which they were passionate and had gifts and to give them leadership within those classes. Almost immediately, we found two men who had never taught confirmation, but they loved the topic of creation. They looked at this class as an opportunity to share their passion and knowledge about this topic. It also gave us a chance to connect them with one of three specific roles we identify in this ministry: lead teacher, small-group facilitator, and behind-the-scenes administrator.

One of the key positions in each course is our lead teacher(s). The lead teacher takes responsibility for the class design, content, and completing the outcomes for each class. The lead teacher is encouraged to design the class around all three learning styles—visual, auditory, and kinesthetic—and to be current, applicable, and interactive within each class. We give lead teachers the freedom to teach the class through different projects and styles, but we ask them to commit to designing their instruction around the predetermined outcomes for the course.

It is important to us that each class is meaningful to those serving as lead teacher. We wanted teachers who could tell real stories or have powerful testimonies in the areas being taught. We want lead teachers who are willing to be appropriately vulnerable in their struggles and experiences in the topic. We did not just want leaders who say, "Scripture says abortion is wrong." Rather, we wanted to bring in a person who could talk about her personal experience with abortion and tell her story.

Lead teachers work with the Confirmation Coordinator if any instruction or class problems arise. We have also teamed up these lead teachers with experienced curriculum writers. These writers help lead teachers overcome the challenge of developing the course outlines. We encourage lead teachers to make the material their own and to teach in a way that honors their style and the gifts God has given them. We also encourage lead teachers to use and team with their small-group facilitators.

In order to keep each small group a manageable and relational size, we try to have one small-group facilitator for every six students. These individuals help facilitate discussions and/or projects that the lead teacher assigns. We encourage each small-group facilitator to intentionally care for the five or six students in that group, which helps facilitate learning. We also encourage them to be the eyes, ears, and evaluators for the large-group leader and to give them helpful feedback in shaping the course. Group facilitators work with the lead teacher as a team, lifting up any individuals or issues that extend the program ministry.

We use two different approaches with our lead teachers and small-group facilitators. We encourage our lead teachers to teach the same course each time it is offered. This way, they can continue to redesign and try new things to make the class and material more effective. We also want them to stay in the topics for which they have passion.

With our small-group facilitators, we encourage them either to stay in the same topic and relationship with the lead teacher and together make that class better or to facilitate in another class that piques their interest. Some of our courses have developed strong core teaching teams, making these classes incredible. Some of our small-group facilitators sign up for different courses and, in a sense, go through their own confirmation experience.

The third role is a behind-the-scenes administrative role. Foundations relies on excellent administration to register people for classes; keep track of the requirements, classes, and retreats completed; and oversee all of the other information and communication of our program. In a congregation our size, this is a formidable task. We identify people with organizational gifts who like to stay behind a desk, enter data, register students, and track attendance.

By keeping the commitment level more manageable, we have seen our adult leadership participation double. People who would not normally teach confirmation found an avenue for their passion and gifts. Some leaders who reluctantly started behind the scenes discovered new gifts and are now serving as lead teachers. Our pastoral staff has the opportunity to develop a five-week course they can teach repeatedly, saving time each week on lesson preparation. It also gives our pastors an opportunity not to teach during especially busy times in the year, such as Advent and Lent.

The shift in adult leadership for the confirmation ministry brought new life and excitement into the program. As we continued to turn over more leadership to our congregational laypeople, we saw our leaders taking more ownership of and pride in the program. We discovered leaders who were passionate about their subject matter and loved to be there; their enthusiasm funneled down to the small-group facilitators and the students. With these changes, we have also seen an increased desire by adults who want to be a part of this program. Even though our required number of volunteers doubled, we have not had difficulty finding enough leaders to fill the spots.

Increased Accountability

Probably the most controversial aspect of the new Foundations program was creating requirements and accountability. Prior to implementing Foundations, we noticed an increase in students whose attendance was inconsistent and whose priorities gave other things precedence over confirmation. We knew we needed to raise the importance and priority of this ministry, while at the same time providing flexibility and options.

Under the Foundations program, each student has to complete thirteen required courses, two elective courses, the required retreat module, and the discipleship module. We allow flexibility for students and parents to complete this program at their own pace. We designed Foundations so that students could complete the program in less than three years by taking five sessions a year (twenty-five weeks of course work). If students choose to take some sessions off in order to participate in sports, theater, or other activity, or if students choose not to take some of the extra courses, they have the option of taking an additional year to complete the program.

Initially, a sizable group of parents objected to this increased accountability. They were used to a church that extended grace when they had schedule conflicts. At the beginning of the program, we had parent meetings, workshops, registration helpers, and one-on-one meetings to help parents understand why we were going to this system. We had great support and encouragement from our pastoral staff and educational staff, which helped ease some tension.

One individual in our congregation who had technology gifts created an accountability computer program to help parents and students see which classes they have completed, which ones they are signed up for, and how much they have completed on their Retreat module and their Spiritual Discipline module. This sheet serves as an important tool for communication and accountability tracking for parents. We identified three to five behind-the-scenes leaders to stay on top of all the data entry. (Remember, we are a large congregation, so we have a lot of data to enter.)

I must note that we tend to rule with grace in many cases, encouraging parents to keep us in the loop about what is going on with their families. We arrange additional options, depending on the obstacles families face. Some families chose to leave the congregation or not complete the program because they felt there were too many requirements. We intentionally followed up with each family and identified other options if our confirmation program did not work for them.

One of the great blessings we have observed is that with increased accountability and emphasis on attendance, our student participation has increased dramatically. Students who come and participate in class have a better chance to learn, grow, and connect with others in their small groups. With increased attendance in worship and at Bible study, we have seen growth in student knowledge as well. At the end of the confirmation process, each person desiring to confirm his or her faith has to participate in a one-on-one personal interview. Since this program began, we have noticed a significant increase in the knowledge and ability to apply faith to life issues. Through these interviews, we are able to identify areas where we need to improve our instruction so we can focus on those classes and content.

Obstacles We Still Face

We are very pleased with many of the changes we have seen in our confirmation program, especially the growth in our students and their families. It took us three years to implement these changes and make minor adjustments as we encountered new issues. We continue to evaluate and make changes in our curriculum, structure, and policy as we see new needs and possibilities arise. Although we are excited about the new structure, as with all changes, when you fix and adjust one area, other issues surface.

In our effort to increase accountability, one major obstacle we still face is the volume of data entry and records that need to be kept. It is easy to miss a detail here and there and frustrate parents who thought their youth had two more sermon summaries done than you have recorded, or that one of their classes was not marked as completed. We encourage parents to track their child's completed requirements and to be understanding and offer us some grace, given the number of kids we are tracking. We try to reconcile these issues with grace, trying not to make the data tracking issue a sour note in our relationship with the parents. Keeping track of all of this has become an enormous undertaking, causing us to form and equip a data team with the gifts required to take ownership in this area.

Another obstacle is connecting with parents who just want their child to go through confirmation but do not give spiritual growth high priority in their own lives. Beginning with our introductory meetings, we encourage parents who struggle with any aspect of the program to communicate with us and work with us on those issues. With parents who accept our encouragement, we are often able to help and support them through the program. However, some parents choose to deal with their issues on their own. In frustration, these families frequently drop out or switch churches, usually without communicating with staff. We try to follow up with these parents when we hear about their concerns, but by that point it is often too late.

Raising the expectations for the confirmation program has caused some families to reexamine the importance and priority they place on their child's faith walk and adjust their schedules accordingly. For some parents who do not make their child's faith formation a priority, we advise them that this program might not work for them and their schedule. Then we help them find another program that does. Still other parents increase their attention to their child's faith development, and in so doing, help their child attend more, connect more, and grow more. We try to let parents know that the more their student participates in the program and in reading God's Word, the more opportunities the Holy Spirit has to reveal truth and help students grow in their relationship with Jesus Christ.

Another major obstacle we wrestled with was finding more ways for kids to connect relationally within the courses. In our previous program, students were in the same small group all year. Relationships within the group were close, but outside of their own small group, students did not get to know others. Changing classes every five weeks, entering a new small group, and joining a new large group does not give students very long to connect with those in their group.

In our fourteen-week Alpha course, we have noticed that by the fifth week students are just starting to gain trust within their group. During the next nine sessions, these students continue to go deeper in discussion because of the trust they are building. We are exploring options for connecting courses in a ten-week session instead of two five-week sessions. We are also investigating the possibility of having small-group facilitators commit to a ten-week time block, following their small group to build on the relationships they have developed during the first five weeks. We have seen some wonderful results in our Alpha course because of those deeper connections.

In every change we make, we have found that it is important to consider all the ripples made by the change. If we do go to ten-week sessions, it will impact some adults who can commit to only five weeks. It may also afford less flexibility as parents try to register for different courses. We are also considering a mixture of both five- and ten-week sessions. We have come to understand obstacles as a good thing; the more we sit down with parents and involve them in the dialogue, the more they understand the decisions and obstacles we face and the more support they offer.

One Size Fits All

In a ministry like confirmation, where people enter with varying needs and expectations, it is apparent that no one program works for everybody. We designed Foundations for our large-church setting. The larger the church, the more flexibility you offer, the more challenging the program. I have been blessed to work with congregations who like our outline and structure but have a smaller number of students. A couple of congregations with smaller numbers of students use the five-week course concept developed for Foundations, but in a regular classroom setting. They establish the course schedule and decide which students need to take each class. This is much closer to the traditional model in which the church staff sets the schedule and expects students to attend each week. Then, they rotate in different lead teachers to run the courses. Some have a seventh grade and an eighth grade track, dividing it by grades. Others have cut the courses down to four weeks to shorten the confirmation program.

One of the things I love about this program is that it is designed to adjust to fit a congregation's culture and size. As with all meaningful ministries, you need to do it in a way that connects with the people you serve. The people in the community of Woodbury are different than the people in the community you serve, so adjustments are key.

Resources We Recommend

One of the great opportunities this program has provided is to depart from a one-size-fits-all confirmation curriculum and workbook. Lead teachers have the freedom, in consultation with our Confirmation Program Director, to look at different resources and curricula on their topic. For example, in our Marriage and Sexuality course, there is an incredible amount of curricula, books, and media resources available. Leaders can utilize different resources, depending on the focus and issue of each class session.

We encourage each lead teacher and small-group facilitator to use real stories and examples of experiences to which students can relate. In our World Religion course, we invite a person from another religion and engage in dialogue. When talking about our Creator, we invite someone from our local pro-life office to show a video of an ultrasound, go through Psalm 139, and talk about how God knits us together in our mother's womb.

We highly encourage videos, movie clips, music, youth stories, testimonies, and other things that bring a visual dimension to learning. We also provide projects and interactive learning for those who learn best that way. The use of creative arts is engaging for youth, so we include the arts as much as possible. Some existing curricula work well for a class like this.

There are great resources, including God Tube, YouTube, and Blue Fish TV, where you can find free or low-cost resources. We use skits and dramas by people like the Skit Guys to introduce topics or create discussions. We have an increased emphasis on creating quiet moments and helping our students slow down a bit. In some classes, we have students take a candle, find a quiet corner, and journal about the topic or answer questions. For our prayer class, we set up a prayer walk, where students experience different stations and are encouraged to reflect on specific aspects of their lives. They draw posters, using Scripture to describe what God says about different issues.

We are thankful that we took the chance and created Foundations. We are seeing some incredible growth, in both our students and their parents. We believe our curriculum and teachers now do a much better job at making classes relevant and exciting. We feel blessed that the Holy Spirit is using us to make a difference in the lives of our families.

Rev. Derek Broten serves as pastor for multi-site ministry at Woodbury Lutheran Church in Woodbury, Minnesota.

Foundations Modules
courses in white boxes are required

Class Module			Action Module	Retreat Module
Required Classes	**Independent Study**	**Electives**		
Shaded classes are required but may be done independently	These modules are done on your own if you choose to take a session off	Choose 2; also find 2 in the independent module	White boxes are required; shaded boxes—do one or both if you'd like	White boxes are required; choose 2 from shaded boxes
101F Foundation Intro (1 meeting with parent)		**E201** Life as a Servant	30 sermon notes (10 per year) from any church	Life of Christ Retreat
102 God's Relationship with Us		**E202** World Religions	Mission Trip	WLC Kick-Off Camp at Camp Omega
103 Creation: The Big Bang		**E204** Relief (formerly called Grief Therapy)	Servant Events or approved projects = to 30 hours (at least 2 sites/events) anything you do that you don't get paid for	Planet Wisdom/Mark Mattlock Conference (7th–12th)
104 Holy Spirit and Life Everlasting	**I308** Holy Spirit and Life Everlasting	**E205** Finding God in Media		Snow Riot Winter Retreat Last weekend in January (7th–9th)
105 Biblical Themes		***E206** How Woodbury Lutheran Works		Jr. High Lock-Out March/April (7th–9th)
107 Baptism: Claimed by Christ		***E207** Defending Your Faith	Attend 39 Sunday School sessions	WLC Youth Ski Trip (9th–12th)
112 Lord's Supper (6th Grade)	**I307** Family/Lord's Supper	***E209** Internet/Video Games and Faith (13/year) or Bible study		Sonshine Music Festival (9th–12th)
109 To Be or Not to Be	**E217** Family/Lent Study (independent study with family)	**E210** You're Made in God's Image (girls only)	Attend All-Dressed-Up drama with parent	TEC Retreat (9th)
110 Family/Our Relationship with Others	**E215** Family Dinner and 5 Movies (independent study with family)	**E211** Healthy Friendships	Invite a friend to worship	Alpha Holy Spirit Retreat (3rd year)
108 Marriage and Sexuality		**E212** Heroes and Role Models (boys only)	2nd year interview	Cornerstone Retreat First Saturday in October (3rd year)
111 Family/Stewardship	Stewardship	**E214** Other Denominations	Interview at completion of 3rd year prior to confirmation	
113 Prayer	**1301** Prayer: Connected	**E208** Tough Questions of Faith		Day Family Cornerstone Retreat (parents must attend with confirmand; 3rd year)
513 Alpha/Testimony (14 weeks+; takes full fall or full spring to complete; 3rd year only)				

9

Module-Based Confirmation Instruction

by Andrew Becker

Overview

In Deuteronomy 6, Moses instructs the people of Israel to impress His Word and Law upon the hearts of their children and to be constantly teaching and modeling and talking about His Word and Law with them. At the beginning of each chief part of the Small Catechism, Luther expresses his desire for the head of the household to teach the things of faith to his family. The home is the center of faith formation, and the church supports, encourages, and equips parents and grandparents for this task. Because we believe strongly in this partnership with the home, our congregation has sought to shift responsibility for the completion of confirmation instruction to the parents, involving them throughout the process.

Five years ago, our congregation switched to a modular, or unit-based, approach to teaching our junior confirmation students. The content we previously taught in a linear, ongoing format from week to week was separated into smaller, stand-alone units called modules. This shift was made to assist in increasing parental involvement and responsibility for faith instruction. Another contributing factor to implementing this switch to a different model was to create consistency for instruction and smaller classes sizes. Due to the hectic schedules so many of our families face, we wanted to provide flexibility by varying when confirmation instruction was offered. Finally, we desired to have others, beyond pastors, teaching classes. The involvement of more adults in teaching meant more faith mentors to positively impact each youth's faith development.

The grade level of participants, as well as the number and type of modules offered, have changed over the past five years. When we first switched to this model, we started with ten four-session modules that participants could complete during their sixth- through eighth-grade years. Each module was offered two or three times each year.

Five of the modules covered the Six Chief Parts, two modules gave an overview of Scripture, and three modules covered areas of Christian life. One of the ways that parents became involved was that they participated with their child on four of the specific modules. These were the ten original modules:

1. The Ten Commandments
2. The Apostles' Creed
3. The Lord's Prayer
4. Baptism
5. Confession and Communion*
6. Old Testament
7. New Testament
8. Practices of the Christian Faith*
9. Worship*
10. Mission and Ministry*

*A parent or faith mentor was required to attend these sessions with the youth.

After a few years, we saw a need for more instruction in Scripture, particularly concerning the life of Jesus. We removed the "Practices of the Christian Faith" module, incorporating the key content of fellowship, discipleship, and stewardship into other units. The new module we wrote, entitled "Jesus Christ," replaced the faith practices module; a parent or faith mentor attended this new module with each child.

We continued to see a need for improvement in the level of biblical knowledge with our participants, so this past year, we removed the three modules on the Bible from the modular approach and developed a program to cover the Old Testament with our fifth-grade students and the New Testament with our sixth-grade students. This leaves seven modules to be completed between the summer before seventh grade and the end of the eighth-grade year.

Below is an overview of how our program is currently structured and when the modules should be completed. The modules in the fifth and sixth grades are taken in sequence. The modules in seventh and eighth grade may be taken in any order.

Fifth Grade

- Creation and Patriarchs
- Slaves to Promised Land
- Empire, Exile, and Restoration

Sixth Grade

- Jesus Christ
- Acts and Revelation
- Letters to the Church

Seventh and Eighth Grade

- The Ten Commandments
- The Apostles' Creed
- The Lord's Prayer
- Baptism
- Confession and Communion*
- Worship*
- Mission and Ministry*

*A parent or faith mentor was required to attend these sessions with the youth.

This modular instruction is part of our church's overall confirmation program. Part of this program includes the junior confirmands serving within the church. During the fifth- and sixth-grade years, this service is limited to acolyte responsibilities. As students move into seventh and eighth grades, they may choose to serve as ushers or nursery volunteers, in music ministry, or on a media team.

When students have completed or are nearing completion of all of their modules, those being confirmed attend a confirmation retreat. This retreat reviews what students have learned, invites them to think deeply about their faith, and helps them talk about their faith with others. Finally, for their examination, each junior confirmand participates in a forty-five-minute interview with one of the pastors, where they share what they believe and what their faith means to them. Parents and an elder are also present for this interview.

Parental Involvement

As stated earlier, we believe parents have the primary responsibility of passing the faith on to their children. With our modular approach to confirmation, we seek to help parents fulfill this role. In fifth and sixth grades, each module is offered once a year at church. Parents are also given the material and training to lead the module in their own homes. Because we desire to have parents integrally involved in faith formation, at least one of the three modules each year is required to be completed by families at home.

As a participant moves into seventh grade and eighth grade, parents are still involved in all areas of instruction. After the schedule of classes is published, parents have the responsibility to register their child for the modules not yet completed. Parents must prioritize their family activities and schedules so that their children can complete the modules. The completion of memory work is also a responsibility given to parents. Most of the sessions also include a family activity. These activities provide parents ways to extend the lesson into the home. For example, after the lesson on the First Article, families are encouraged to go on a nature walk and talk about all of the things God has made. Parents also participate with their child in four of the modules. These classes allow parents to learn (or relearn) essentials of the faith. Throughout instruction with the modules, parents are learning and interacting with their child, allowing them to have essential faith conversations with their child. Parents are given instruction, ideas, and practice on how they can teach and model faith in their homes, including prayer and devotions. Parents are also encouraged to work with their children to prepare for their confirmation interview.

Class Size

As a larger congregation, we struggled with large class sizes. Typically, there are twenty to thirty participants per grade level. Depending on the format, we had a room of forty to fifty seventh and eighth graders receiving instruction at one time. Individuals could get lost in the class, and it was difficult for the instructor to have meaningful time with each participant. Because the modules are offered multiple times each year and participants' schedules allow them to take only so many modules in a given term, we were able to make our class sizes smaller. We now have classes of eight to twelve confirmation students (twice as many in classes where parents attend).

Smaller class sizes allow for increased development of relationships. The teacher and the participants are able to connect more in a smaller class. This means that the participants really sense the care and hear about the faith of the teacher. The teacher is also able to connect with and help individual participants in a personal way. Additionally, the smaller class size makes it more conducive for participants to get to know one another better in a nonthreatening environment.

Smaller class sizes also allow for a broader range of activities that would not be possible with a larger class. For example, this may include baking activities to reinforce the lesson; this would be too difficult to do in a larger class. It also allows for us to all come together and pray in a more intimate and less time-consuming fashion.

Module Leaders

It is helpful for the faith development of youth for them to observe a variety of people as examples of faith. Because of this, adults from the congregation, in addition to the pastors, are involved in confirmation instruction. We involve others in leading modules so students can hear the message of faith from teachers with a variety of backgrounds and experiences. In our context, besides pastors, we have had our director of Christian education, children's ministry director, seminary students, elders, and Sunday School teachers lead modules. Depending upon the education, experience, and knowledge of each of these individuals, the training for these individuals varies.

When we recruit and assign leaders, each person is assigned a specific module. That person becomes the only individual who teaches that specific unit. Because of this, each teacher has the opportunity to connect with each participant throughout his or her years of confirmation training. For example, I, as a pastor, am able to teach two modules. One of these modules involves the parents; the other has just the youth participants. I have the opportunity to teach a class to each participant both when their parents are involved and when they are not. This helps me to better build relationships with each participant. I also am able to connect in a deeper way with at least one of his or her parents. Because we have a specific teacher for each module, each participant will learn about the faith from many different individuals.

Flexibility

One of the strengths of this model of instruction is that it provides flexibility of schedule. When participants are in seventh and eighth grades, their families are given a course schedule of all of the modules being offered each term. Those modules are taught at various times and on different days, depending on the availability of our teachers and the schedules of our students. For example, one module might be on Wednesday afternoons in the month of September, while another module might be offered on Tuesday evenings in October. Families sign up for the modules that fit within their schedules and other commitments. By offering varied times and days, families are able to make confirmation a priority in their schedule without greatly impacting their participation in sports, scouts, or band.

Families also have the flexibility of knowing they will have multiple opportunities to take a specific unit. All of the modules are offered two or three times each year. All of the modules are offered sometime between August and December. All are offered again between January and April.

Most are also offered during the summer, depending upon teacher availability and the need for the specific module.

Counting the summers, seventh- and eighth-grade students have six different terms to complete the modules. Families manage the load by taking one or two modules each term. Below is an example of a module schedule for a specific term.

In the younger two grades, the flexibility is provided for families by empowering parents to lead the module at home. Because the base content for these modules is the Bible, we desire to have them taught in a chronological sequence. In the fall of the year, the first module is taught at church. If parents are leading this module in their home, they have from August to Christmas to complete the module. The second module is taught in the winter. If the parents are leading the module in their home, they have from January to March to complete the module. The third module is taught in the spring, usually after Easter. Parents have from April to July to complete this module if they are leading it in their home.

The Ten Commandments	Wednesdays 4:00–5:30 p.m.	January 5–26
The Apostles' Creed	Wednesdays 6:30–8:00 p.m.	February 2–23
The Lord's Prayer	Wednesdays 6:30–8:00 p.m.	January 5–26
Baptism	Wednesdays 4:00–5:30 p.m.	February 9–March 2
Confession and Communion	Tuesdays 6:30–8:00 p.m.	February 8–March 1
Worship	Sunday, March 13, 5:00–8:00 p.m.	Saturday, March 19, 4:30–8:00 p.m.
Mission and Ministry	Saturday, February 26, 9:30–11:00 a.m.	Saturday, March 5, 7:30 a.m.–1:00 p.m.

Participants in fifth and sixth grade must take one module at church and one at home, leaving the third module that year to be taught in whichever context the parents choose.

There is also flexibility within each module. Modules have four ninety-minute sessions. Normally, each module is taught over a period of four weeks, with one session taught each week. If, for some reason, a participant misses a session of a particular module, he or she makes that session up when the module is offered again.

Let's look at an example. Tim is a participant entering the seventh grade. During the summer, he took "Mission and Ministry." In the fall, his parents register him for "The Apostles' Creed" and "Confession and Communion." He was able to attend all of the sessions for "The Apostles' Creed," but he missed the third session of "Confession and Communion" due to illness. Over the next year and a half, "Confession and Communion" would be offered four more times, and Tim would have the opportunity to make up that third session any of those times in order to complete the module.

Families have varied structures and schedules—single families, families where both parents work, grandparents raising grandchildren—all having varying needs. Confirmation students are involved in many activities. Module-based confirmation offers them great flexibility. Some participants take three or four modules in a term, and some even finish all of the modules by their seventh-grade year and are confirmed at that time.

In order to offer all of these modules during the same term, pastors are not the only leaders of these modules. This allows flexibility in scheduling around the teachers' schedules as well. If teachers are gone for a conference, have another program in the church that they are heavily involved with at certain times of the year, or have any other conflicts, they can schedule their module for days and times that work best for them. Depending on the modules, some teachers have even scheduled multiple sessions of the same module on the same day, effectively turning the module into a mini retreat.

In the context of a busy culture, a module approach to confirmation instruction allows for great flexibility. Families are able to work with the schedule to make confirmation a priority. Instructors are also able to work with their families and work schedules to teach at times that fit with their many other time commitments.

Focus

Having modules provides a specific focus for each unit. Teachers, participants, and the overall curriculum all benefit from this focus.

Because most teachers teach the same module year after year, they are able to hone the modules over time. This enables them to dig deep, not only into the content, but also into how to teach the lessons creatively. Each instructor, regardless of his or her training, becomes an expert in a specific area. While given curriculum, teachers are encouraged to bring other activities and resources to help the participants engage even more in the lesson. Because of the narrow but deep focus that our teachers have, it has been easier to recruit and train teachers.

Because of the focus of the units, we are able to offer our participants consistency. All of our confirmation instruction happens within these modules. Whether a participant has attended our Lutheran Day School, Sunday School, or Vacation Bible School, all participants take all of the modules. This consistency has helped to break down barriers between these participants with varied instructional experiences. Also, because the units are taught by the same teacher, the content and presentation from term to term is very consistent.

While maintaining its focus, each module also appeals to different learning styles. Throughout a given unit, participants may be reading God's Word, doing group work, completing individual work, listening to a lecture, incorporating drama, presenting a story to others, cooking, or being artistic with colored pencils, markers, or play dough. Participants use their senses to smell, taste, touch, hear, or see in a variety of activities. Because of the focus of each module and how they have been designed, the student is able to learn in a variety of ways.

A modular approach is also adaptable because it allows for units to be added and created where more emphasis is needed. For example, we added more emphasis on scriptural knowledge. Others may want to have a module on church history or apologetics. Finally, because each unit is only four sessions long, teachers and students are more likely to remain engaged throughout the module.

Challenges

While this approach has been a blessing in our ministry context, it is not without some challenges. By God's grace, through excellent people who work with our confirmation curriculum, and by discerning our priorities in the program, we continue to improve every year.

One of the struggles of this approach has been a lack of class cohesion. Because participants in multiple grade levels can sign up for modules that work best for their schedules, all of one class is never together for confirmation instruction until the whole class meets for the preconfirmation retreat. While we offer many church and youth activities, it is difficult to develop into a close-knit group. Instead, our focus has been on encouraging and supporting the families so that they can build one another up even when the confirmation instruction has finished.

Another challenge actually stems from one of the strengths of the program—flexibility. Because of the great flexibility this program provides, confirmation class is not a constant on the weekly church calendar or on the family calendar. Parents need to take an active role to ensure that their child is signed up and comes on the correct evening. They also need to remember when they are attending with their child. Even with regular communication, some families seem to struggle with the varied schedule.

The administration of the program can also be a challenge. One of our staff members administrates the program. Each term, all the modules need to be scheduled. This is a process that involves communicating with each teacher to see when he or she is available to teach, working with the individual teacher to make sure that the class is offered at different times, and then working with all the modules at the same time so that most do not conflict. Once the schedule has been made, parents are given the schedule and a reminder of which modules their child has completed. Timely reminders throughout the term about when new modules are starting are an additional administrative task. Good record keeping and frequent and clear communication are essential to the success of a modular approach to confirmation.

Finally, while we strive to encourage, equip, and train parents to be the faith leaders in their homes, sadly, some parents choose to abdicate this leadership to the church. They struggle to work with their child to do home activities that enhance the lesson. Sometimes, the support is not there for the accomplishment of memory work, or they may not be timely or proactive in registering their child for modules. Occasionally, a parent may come begrudgingly with his or her child to modules where parents participate. A few of them struggle to understand this different approach to confirmation, which is a little more complex. This is by far not the majority of our parents, but it still poses a significant challenge.

Different Contexts

Although designed with a large church in mind, this approach could be modified to work well within a different context. Because the pool of teachers might be smaller, or the number of students smaller, each module could be offered only once a year instead of two or three times each year. While this diminishes some of the flexibility, in a smaller congregation, the schedules of more families may be known. Also, depending on the lesson, parents could be empowered to teach some of the modules at home, allowing the program to retain some of its flexibility while supporting the parents in their role as spiritual leaders.

Some congregations have a set time when confirmation, Midweek School, or other education programs happen. This modular approach could also be modified and used within a context where confirmation is always at the same time. Modules could also be sequenced and placed within this context. This would allow the opportunity for focus, other teachers, and even parental involvement in some of the modules, even if some flexibility may be lost.

Conclusion

A modular approach to confirmation has been a benefit to our congregation. Parents have become an integral part of the confirmation process. Not only are our youth participants growing in their faith, but their families are also growing on this journey together. The flexibility has allowed families to make confirmation a priority and has allowed for many adults to be involved in the instruction process. The classes continue to be modified and improved to better convey not only the truths of God's Word and our Lutheran doctrine, but also to provide opportunities to help deepen the personal faith of all of our participants.

Rev. Andrew Becker is associate pastor of St. John's Lutheran Church in Arnold, Missouri. Andrew is a 2010 graduate of Concordia Seminary in St. Louis.

10

Retreat/ Small-Group Model

by Krista Young

A Different Situation

Hope Lutheran Church in Wake Forest, North Carolina, may not be your typical Lutheran Church. For starters, our congregation is relatively young, both chronologically and demographically. Second, there are fewer LCMS congregations in the entire state of North Carolina than there are in some major Midwestern cities. This lack of tradition allows us to explore new ideas and directions for ministry. One of those areas involves the instruction and practices surrounding confirmation.

Confirmation instruction at Hope takes place during fifth and sixth grades, with the Rite of Confirmation administered at the end of sixth grade. We also moved away from a traditional classroom style confirmation instruction in favor of a combined retreat/small-group model.

An Overview

The key goals for our confirmation ministry are both instructional and relational. In developing Hope's confirmation program, we identified a list of outcomes that we desired for students. From those outcomes flow seven modules (or teaching components) on which we focus during the two years of instruction.

Outcomes

- Youth develop a positive relationship with their Lord, the pastors, the director of Christian education and youth ministry, and the church.
- Youth develop meaningful relationships with one another, forming a spirit that sustains the group as they move through the youth ministry program at Hope.
- Youth deepen their understanding of the Christian faith through an introduction to the Six Chief Parts of Luther's Small Catechism.
- Youth are expected to proclaim and live the Word and love of Christ.
- Youth are confirmed in the sixth grade year, either on Pentecost Sunday or the Sunday of the Holy Trinity.
- Parents join their youth in the journey of confirmation as partners with the church staff in teaching, leading, and praying for their children.

The Confirmation Instruction Modules

Module 1—Jesus in Your Heart and Life

- Connect youth to who Jesus is and what He has done for them.
- Connect youth to the power of their Baptism.
- Deepen youth's understanding of the power and authority of God's Word.
- Connect youth to the daily difference Jesus makes in their lives as they relate to their world, family, and friends.
- Provide youth with a sense of the "big picture" in the Bible, connecting the Old and New Testament message to the reality of Christ in their hearts and lives.

Module 2—Connecting to the Power Source

- Youth are introduced to the concept of the Means of Grace.
- Youth affirm the way in which God shares His undeserved love and mercy through Word and Sacrament.
- Youth deepen their knowledge of the meaning of Holy Baptism, affirming God's covenant promises made at their Baptism.

Module 3—Preparing for the Lord's Supper

(This is a spring retreat for the sixth graders and the nonconfirmed seventh through ninth graders)

- Youth discover the special gift of pardon and peace offered to them in Holy Communion.
- Youth are prepared for first Communion.

Module 4—Meaningful Life in the Church

(This is a parent/youth module for the sixth graders and the nonconfirmed seventh through ninth graders)

- Youth and parents grow in their understanding of the importance of faith, fellowship, and service.
- Youth and parents share their faith story.
- Youth and families are encouraged to stay connected to meaningful worship.
- Youth and parents affirm that confirmation isn't graduation.

Module 5—Keeping Your Relationship with Jesus Strong through Prayer

- Introduce the relationship youth can have with Christ through prayer.
- Use the Lord's Prayer as the teaching model.
- Form youth prayer groups.

Module 6—Getting Up Close and Personal with God

- Youth explore the deeper meaning of their confession of faith in God—Father, Son, and Holy Spirit.
- Use the Apostles' Creed as the teaching model.

Module 7—Loving the Lord with All Your Heart

- Youth discover the deeper meaning of the Ten Commandments and how to apply them to daily life.
- Youth explore what difference it makes when they know God's will and way.

We schedule the modules to flow in a specific order following a two-year cycle as follows.

Year 1 Schedule	
Fifth Grade	**Sixth Grade**
Module 1—Jesus in Your Heart and Life	**Module 1**—Jesus in Your Heart and Life
Module 2—Connecting to the Power Source	**Module 2**—Connecting to the Power Source
	Module 3—Preparing for the Lord's Supper
Module 5—Keeping Your Relationship with Jesus Strong through Prayer	**Module 4**—Meaningful Life in the Church

Year 2 Schedule	
Fifth Grade	**Sixth Grade**
Module 1—Getting Up Close and Personal with God	**Module 1**—Getting Up Close and Personal with God
Module 2—Loving the Lord with All Your Heart	**Module 2**—Loving the Lord with All Your Heart
	Module 3—Preparing for the Lord's Supper
Module 5—Keeping Your Relationship with Jesus Strong through Prayer	**Module 4**—Meaningful Life in the Church

Retreats as a Necessity

In its brief history, our congregation has outgrown its building twice. As a result, at one point, our facilities no longer allowed all the youth to meet in one room for instruction. Even though the next phase of expansion was in the works, we needed a more immediate solution.

Our leadership team felt it was vitally important for the pastors and DCE to have "face time" with the students in order to build relationships. So we designed retreats for the beginning of each confirmation module. During these retreats, the pastor or DCE teaches the core module content. For several weeks following each retreat, students meet in small groups to continue building relationships and process the information on a more personal level.

Our retreats change in format depending on the module and time of year. In the fall, we start with a Day Retreat at church. We meet from 9:00 a.m. to 2:00 p.m., with a break for lunch. This allows for three teaching sessions as well as breaks and community-building activities.

Day Retreat Sample Schedule

9:00 a.m. Arrive and get settled

9:15 a.m. "Getting to know you" activities and games

10:00 a.m. Jesus in YOUR heart and life

10:45 a.m. Break

11:15 a.m. Where do YOU turn for answers—the B-I-B-L-E!

12:00 noon Lunch

12:45 p.m. What do you KNOW about the Bible?

1:30 p.m. Closing devotion, prayer, and sending

Overnight Retreat or Lock-In

In the spring, we host our sixth graders at a nearby camp for a retreat based on Module 3—Preparing for the Lord's Supper. The youth especially enjoy the time in the woods and the camp atmosphere. We plan several breaks so they can get outdoors and enjoy God's creation.

Be sure to gather vital information before taking youth on a retreat or having them stay overnight at the church. Parent contact and emergency information should be with you at all times. Our parents fill out an emergency information form at the beginning of the confirmation year. We take these forms with us to each event so that we have vital information in case of an emergency. In some states, hospitals will not start treatment on a minor without parental consent. It's also a good idea to have your emergency forms notarized to avoid any questions.

We ask parents and youth leaders whom we trust and who relate well with young teens to help chaperone retreats. Before the trip, we run background checks on these volunteers. These leaders build relationships and help behind the scenes while the lead teacher conducts the lesson. Volunteer leaders frequently conduct small breakout discussions.

Overnight Retreat Sample Schedule

Friday

5:00 p.m.	Arrive at church
5:30 p.m.	Vans leave from church (McDonald's along the way)
7:30 p.m.	Fellowship and fun activities
8:00 p.m.	Focusing on the Sacraments
9:00 p.m.	Break and snacks
9:20 p.m.	Focusing on the Sacraments
10:15 p.m.	Evening devotions
10:30 p.m.	Quieting down time
11:00 p.m.	Good night!

Saturday

7:30 a.m.	Up and at 'em
8:00 a.m.	Breakfast
9:00 a.m.	Morning devotions
9:15 a.m.	Focusing on the Sacraments
10:15 a.m.	Break
10:30 a.m.	Group activity
10:45 a.m.	Focusing on the Sacraments
11:45 a.m.	Break
Noon	Lunch
12:45 p.m.	Group activity
1:15 p.m.	Closing Focusing on the Sacraments
2:00 p.m.	Closing devotion
2:30 p.m.	Pack up and leave
4:00 p.m.	Parents pick up youth at church

Small Groups

Our small groups meet on Wednesday nights as part of a program called Wednesday Night Alive. Our Wednesday Night Alive schedule has three seasons—Fall, Winter, and Spring. We break for the Advent and Lenten seasons. The Wednesday Night Alive program combines all music groups, children's ministry, adult education, and youth ministry in one place at one time. It begins with family dinner time from 5:30 to 6:15 p.m. During the dinner hour, musical groups rotate meeting times so participants can eat dinner before or after their practice. Our musical groups include children's choir, children's bell choir, and youth praise team. The adult choir meets at 7:30 p.m.

The "education time" goes from 6:30 to 7:30 p.m. Small groups meet in areas around the building. Each group follows the same outline. For Module 1—Jesus in Your Heart and Life, we use *God's Action Plan.* The lesson gives students memory work and ways to connect to the home. The group time consists of three main components:

- Group building

- *God's Action Plan* workbook
- Prayer

We conduct small-group leaders training at the beginning of the year and continue meeting quarterly throughout the year for support, encouragement, and training.

I cannot overstate the importance of training your small-group leaders. You cannot assume that leaders know how to effectively build group dynamics. There are a variety of Christian resources for training effective small-group leadership. Find and/or adapt one that works well in your setting.

We also found it helpful to establish a small-group code of conduct. Any number of possible codes may be found. We use the code outline to help lead the discussion—the youth come up with areas of concern, and we add or revise as needed. Our code of conduct looks like this:

Youth Ministry Code of Conduct

Who are we?
Why are we here?

"The people of Hope Lutheran Church are committed to proclaiming and living the Word and love of Christ."

The purpose of youth group (confirmation):

- Grow in faith
- Build friendships
- Have fun (the only way for everyone to have fun and be safe is by knowing and living within the following guidelines)

What do we do while we are here?

We study God's Word together, play games, watch movies, talk and listen (Acts 2:42–47), serve others, and grow in friendship.

How do we treat each other?

- Show love and respect (John 15:12)
- Understand that this is a "safe place" for everyone (physically, emotionally, and spiritually)
- Listen to one another; one person talks at a time (Proverbs 18:13)
- Care for one another—show sympathy or joy when appropriate
- Put the best construction on everything—no name-calling (Philippians 4:8; Proverbs 18:21)

- Show respect for the adults who are here (Leviticus 19:32)

Nonnegotiables:

- Illegal activities (drugs, alcohol, weapons)
- Total disrespect and rudeness
- Physically or emotionally hurting someone else

Each year, we begin with the discussion of who we are and why we are here. It helps remind the students of our expectations for our time together. Parents and youth sign a covenant at the beginning of the confirmation journey. That covenant states that they are committed to the confirmation time, and it maps out the expectations for their commitment to the group times. Each small group spends time together discussing how they will function as group.

Questions for small-group discussion include how we explain these guidelines when we bring friends to visit. It is our job to help them know what is appropriate here. It is also our job to remind one another of how we act here.

The small-group leaders have been impressed with the model we have adopted. In fact, they usually thank us for asking them to be leaders because they have so much fun and learn much in the process as well.

Confirming Youth Outside of the Plan

On occasion, we have older (junior high or high school) youth join our congregation who for one reason or another have not been confirmed. The pastors and director of Christian education and youth ministry attempt to identify youth in these age groups (grades 7–9) who have not been confirmed and work with them to complete confirmation through a special small-group process. Students in grades 10–12 who have not been confirmed are expected to attend the adult membership class. We try to schedule a separate confirmation date for these students rather than confirming them with the younger students.

Krista Young served ten years as director of Christian education and youth ministry at Hope Lutheran Church in Wake Forest, North Carolina. She now works with LCMS World Mission as a volunteer coordinator in Addis Ababa, Ethiopia.

11

Youth Ministry as Confirmation

by Steve Christopher
and
Timothy Potthoff

It's Wednesday evening shortly before 6:30 p.m., and the door to the gym at Our Savior Lutheran Church is unlocked by the youth director. Already waiting outside the door are Jeffrey and his twin sister, Annie. As the lights come on in the gym, these two quickly grab a basketball and start shooting some hoops. The youth director begins a conversation with them that gets him caught up on their recent trip to Mexico, their current athletic activities, and their musical interests.

Before long, the gym fills with over two dozen seventh and eighth graders. More basketballs are brought out; Nerf balls begin flying every which direction, hitting the kids with friendly affection. At 6:45 p.m., the family minister from Our Savior comes into the gym and begins interaction with the youth, getting hit by an occasional Nerf ball himself. And yet, in the midst of what looks look total chaos, other young people sit along the side of the gym on benches, enjoying friendly conversation.

Around 7:05 p.m., when it appears that most of the students have arrived, the youth director calls the kids to form a circle in the middle of the gym, has an opening prayer, and welcomes them to another evening of confirmation. He then explains the first activity for the evening, a game of Capture the Flag out on the grass field behind the gym. Some of the young people petition for a game of dodgeball but are quickly told that it is a nice evening outside and that dodgeball will be played in the coming weeks when it gets darker sooner.

So, out the door go the youth director and the two dozen plus group of adolescents—releasing much pent-up energy. The other ministry staff member goes to the church kitchen, located just off the gym, and begins preparing the snack, brought this evening by a member of the second-year class. In over two years, not a single person has forgotten to bring the snack, thanks to the church office staff that regularly sends out reminder postcards and emails.

Once the game has ended outside, the players come running in and over to where the snack is being served. Most of the time, they wait patiently to get a cookie, a bag of chips, or a granola bar and a drink. Upon receiving their treat, they gather again in a circle in the middle of the gym. As they eat, they hear about upcoming youth events from the youth director. They may also get an update on the paperwork they owe regarding worship service reports during the current confirmation quarter. One student raises his hand and indicates that he cannot acolyte this coming Sunday as scheduled and requests the opportunity to switch his date with someone else so that he can cover this required service activity.

Upon dismissal from the snack time at around 7:40 p.m., the students gather up their Bibles and catechisms, personal belongings, and confirmation notebooks, and go to their respective rooms as first-year students (usually seventh graders) and second-year students (usually eighth graders). Once there, the instructor begins the lesson on one of the Six Chief Parts of Luther's Small Catechism. This evening, the first-year students have a lesson on Baptism taught by the youth director, and the second-year class is taught the Ten Commandments by the family minister.

Later in the year, the senior pastor will teach Communion to the second-year students, and the family minister will teach the Apostles' Creed to the first-year class. In the course of the two-year program, these students will experience eight components over fall, winter, and spring quarters, covering the Six Chief Parts of Luther's Small Catechism as well as the units An Introduction to the Bible and Being a Christian Witness.

It is just about 8:30 p.m., and the class instructors wind down their lessons and close the teaching session with a word of prayer. Students grab their personal belongings and head out the door, parting company with "See you tomorrow at school" or "See you Sunday." The youth director and family minister clean up their rooms, head to the gym to make sure things are in order, and then go out to the parking lot to make sure students are picked up in a timely manner, giving them another chance to touch base with parents on individual concerns or scheduling matters for the week ahead.

The above account is a true story of a typical evening of confirmation at Our Savior Lutheran Church in Livermore, California. Even some of the names have not been changed. This is the same structure that has been used for confirmation at this church for over fifteen years. It may not look like confirmation to some. It may appear more like a youth night, and that is the express purpose of this design entitled Youth Ministry as Confirmation.

Purpose

The purpose of the confirmation instruction program at Our Savior Lutheran Ministries is to help nurture the faith of young people and see them grow toward more mature expression of their faith in word and deed.

Content

We use eight teaching components based on the instructional format of teaching the Six Chief Parts of Luther's Small Catechism, as well as additional Christian teaching vital for the development of faith in God's people.

Year 1: Usually as a seventh grader

- **Intro to the Bible**—Survey of God's Word in the Old and New Testaments
- **Baptism**—Sacrament of belonging and welcome to the Lord's family
- **Prayer**—Study of the Lord's Prayer and personal prayer life
- **What We Believe**—Apostles' Creed, key Church teachings
-

Year 2: Usually as an eighth grader

- **Christian Living**—Study of the Ten Commandments
- **Communion**—Sacrament of renewal and forgiveness
- **Worship and Confession**—Understanding how and why we worship as we do as Lutheran Christians
- **Sharing the Faith**—Our Christian witness and faith expression

Structure

We cover these eight components over the course of two years in six quarters, a fall-winter-spring schedule with time off for holidays. Classes meet from September until June. Class meetings are held on Wednesday evenings from 7:00 to 8:30 p.m.

Curriculum

Instructors create their own lesson plans based on their experience with and insight of the assigned component. Usually, handouts are given to the students, with overhead or PowerPoint outlines used to present the lesson. The teaching-learning design is purposely interactive between students and instructors, as we desire to see the faith "caught" by the students as well as the information "taught" by the teachers. The teaching staff includes the senior pastor, family minister, and youth director. A $25 fee covers the cost of a Small Catechism, three-ring notebook, and other program materials.

Format

The schedule remains fairly constant throughout the year. A typical evening:

7:00 Welcome and settling time in gym

7:10 Organized group-builder activity in gym or outside (see addendum for examples of these activities)

7:30 Snacks, provided by parent(s) and served in gym kitchen

7:40 Separate class sessions for Year 1 and Year 2 classes

8:30 Dismissal

Requirements

Class Attendance

We expect students to be in class on a regular basis and on time. If they need to be excused, they phone or email the church office.

Class Participation and Cooperation

We expect students to behave, to cooperate with their instructor, and to engage in the class process and content.

Worship Application Report

Every Sunday, we have several worship services offered at Our Savior. It is our hope that students will be in attendance every week. Worship is a central experience for Christ's disciples. To help facilitate a better understanding of the value and importance of worship for our confirmands, we ask for them to write a report of two worship experiences during the fall quarter, two during the winter quarter, two during Lent, and two during the spring quarter. Special forms/worksheets are available in the back of the church every Sunday. See addendum for an example.

Faith Expression (Second-Year Students)

In the past, confirmands at Our Savior have given a verbal faith statement or personal testimony during the annual confirmation banquet. We now offer other options for that faith expression, such as a video, a PowerPoint presentation, the singing of an original song, the writing of a poem or story, a drama production, or a visual work of art, in addition to the traditional speech/faith statement, all of which are based on the student's assigned confirmation verse. The presentation of these faith expressions takes place in the sanctuary on the evening of the confirmation banquet. They may also be shared in various ways with the wider community of faith here at Our Savior as deemed appropriate.

Banquet Arrangements

The families of the first-year students host a confirmation banquet for the confirmands. This project continues a long-standing tradition at Our Savior. The first-year parents and students plan the menu, set the tables, cook and serve the food, and do the cleanup as a gift in honor of the confirmands.

Acolyting

Acolytes assist in Sunday worship services. They light the candles as the service begins, collect Communion trays, and snuff the candles at the end of the service. Training is provided during confirmation class time at least once during the course of the year.

Some Final Thoughts

Parent Involvement

While the church staff directs the majority of the activities and does the classroom instruction, parents are expected to make sure their children attend church in order to complete the required number of worship reports and to reinforce the worship experience at home. Parents are also involved as snack providers and kitchen crew in the planning and serving of the banquet. Second-year parents support their child's faith expression project at the end of the second year.

Interchangeable Leadership

Over the course of some fifteen years that this model has been used, it has involved two senior pastors, an interim pastor, two youth directors, a DCE intern, an elder, a teacher from the Lutheran elementary school, various other congregational leaders, and a family minister. Because of the component teaching schedule, instructors can be scheduled at different times with varying topics so that they can teach to their strengths, and the students can experience the personalities and faith perspectives of a number of adult models during their two years in the program.

Family-Friendly Schedule

We offer a system of three distinct quarters: fall, winter, and spring. The last class of the fall quarter is the week before Thanksgiving, with classes not resuming again until January. This break gives families a time to catch their breath and offers them the gift of time during the busy holiday season. While we may lose class time with this long seasonal break, it seems to be offset by the goodwill created by giving families such a break. The same type of schedule break occurs during Lent, when our congregation offers a first Communion program on Wednesday evenings following Lenten worship. The confirmation program takes a break and starts up again after Easter vacation. Formatting confirmation in this way fills the niche of a regular youth night for this age group—no other junior high or middle school youth group night is scheduled, thus reducing the pressure on families to come to the church several times during the week.

Relational

This structure has a relational focus, where a high value is placed on students interacting with one another and on building supportive relationships for both the present and the future. Our community, while large in size, has a small-town feel, and with only two high schools, these students will likely have a number of their fellow confirmands as classmates during high school. After two years of being together in this setting, we hope that students develop strong relationships among themselves and the church staff members who will support them during the challenging high school years. The involvement of the youth director is integral to this process. He is always present at these Wednesday night gatherings in a leadership and mentoring role, establishing a strong connection with the students that can be built on in the years ahead. One delightful surprise has been the desire of students to bring their friends to these Wednesday evening gatherings, just as they might bring them to a youth night. We have seen some of these friends attend the program and eventually become baptized and confirmed members of the congregation.

Worship Report **Confirmation Program**

Name ______________________________ Date ____________________

What was the theme of the service?

How was the theme presented in various parts of the service?

Where were the elements of Law and Gospel present in the worship service?

How did the message/sermon stretch your perspective of faith?

What changes in your life might you consider as a result of the message?

What other points of life application did the service present?

Our Favorite Community-Building Activities and Group Games

Get-to-Know-You Games

Signature Scramble

Materials: One pen or pencil per person
One copy of the signature list

Hand out a pen or pencil and the signature list to each youth. Have the youth go around and obtain the necessary signatures. You can sign another person's form only once (unless your group is too small).

Example of a signature list:

- Has the same birthday month as you
- Likes the same flavor of ice cream as you
- Has the same hair color as you
- Likes the same favorite professional sports team as you (baseball, basketball, hockey, soccer, football)
- Writes with the same hand (left or right) as you
- Likes the same kind of candy bar as you do
- Has the same number of letters in their first, middle, or last name as you
- Likes the same favorite type of ethnic food as you
- Has the same color eyes as you do
- Parts their hair in the same place as you

Indoor Quiet Games

Clumps

Materials: None

This game can be played with a large or small group. Have some music playing as the youth walk around shaking hands. Stop the music, and call out a random number. The youth then need to get into groups of that number. When they have done so, have them sit down. In that group, they are to say their name and then answer a question that you call out. Examples of these questions: favorite food, favorite holiday and why, favorite color, something you are good at. When all groups have shared their answer for this round, have them stand, and then repeat the process.

Two Truths and a Lie

Materials: One 3 × 5 note card per person
One pencil or pen per person

As the youth enter, hand them a note card and a pencil or pen. Ask them to write on the note card two things about themselves that are true and one thing that is not true, but is believable. Get the group to sit in a circle. Have one youth at a time read the three items, and have the rest of the group guess which one of the three statements is the lie. If your group is large, separate them into small groups.

Outside Field Games

Capture the Flag

Materials: Enough cones to divide the field in half, to designate a flag area and a jail
Two different colored bandanas to use as flags

Before students arrive, set up the field with cones separating it in half. On one side, set one cone with the flag on it with three cones in a triangle about three feet around the cone with the flag. On the same half of the field on the opposite side of the flag, create a rectangle with cones to designate the jail. Do this for the other side also.

Rules: If a member of the opposite team is in the triangle around the flag, he cannot be tagged. If a member of the opposite team is on your side of the field and is not in the triangle around the flag, and gets tagged, she goes to jail. Once in jail, players wait for a member of their team to run to them, without getting tagged, to free them. Once this happens, the two of them get a free pass to walk to their side of the field. Once on their side of the field, they can go after the flag.

To win, a team must go over to the opponent's side and get the flag across the center line to their side without getting tagged.

Separate the youth into two teams. The teams should be as equal in number and athletic ability as possible. Play the game.

Extreme Steal the Bacon

Materials: Something to use as the "bacon" (hand towel or scarf)

Separate the youth into four equal teams. Have the teams stand in a straight line so that if you looked at the four teams from above, it would look like a square. Number off the youth on a team from one to however many are on the team. Make sure that you do not have the same number in the same corners of the square (i.e., number 1 from one team is not standing next to number 1 from another team). Place the "bacon" in the center of the square. Call out a number. Every person with that number enters the playing area and tries to get the bacon to his or her side of the square without being tagged by the other team. Those who succeed in getting across the line get a point. If they get tagged, no points are awarded. After each round, make sure the "bacon" gets put back into the center of the square. To make it more interesting, call out more than one number per round. Continue this until you want to end the game.

Three-Ball Soccer

Materials: Three different colored soccer balls
Two goals

Divide the youth into two teams with about the same athletic ability. Assign one team one goal and the other team the other goal. Distinguished by color, one of the soccer balls is a girls-only ball—only girls can kick that ball; another is a guys-only ball, which only guys can kick; and the third color is all-play, and anyone can kick that ball. Play the game like regular soccer with the standard rules applying.

Indoor Large-Room Games

Dodgeball

Materials: Foam or other soft balls that do not hurt on impact

Divide the youth into two teams and define the play area. Set the balls on the center line of the play area. To start the game, have each team go to the line on their side of the play area that is farthest from where the balls are. Shout "Go" or blow a whistle to start the game; the two teams will run and get the balls and throw them at the other team. If a youth gets hit by a ball on the fly, he is out. Define a place for those players to go and wait until a person on their team catches a ball or the game is over. If a player catches a ball, the one who threw the ball is out, and a member of the team that caught the ball can return to the playing field. Players who cross over the center line are also out. During the game, you can yell "Jail break," which allows anyone who is out to reenter the game. Use soft balls because head-shots can happen during this game. Volleyballs, basketballs, and shot puts are not recommended. If head shots get out of control, change the rule so that the one who threw the ball that hit another player in the head is out.

Ultimate Basketball

Materials: Minimum of one ball, up to as many as you want
Two basketball goals (indoor or outdoor court)

Rules:

- When a player has a ball, he or she cannot move

- To shoot, you must be outside of the key (of the basketball court)
- Shots scored outside of the three-point line are worth two points
- The goal is set on the out-of-bounds line
- There is only one goalie

Separate the youth into equal teams in number and athletic abilities. Assign one team to each of the two goals. After the teams are made and the sides are given, start the game with a jump ball in the middle of the court. The team that wins the jump throws the ball to other teammates, who move the ball down the court to get into position to shoot. The other team tries to intercept the ball.

This can be a highly competitive game for athletic guys. To keep the girls involved, have a rule that (x) number of girls need to throw the ball before a team can shoot. To add another level to the game, throw out more balls as the game goes on. Throwing out more balls quickens the pace of the game. The number of balls thrown out depends on the number of youth playing.

What Are We?

Materials: Nothing

Separate the youth into teams of five or six players. Each team is to create the image that you give them as it would look from above. Every member of the team must be part of the image. You and a couple of other leaders are the judges.

Examples of shapes (pick ones that can be successfully completed with the number of youth available in your group):

- Your home state
- A dog
- A cat
- Your church steeple
- A car
- A duck
- A tree with fruit
- A shark
- A baseball hat
- A pair of sunglasses
- Your youth group leader

Smaller-Room Games

Shuffle Your Buns

Materials: A chair for every youth

Put the chairs into a circle and have everyone sit in a chair. Choose a youth to leave a chair to be in the center of the circle, leaving one chair open. The game starts with the person to the left of the open chair moving into the open chair. The chair vacated by this youth is filled by the youth to the left. This keeps going on around the circle. While the youth are filling the open chair, the person in the middle is trying to get into it before the next person in the circle does. To create a chance for an opening, the leader can shout "Left" or "Right" as desired to change the direction of the group. If the youth from the center of the circle makes it into an open chair, then the youth to that person's left must stand up and be in the center of the circle, and the game starts again. Be sure that you have sturdy chairs, or replacements may have to come from the youth budget.

Give Me—Give Me

Materials: Nothing

Create teams with equal numbers of people. (If there are fewer than ten youth, have them all as one group.) Have each team come up with a team name. To begin, say, "Give me, give me (something that the group could give you)." A member of the group goes to where you are with the item or skill you asked for. The group that either does it first or has the most of the thing you called wins that round.

Continue for at least seven rounds.

Examples of things to ask for:

- $1.37 in exact change
- A person who can name the four states of the U.S. that begin with *W*
- A person who can recite the Fifth Commandment
- The person with the largest foot
- The person with the longest fingernails
- The person with the most letters in both first and last names

Musical Spoon

Materials: Plastic spoons
Jars of baby food
Recordings of Christian music

Have youth stand in a circle. Give them one plastic spoon. Start playing music. As the music is playing, the youth pass the spoon to their right. Stop the music whenever you want. Whoever is holding the spoon when the music stops has to reach into a bag and pull out a jar of baby food and a clean plastic spoon. This person is required to eat a portion of the baby food and is then out for the rest of the round. Continue the same process until you have a winner. The stranger the flavor of baby food, the more hilarious the facial expressions! For real fun, take off the labels so students will not know what they are eating.

Dr. Steve Christopher serves as the director of the Family Life Program at Concordia University, Ann Arbor, Michigan.

DCE Timothy Potthoff now serves as director of youth ministry at Hephatha Lutheran Church in Anaheim, California.

Section 3

Beyond Confirmation Instruction

Confirmation involves so much more than just instruction in the Six Chief Parts. In this section of *Confirmation Basics,* we explore some of the issues surrounding confirmation practice in your congregation.

12

When Is Confirmation?

by Jeremy Becker

When Is Confirmation?

It seems there are as many different confirmation models as there are Lutheran congregations. In recent years, many congregations have been rethinking long-standing traditions about their specific confirmation programs, especially concerning the *when* of the Rite of Confirmation. They want to determine if the timing of the rite makes a difference.

Nearly ten years ago, the time of year in which we celebrated the Rite of Confirmation in our congregation was drawn into question. Could it be that the traditional spring date was actually *preventing* spiritual growth opportunities for our confirmands? Was the Rite of Confirmation being confused or combined with graduation from eighth grade? How could we keep our youth involved in church after confirmation? These questions, and others, were asked. These questions, and others, created a movement toward changing the date of the Rite of Confirmation.

"Does the date when the Rite of Confirmation occurs have any affect on those involved?" It appeared to us that the answer was yes! Some parents of our youth were concerned that confirmation in the spring looked a lot like graduation. These concerned parents did not want their son or daughter to get the idea that confirmation was a "graduation" from church. Our research told us that this perception of graduating was very real. Statistics proved that youth stopped coming to activities after they went through confirmation. By the time our students became high school freshmen each fall, the percentage of active, involved youth dropped dramatically compared to our eighth graders. We found ourselves asking, "If confirmation was moved from the spring of eighth grade to a different time, could we resolve the loss of involved students as they transitioned into high school?"

Another question we asked was "Do youth going through confirmation feel pressured to make promises and be confirmed because it's the 'thing' to do?" Do students in a traditional confirmation program really want to make these promises at the Rite of Confirmation, or are they just going through the motions because of pressure from parents or the situation? If confirmation was at a different time of year, would youth feel more inclined to make promises because they want to?

With confirmation in the spring, our students finished their instruction and were confirmed almost immediately afterward. Our traditional confirmation instruction included few, if any, opportunities for parent and family involvement. If confirmation occurred at a different time of year, separated from the culmination of instruction, could we provide enhanced parent and/or family components?

Time for Change

The more we talked about keeping confirmation in the spring, the more we realized we needed to make a change. We decided that the Rite of Confirmation needed to move to the fall. This would mean that students would be confirmed in the fall of ninth grade instead of in the spring of eighth grade. We hoped and prayed that this change would provide many new positive outcomes. The decision to move to fall provided a number of additional opportunities.

Reformation Confirmation Celebration

Confirmation was not simply moved to any date in the fall; rather, we specifically chose Reformation Sunday. In choosing this date, we linked the Rite of Confirmation to a significant historic celebration in the Lutheran Church. Because we have a large number of confirmation students, we instituted a special afternoon service on Reformation Sunday for confirmands to make public promises of faith to God, their family and friends, and the church.

Growth in Maturity

We hoped that the extra five to six months would allow confirmands to mature a little more. One might not think that a typical freshman is very mature, but when you compare their thoughts on faith and their relationship with God from their eighth-grade year to their freshman year, it's amazing to see the maturity that occurs in that short span of time. Special summer events and new experiences on entering high school cause the young people to mature quickly.

Forced Faith Conversations

We wanted to create forced faith conversations in the high school setting. With the accelerated schedule of high school, confirmands are forced to decide how, or even if, they want to involve faith in their list of priorities. Many youth make promises in eighth grade not knowing that in high school they might not be able to live up to them or even remember what they said at confirmation. They find themselves forced to make a choice between some high school activities and their faith life or church life. By walking alongside students as they faced these struggles, we hoped to help them deal with the bigger conflicts they would face later in life.

A Hook for High School Youth Involvement

We often found ourselves asking, "How do we keep kids involved after confirmation?" By moving confirmation into high school, we hoped to establish a pattern of involvement by the high school youth in a group setting. We knew that our confirmands attended a wide variety of high schools in our area. Confirmation activities that we would plan for the fall of freshman year would help students realize that the youth group could be a place to get together and celebrate faith together, regardless of where they attended high school. By the time the Rite of Confirmation was celebrated, these students would have established patterns of behavior toward more active participation in youth ministry.

Confirmation Is a Beginning, Not a Graduation

Through our study, we found that if it *looks* like graduation, *feels* like graduation, has a *robe* like graduation, and is about the *same time* of year as a graduation . . . it must *be* graduation from church. This was a huge problem. The Rite of Confirmation should mark the beginning of one's adult life as a Christian. By moving confirmation to the fall, we hoped the activities surrounding the Rite of Confirmation both inside and outside of the church served as reminders of beginnings and fresh starts, which helped reinforce the idea of confirmation as a beginning rather than an ending.

Forced Confirmation versus a Choice

We hoped that moving the date of confirmation to the fall would give the youth a little more time to honestly and seriously commit to the promises of confirmation. We don't want youth making promises halfheartedly because they have a mom or dad forcing them to move through the program. By separating the Rite of Confirmation from the spring instruction, we hoped the youth would feel less forced and that they would question whether they wanted to make these promises. Our hope was that all the confirmands would choose for themselves if they wanted to make these promises. If youth were to decide they did not want to be confirmed, we were prepared to walk with them through continued instruction, study, and conversation in hopes that they would eventually feel prepared to make these significant promises to God.

Increased Family and Parent Involvement

Our former confirmation program had very little intentional parent or family involvement. With the move to fall confirmation, we knew it would give us some time to be intentional in how parents and families plug into the process leading up to the Rite of Confirmation. We planned activities at church and take-home pieces for each confirmand that involved parents and sometimes the whole family. These included service project ideas, faith conversations, home devotions, and other activities. We wanted to help parents be involved so that they would have an active role in the confirmation process and beyond.

A Plan for Action

In order to achieve our desired outcomes, we needed a detailed plan to make the change. It was decided that we would not change anything about how we currently lead instruction up through the end of the eighth-grade year. However, we put into place several pieces that would help transition through the summer and into the fall.

The summer plan included a family component, class connections, and a congregation module. Through these three pieces, we worked to involve the parents and family in the confirmation journey, brought the class together as a peer faith-support group as they headed into high school, and connected the youth to the greater congregation outside of the youth ministry area. There were scheduled activities and meetings, along with flexible programs and resources for confirmands to use in their home.

We created three intentional events for the fall, right as high school started, which required the class to work together as a whole. The first of these three events would be a confirmation retreat. At this retreat, the confirmands reviewed key pieces of their confirmation instruction that took place in junior high. The second event would be a public affirmation of faith. This public affirmation would take place during the regular weekend services the week before Reformation Sunday, allowing the congregation to hear, affirm, and pray for the confirmands. This event replaced our traditional questioning night. The last event, scheduled for the day before confirmation, provided time for a Baptism celebration with family and godparents, while also serving as a quick logistics practice for the Rite of Confirmation service. We planned this last event to help families encourage their child as they prepared for this major step in their faith journey. By including both parents and baptismal sponsors (when possible), confirmands were surrounded by their faith mentors on this night before publicly professing their faith.

With the plan in place, we began meeting with leaders of the congregation and, more important, with parents of the confirmands. We held several meetings throughout the fall, one year before the new Rite of Confirmation date was scheduled to occur. At these meetings, we were careful to articulate the goals and desired outcomes we had in mind by changing the date. A small group of parents were very much in favor of the change. We used them to share the excitement they had from a parent's perspective to help "sell" the new plan. We knew that 100% buy-in from all parents was not going to happen, but for the most part, parents were excited about the change.

During the first two years of the transition, we were deliberate about sharing our reasons for having the Rite of Confirmation in the fall in any and every meeting and gathering of confirmation parents. Communicating these values repeatedly helped ensure that everyone knew why we were making the change. Another key to the success of the date change was that we provided opportunities for people to express their thoughts and reactions throughout the change process. We listened to parents and the feedback they provided. We went out of our way to follow up with families who were not excited about the change to make sure they knew we still cared about them and valued their opinions. We remained open to changes or tweaks in the plan if it did not prove to be successful.

A Plan Becomes Reality

What we envisioned in the new confirmation date became a reality. Just three years after first celebrating the Rite of Confirmation in the fall, youth and families did not even mention the change. Our leadership team was excited that after only three years, confirmation on Reformation Sunday had become the new tradition.

The goals and desired outcomes have all played out. We retain more youth in high school ministries since the date change. Families are more involved in the process because of the added components. We have a great celebration on Reformation for the congregation, confirmands, and their families. Some youth decided they weren't ready to make promises with their class, but many of these youth continued in their study and confirmed their faith later in high school.

The two things that have impressed me the most regarding the date change include the maturity of the freshmen regarding issues of faith and doctrine, and the way it feels more like a beginning than an ending. I was overwhelmed by the difference in conversations with confirmands as freshmen compared to eighth graders in the spring. The experiences they encounter in the first few months of high school seem to challenge their faith in more ways than they expected. By "forcing" these faith conversations in high school, students think through decisions a little differently. It sets up a better pattern for Christian living and creates a peer setting in which students feel comfortable talking about these issues.

Confirmation feels more like a beginning now than when we celebrated it during the spring graduation season. As these young people begin a new chapter in their life as high school students, they are making promises to live as Christian young men and women.

As you ask the question "When is confirmation?" consider the long-term effects and impact of the date in the lives of these youth. For our congregation, the move from spring to fall has proven to be a positive change, not just for the confirmands, but for their families and the congregation as well.

DCE Jeremy Becker wrote this chapter based on his service at Concordia Lutheran Church in Kirkwood, Missouri. Jeremy currently serves St. Paul Lutheran Church in Weston, Florida.

13

Students with Special Needs

by Andrew
and Susan Bailey

Meeting the Needs

God desires His Word to be shared with all people, but how can you confirm in his or her faith an individual with special needs? Don't panic and worry that you are inadequate to share our chief articles of faith with this person. You don't need years of special training to help this child of God. By being attuned to the strengths and needs of the individual and refining your present skills, you will not only nurture this student, but you will more effectively reach your other students as well. The same basic rules and guidelines apply to teaching all students; they just apply all the more when teaching someone with a special need. This chapter will provide some general tips for teaching people with special needs (whether children, adolescents, or adults); list various specific special needs and offer suggestions for aiding these people in their growth; and share information about agencies, resources, and websites that can provide additional support.

In many cases, students with special needs can be taught in the regular confirmation class with some modifications or accommodations. At other times, it is best to teach the student individually or in a small group due to the need for more significant modifications or accommodations.

Modifications refer to changes in *what* students are expected to learn. Modifying the curriculum is done when the expectations are beyond a student's performance capability. The changes provide students the opportunity to participate actively and productively in the learning experiences at their pace and level of ability. Examples of modifications include requiring less detailed information and terms for the Six Chief Parts, being allowed to restate Bible passages or the Commandments with simpler words and phrases rather than memorizing them word-for-word, or having different criteria for class projects and assignments.

Accommodations are changes in *how* students gain information and demonstrate the knowledge they have learned. People learn and share information in a variety of ways. Changes or adjustments to classroom instruction allow a student to acquire knowledge and have the opportunity to express it in the way that is best for him or her. Accommodations include allowing oral answers rather than written for a test, having a study buddy for assistance and keeping on task, using a braille catechism, or having a sign language interpreter.

Regardless of whether you are teaching a confirmand with special needs individually or in a regular class, or whether significant or few modifications or accommodations need to be made, some general rules and guidelines should be considered. First and foremost, pray for your students by name. It is God who opens the hearts and minds of all believers. Ask God to guide you as you have the privilege to be His messenger to a new generation of believers.

Next, be caring and patient; teach by example. Loving patience and care are the greatest ways to show God's loving patience and care to your students, so they can see how they can live as forgiven, loving, patient, and caring children of God. Your examples of prayer; Bible reading; trust in God; repentance; regular remembrance of God's promise to you in your Baptism; regular worship and receiving of the Lord's Supper; stewardship of time, talents, and treasures; and general Christian living are the best lessons for all young believers. Special-needs students are especially impressionable. Your actions and example will speak volumes.

Talk with the parents and the child with special needs to learn about that child's needs, strengths, and interests. The parents, the child, and the child's teacher or special education support person are good sources of information for appropriate modifications and accommodations to use in confirmation class. Feel free to ask specific questions so you can present our faith in Christ and the catechetical instruction in the best way possible for the student. Also, use the websites and resources listed at the end of this chapter, or search the student's specific need online for many other ideas and suggestions to aid the child and open God's Word for him or her.

Getting Started

There are four steps you should follow for each class period. First, list the specific objectives you want your students to accomplish: the information, concepts, or abilities they should know, be able to do, or believe. At the start of each class session, tell your students what the objectives are. Then use the activities of the class period to teach and share the specific information, concepts, and/or abilities to your class. Finally, assess how well the students have accomplished the objectives.

When planning your objectives, carefully determine what key element should be taught each class session, and focus on that concept. Keep lessons simple and clear, with classroom activities pointed toward the most important idea to be shared. Think about what your student *can* do and what interests she *does* have, as opposed to what limitations she has and what she cannot do. Then adjust your lessons to her capabilities, always showing her specific and concrete ways in which God declares His love for her so she can declare God's love to others in her own genuine and honest ways.

Consider the modifications needed for a student to be successful in growing in his faith. Must he recite the Seventh Commandment and its explanation word-for-word, or can he simply know "I should not steal and, in fact, I should help people around me"? Does a child need to list all of the names, places, and details of David, Bathsheba, Uriah, and Nathan, or can she state that we all sin, but when confronted with our sin, like David, we can turn to God and trust in His forgiveness? We have a lifetime of information to share about God and His love for us, but so few lesson periods in which to share it. Be patient. Share one key point at a time, and marvel how God lays the foundation and, brick by brick, builds a solid structure of faith in a person.

Individual treatment is important for special-needs students. Each student is unique in the ways he or she can and cannot learn. Get to know your students as individual children of God. Listen closely to each child and observe carefully his unique interests, needs, likes, and dislikes, as well as his learning strengths and weaknesses. Place yourself in the shoes of the individual you are teaching. What assistance would you like or need in order to be successful, more fully understand the lesson, and be able to participate in class? Use activities and teaching techniques that center around a child's strengths. A student who has trouble expressing ideas orally may not be able to define God's grace, but may be able to draw a picture that shows she understands what the term means. Another may not be able to write anything for a short-answer question, but can answer the question orally. A third may have difficulty reading, but can role-play a Bible story. Audio and video Bibles may help some students focus and thus better hear and understand the lesson. Treating each student as an individual also helps you avoid stereotyping a person. Two children may have similar learning disabilities, yet have totally different likes and dislikes and ways of actually learning. Likewise, two teens may be deaf or blind or paralyzed, but have completely different personalities, aptitudes, and abilities. They need to be treated as individuals. Note once more, through this entire endeavor, that prayer and caring patience are vital.

Trying to individualize each lesson may seem difficult, even overwhelming at times, with one or two special-needs children in a classroom with a dozen other students you desire to teach. However, regularly using a variety of methods to teach a concept over a course of some time provides opportunities for students to experience their best method of learning, as well as receive needed repetition of the information. A person frequently does not learn an idea, fact, or piece of information the first time it is shared with him or her. We all need to hear, see, and experience a concept over and over again for it to sink in. This is even more true for a person with a special need. One reason for the repetitive cycle of the Church Year is so the basic stories of God's everlasting love can sink into us through a variety of means over time. Note the colors, symbols, special words, hymns, prayers, and Bible verses associated with the different seasons of the Church Year. Use these elements and the ideas behind them as you develop a cycle of information and faith-sharing experiences for your class. Review, readdress, and repeat concepts again and again. Varying your teaching methods and class activities can be invigorating, not boring; can help refocus the attention of the students; and can help all in your class gain a fuller understanding of each facet of God's redeeming love.

Making It Concrete

It is better to use concrete descriptions and ideas rather than abstract ones. Yet many theological concepts, such as faith, God (especially a three-in-one God), original sin, atoning sacrifice, eternity, the special nature of the Sacraments, forgiveness, and similar terms can seem very abstract. Consequently, throughout the ages, God Himself has made His enduring love for us as concrete, physical, and visible as possible. Israel's slavery in Egypt and God's physical redemption of them mirrors our slavery to sin and God's spiritual and physical redemption of us. Water is a powerful, cleansing, and refreshing tool God uses to wipe out evil and save Noah in Genesis, to free Israel from their enemy in Exodus, and to give us new life in Baptism. Like water in Baptism, bread and wine in the Lord's Supper are God's means to tangibly enter our lives. Jesus, God's Son from eternity, became human, exactly like us, to live for us through all our stages of life, from fetus to infant, toddler, child, tween, teen, young adult, and adult, so now we can truly live. Jesus used parables to describe the kingdom of God, the judges lived out God's redemption of His people from evil, and the prophets used illustrations of courtroom and marketplace scenes, potters working with clay, deserts blooming with life-giving water, marital faithfulness and unfaithfulness, and the like. From the earliest days of the Christian Church, believers used symbols and colors to visualize, express, and explain abstract concepts. Use these tangible elements, which students can see, hear, touch, taste, and smell, so they can understand the real and uniquely tangible ways in which God shows His redeeming love for us.

For instance, to illustrate that Christ is the solid rock in whom we can always trust, present an object lesson of the parable of the house built on the rock and the house built on sand (Matthew 7:24–27; Luke 6:47–49). In a roasting pan or automotive oil pan, pile a large, flat mound of sand, and also set in a stable rock (a brick will do). Have the students build two houses of interlocking blocks, toy logs, or other items, and set one on the sand pile and the other on the rock. Then pour in some water. Soon the sand will shift, and its house will tumble into the water, while the rock remains firm, supporting the house built on it. So Christ is the solid rock on which our faith is firmly anchored. And it is not we who made the rock or who anchored ourselves to it. It is our solid, ever-loving God who has done that. Still, God gives us a free will regarding the type of house we build on Christ (see 1 Corinthians 3:10–17, which is an entirely separate lesson that can be illustrated by reading or acting out the story of the Three Little Pigs).

Law and Gospel

As with any confirmand, if you have a child with a special need, it is important to share both Law and Gospel, not just one or the other. Do not make the lessons a moralistic practice of learning right from wrong. Because the Law is a concrete concept (do this, don't do that), while saving faith is abstract, we easily fall into the trap of teaching the Law without sharing the Gospel. However, God does not save a child because she is blind or deaf, struggles with reading or understanding, or has some other disability. Likewise, we are not saved by learning to do good works. It is only by faith in Christ's life-giving sacrifice and victorious resurrection that any of us are saved from the punishment of death and condemnation we deserve for our rebellious, sinful life. All of God's children are capable of growing in faith when people of faith live, talk, sing, act, and pray in that faith around them. Someone may plant, another may nurture, but it truly is God who makes faith grow in us (1 Corinthians 3:6–7), and He can and does work His miracle of faith in any one of us.

A family we knew in Michigan discovered during the second month of pregnancy that the skull of the fetus, their second child, was incomplete and would not close. As long as their daughter was in the protective environment of her mother's womb, she would grow and flourish. But once born, she would live only very briefly if she was not stillborn. The parents chose to go full term with their child rather than have the recommended abortion. Their son named his sister Angel. The family was regular in prayer, family devotions, and worship. And Angel worshiped with them. Angel regularly kicked and moved in her mother's womb when hymns were sung in church and when people responded with prayers and the Creed. She also moved when her parents or brother talked to her. When she was born, Angel lived only a few minutes, long enough to be held and be baptized. But Angel continues to be a powerful witness (for which the Greek word is *martyr*) of God's life-saving love and gracious gift of faith to her family, the congregation, us, and others. Indeed, God can make faith grow in any one of us, and He generously lets us be the instruments He uses to share that faith.

Even so, we should not ignore the Law, teaching only the Gospel. As Paul states, "Yet if it had not been for the law, I would not have known sin" (Romans 7:7). God gave us the Law so that we see our need for a Savior and learn how we should live as redeemed children of God. Special-needs children, too, are capable of learning and following God's Law. Use the brief answers and Bible verses in *Luther's Small Catechism with Explanation* and your knowledge of your student's life circumstances and abilities to guide you in determining how simple or deep you should make the study of each commandment and the need for repentance.

More Modifications

Though memory work may be modified, it still can and should be done with students with special needs. This is not to make a tedious, burdensome task for the students and teacher, but to create a joyful, expressive way to remember our God, give Him thanks and praise, and hear His words of guidance for our lives. Using music and repetition are the best ways to memorize. (Note how well this combination is used with commercials.) This is how our Old Testament forebears learned the Psalms and much of Scripture, and it has been an important reason for the use of the liturgy in the Church from its early days until the present. Many songs and hymns are Bible verses set to music and are excellent for memorization. For reinforcement, consider having a recording of these songs playing during times used for study, projects, or activities. Repetition and the regular use, in class, of memory verses, the creeds, and prayers makes it easier for students to remember these items in the future. Besides these ideas, you can break memory work into small chunks, slowly building to a whole. Do fill-in-the-blank memory games so a child recognizes and remembers key words and phrases. Play Hangman, using words from a memory verse instead of letters for a word, and for each word the student selects out of order, another stick is added to the Hangman.

Assessment, the final step for each class period, is any method of measuring or judging if a student accomplished an objective. This includes tests, quizzes, oral or written answers, role-playing, knowledge shared while playing a game appropriate to the lesson or unit, information shared during discussion time, and pictures or other art pieces made. An assessment is one way to check that your class goals are realistic and obtainable, and it gives you the opportunity to adjust these to fit the needs and abilities of your students.

Do not fault a child for not doing well on items you are not teaching, such as spelling, grammar, math, speaking clearly, sitting still, or understanding precise dates, terms, or names. Do not be afraid to let students know how they are doing in your class. Give feedback to your students as immediately and frequently as possible. They will not correct a mistake if they do not know it is a mistake. Praise and encourage your students for the goals they accomplish and learn. Recognize small, even minuscule, increments of growth, and offer genuine praise for each bit of progress. Especially show them the ways they live their faith and shine forth with the true wisdom of God. This, in fact, is the purpose of confirmation, to *confirm* to a person the true faith in God.

Consider these additional accommodation ideas and general information for teaching confirmation to individuals with special needs. If a special-needs child is in your regular confirmation class, do not seat that child where you can forget or "lose" him. Be attentive to the child, fully involving him in classroom activities and experiences. Make regular eye contact, and call on the child by name. Experiment with various seating arrangements to meet individual needs, placing the student near you as you teach or with space between neighbors if behavior interferes with others or nearness to classmates distracts the student.

Though a variety of teaching strategies, seating arrangements, and classroom activities are used, it is important to have a routine, an overall, consistent structure for your class. Knowing the basic procedures for class activities, whether starting and attendance routine, devotion time, quiet lesson period, or free-flowing discussion opportunities, students can anticipate what comes next through each stage of class. This relieves anxiety, provides security, and enables the student to focus better on the present task.

If you use the buddy system to assist a special-needs child, select a respected peer (older, younger, or a contemporary, depending on the situation) who can provide more individual and instantaneous assistance to the person in need. If a child has trouble writing, the buddy can share class notes with her or write down her oral answers for a worksheet. The buddy can read to one who has trouble reading or help a classmate review memory verses. A buddy can help a distractible child stay focused and on task. For physically disabled students, a buddy can help move the wheelchair, carry class supplies, guide a blind student through the hallways or around desks, or alert you to any special needs during class.

Let your class space and your presence be a safe haven for children with special needs. They may experience spiteful teasing or bullying. Do not tolerate it among any students in your class or presence. Pay attention to the words, actions, and body language of students as they interact with one another. Have a clear discipline policy, which gives the bully ownership of the problem while preserving his dignity. Many helpful tips can be found by searching online for "bullying" or "bully prevention."

Any copies or handouts you use should be clear, crisp, and legible. This is true not only for material you make, but also for commercially purchased products. Often, pages are too busy and the print is hard to find or follow. Similarly, be sure any information, directions, or instructions you give to a child or a class are clear, concise, and in words they can easily understand. Give only one or two steps of instruction at a time; do not expect students to remember a half dozen or more directions at one time.

Use specific interests of your students in your lessons. This will help hold their attention and connect each lesson to their everyday lives.

Create flash cards with a picture or name of a biblical character on one side. On the other, write the book of the Bible in which the character is primarily found or a description of that person's life and activities. Or make flash cards of a theological concept or term and the Church symbol that goes with it. You can quiz students with the flash cards, or they can take turns quizzing one another.

Have a reading time to acquaint students with reading from the Bible. You can read aloud to the students, or they can do the reading—either as a class or in small groups. Use simpler Bible translations or paraphrases for struggling readers. Adjust the reading length to the ability of the student. Do not force a student with poor reading ability to read aloud. Do encourage students to follow along as another reads. If you are teaching just one or two students, feel free to use your finger so they can see from where you are reading. Some students read better while moving around; others may need to use a colored overlay, hold the book upside-down, or block all but the portion from which they are reading. Be flexible, and encourage any reading they can do.

The variety of teaching strategies and accommodations is virtually endless. You can use games, small groups, puzzles, clay maps, cardboard images, puppets, large print, tape recorders, rice trays, posters, dance, and the myriad of other suggestions found on the websites listed at the end of this chapter. The key is to stimulate as many senses as possible: hearing, seeing, touching, smelling, and tasting, so more parts of the brain, heart, and soul are engaged in the learning and faith-building process.

Finally, be patient, caring, and prayerful with your special-needs student. He or she can learn many things, though it may take more time and a wider variety of methods. Still, the joy of watching a child of God grow in her faith is worth it. And the benefits for all students can be eternally joyous as well.

Specific Special Needs and Suggestions

Disabilities have strict medical and legal definitions for medical, insurance, and educational purposes. For medical and insurance purposes, cognitive disabilities are governed by the *Diagnostic and Statistical Manual of Mental Disorders, 5th edition* (Arlington, VA: American Psychiatric Association, 2013), commonly abbreviated DSM-5. For educational purposes, disabilities are legally categorized and defined by the federal government through the Individuals with Disabilities Education Act (IDEA). Section 504 of the Americans with Disabilities Act (ADA) uses broader definitions of what constitute disabilities for general societal and additional educational situations. Meanwhile, states and local school districts use various names to describe the same disability, such as mental retardation, educable mentally impaired, and cognitively impaired. In addition, "special needs" is a non-legally binding, very broad, catchall phrase generally used to describe children who do not have an identifiable disability and do not qualify for special education services, but do require additional help and support of some sort in order to learn and succeed in school. Consequently, confusion occasionally arises when a pediatrician or psychiatrist describes a disability based on the medical treatment, the school psychologist and teachers use the educational terms, lawyers and courts sometimes use narrow definitions and other times broader ones, and a family moves from one state to another and tries to describe their child's special needs.

Fortunately, for our purpose to provide confirmation instruction to all eligible individuals, the definitions of each disability need not be so precise and limiting. Our concern is to recognize that people can have a variety of special needs and to see how the need can be overcome so the Gospel can be proclaimed.

In general, a person with special needs has limitations in one or more of the following areas of ability: physical, cognitive, communication, social or emotional, or adaptive. For educational purposes, IDEA lists thirteen groups of disabilities: specific learning disability, speech or language impairment, visual impairment, hearing impairment, deafness, autism, emotional disturbance, mental retardation, orthopedic impairment, traumatic brain injury, other health impairment, deaf-blindness, and other multiple disabilities.

Physical disabilities include being deaf or hard-of-hearing; blind or visually impaired; having an orthopedic impairment such as cerebral palsy, muscular dystrophy, poliomyelitis, arthritis, paralysis or missing limbs; suffering from chronic diseases such as sickle-cell anemia, hemophilia, AIDS, HIV, other auto-immune diseases, diabetes, leukemia, and cancer; or coping with any other situations affecting one's muscles, body, and physical response. Physical limitations do not imply mental limitations. Physical accommodations and adaptations, however, may be needed. Examples include sign language interpreters; amplification systems; braille or large-print Bibles, catechisms, and other literature; hand rails; soft chairs; limited walking; class sessions done in the home; and a flexible schedule to enable instruction despite frequent absences.

Cognitive disabilities occur when the chemical, electrical, or other systems of a person's brain or nervous system do not function properly or optimally. Cognitive disabilities include learning disabilities, speech and language disorders, behavioral disorders, and mental impairments. Learning disabilities, speech and language disorders, and autism are communication disorders as well as cognitive disabilities.

Learning disabilities include reading, language, math, and attention deficit disorders. A child with a learning disability is not mentally retarded or slow. These students often have average or higher intelligence coupled with an inability to process or store information completely or efficiently. Consequently, they have very active, innovative minds, while struggling with reading (dyslexia), writing (dysgraphia), using numbers (dyscalculia), memorization, and/or recalling information. They also often have difficulty understanding abstract concepts. Their minds are full of ideas, but they may have trouble expressing those ideas or understanding ideas expressed to them. As a result, some are unable to focus their attention for more than a few minutes. Note that there are several types of learning disabilities. Individual children will not necessarily have all of these problems or have them with equal severity.

People with dyslexia or a learning disability, along with the blind and visually impaired, are eligible for free recorded books. For details, contact your local school district or library or Recording for the Blind and Dyslexic (listed at the end of this chapter).

Attention Deficit Disorder (ADD) can occur either with hyperactive behavior or with passive, underactive behavior. Likewise, a child with ADD may or may not have additional learning disabilities or other special needs. The root cause of ADD is not over-activity but poor concentration. The inability to focus can lead to other behavior problems, such as distractibility, disorganization, and impulsiveness.

Speech and language disorders are two very different categories of impairment. A person has a language disorder if she has difficulty expressing her ideas to others or has trouble understanding the connotation or denotation of words spoken to her. Language disorders are types of learning disabilities. If a person has difficulty producing speech sounds correctly or fluently, or has problems with voice fluctuation and articulation, then he has a speech disorder. Lisping, stuttering, and slurred speech are examples. Selective mutism is an anxiety disorder, not a speech or language disorder. The parents, or perhaps the child in a nonclass setting, can share communication methods with you.

Students with a behavioral disorder exhibit inappropriate behavior or feelings under normal circumstances. They have great difficulty making or keeping friends or establishing or maintaining basic interpersonal relationships with peers or others. They need a rigid class structure with clear, consistently enforced rules and an established routine that is regularly followed.

Tourette syndrome is a condition that many in the general population consider a behavior disorder; however, it is not. It is suspected to be a genetic abnormality of a person's neurotransmitters, the chemicals that carry signals between nerve cells. Sufferers have involuntary muscle movements and vocal utterances, which can be disruptive in group settings, especially if others are unaware of the cause. The Tourette Syndrome Association website listed below has excellent suggestions for assisting a child in class.

Mental impairments, also called developmental disabilities or adaptive impairments, include mental retardation, Down syndrome, and autism. A person with one of these conditions has difficulty learning and adapting to work, life skills, and the general culture around him. Mental retardation is usually divided into three categories based on a person's abilities: educable mentally impaired, trainable mentally impaired, and severely mentally impaired. Down syndrome is a congenital mental deficiency caused by an extra chromosome and can have a mild to severe effect on a person.

Autism significantly affects verbal and nonverbal communication and social interaction. Autistic individuals often engage in repetitive activities and stereotyped movements, resistance to change in their settings or daily routines, and unusual responses to sensory experiences. The autism spectrum, likewise, ranges from mild to severe, and includes Asperger syndrome and pervasive developmental disorders.

Many, perhaps even most, individuals with developmental disabilities can be confirmed. However, it is important for the pastor, the parents or guardians, and the individual with the disability to consider if that person can properly examine himself or herself for Communion. Similar consideration needs to be made for those who have suffered a traumatic brain injury. Significant modifications to the curriculum may need to be made. Accommodations can include the use of flashcards with symbols for key concepts and terms; allowing very simple answers, such as "not steal" for the Seventh Commandment or "Jesus loves me" for what God has done for the student; or allowing the student to point to answers on a communication tray.

Students afflicted with schizophrenia and other psychotic disorders can be very lucid and have no problem in a regular confirmation class. They also may have serious delusions that prohibit them from actively being involved in confirmation. As with students suffering from chronic physical illnesses, so, too, students suffering from chronic mental illnesses may need a flexible schedule to enable instruction despite frequent absences.

Much more specific information and details regarding various modifications, accommodations, and teaching strategies can be found with the resources below or by conducting an online search.

May God bless your words and actions so these children may truly hear and understand God's love for them and grow in His grace and keeping. And may you have the beautiful feet God provides to carry you into their presence to share God's saving Word with them. "How then will they call on Him in whom they have not believed? And how are they to believe in Him of whom they have never heard? And how are they to hear without someone preaching? And how are they to preach unless they are sent? As it is written, 'How beautiful are the feet of those who preach the good news!'" (Romans 10:14–15).

Andrew and Susan Bailey have been active in Lutheran education and volunteer ministries for over thirty years. Andrew has an MAR in historical and exegetical theology; Susan has an MA in special education.

Resources for Further Study

Concordia Publishing House neither endorses nor disclaims any of the information available through the following sources. This resource list is provided simply for your information. Web addresses were accurate at the time of printing.

General

Books

Three excellent books that share many practical ideas and suggestions and are easy for a layperson to use:

Cherne, Jacqolyn. *The Learning Disabled Child in Your Church School.* St. Louis: Concordia Publishing House, 1983.

Haag, Kimberley, Keith Kaspar, Elizabeth Dziak Kryst, and Edith Young. *Common Solutions for the Uncommon Child (K–8).* St. Paul, MN: JIST Publishing, 1995; Danville, IL: The Interstate Printers and Publishers, Inc., 1982.

Bethesda Lutheran Homes and Services. *Building a Developmental Disability Ministry: A Manual for Congregations.* Watertown, WI: Bethesda Lutheran Homes and Services.

Organizations

Lutheran Special Education Ministries (LSEM)
6861 E. Nevada, Suite 2, Detroit, MI 48234, 888-488-LSEM (5736)
www.luthsped.org • lsem@luthsped.org

LSEM's website is an excellent portal with links to thirteen of the sites listed below. Its National Resource Center responds "to inquiries with ideas, strategies, advice and counsel," and provides "instructional materials and consultation services that accommodate children with special learning needs in confirmation class, Sunday School, and Vacation Bible School."

Bethesda Lutheran Homes and Services
600 Hoffmann Dr., Watertown, WI 53094, 800-369-4636
www.blhs.org/resources • ncrc@blhs.org

Bethesda operates the National Christian Resource Center, which provides "resources worldwide to families of people with developmental disabilities, and to pastors, volunteers and professionals in the field of developmental disabilities." They publish *Breakthrough*, a free quarterly magazine of resources and ideas for providing Christian training to individuals with developmental disabilities. Bethesda's Religious Education Catalog includes a Bible study curriculum package for adult individuals with developmental disabilities, *Exploring Faith and Life*, which is very useful for confirmation instruction. The NCRC and Bethesda's catalogs offer many other resources, including the book *Building a Developmental Disability Ministry*. Its website includes links to a variety of "other sites with spiritual and secular information on developmental disabilities."

The National Dissemination Center for Children with Disabilities (NICHCY)
P.O. Box 1492, Washington DC 20013, 800-695-0285
www.parentcenterhub.org/nichcy-resources/ • nichcy@aed.org

This site provides much general information for supporting those who assist children with disabilities, as well as "research-based information on effective educational practices."

National Institute of Neurological Disorders and Stroke (NINDS)
www.ninds.nih.gov

NINDS is part of the National Institutes of Health. Its website contains excellent, brief descriptions for hundreds of neurological disorders, with links for each disorder to numerous other institutes and support associations.

Local Lutheran Special Education Organizations

Milwaukee

Lutheran Special School and Education Services (LSSES)
9700 W. Grantosa Dr., Milwaukee, WI 53222, 414-461-8500
www.lsses.org • info@lsses.org

St. Louis

Lutheran Association for Special Education (LASE)
3558 S. Jefferson Ave., St. Louis, MO 63118, 314-268-1234
www.lutheranspecialed.org • lori.christiansen@lutheranspecialed.org

Local Public School Districts

Most local public school districts are very willing to help members of their community with ideas for modifications, accommodations, and resources to serve and support children with special needs. If the child is receiving service from the local school district, his parents can put you directly in touch with his special education teacher or consultant (signing a waiver may be required) so you can receive specific advice regarding effective learning strategies and teaching techniques. Otherwise, contact your local school or district office, indicate you are a volunteer who will be helping to teach a child with a special learning need, and ask to speak with a special education consultant. States also have broader educational service agencies that often provide certain specific special education services to groups of local school districts. Depending on your state and location, these may be called Intermediate School District (ISD), Cooperative Educational Service Agency (CESA), Regional School District (RSD), Educational Service District (ESD), and the like. Feel free to contact them for advice and guidance. Your state department of education website should have information for and links to these agencies.

Other Educational Resources

Lutheran School Portal
www.lsportal.net • membership@lsportal.net

Lutheran School Portal is an excellent resource for Lutheran educational ministries. Though primarily geared toward day schools and early childhood centers, several links and resources offer great support for any volunteer educational ministry in Lutheran congregations, including confirmation instruction of special-needs individuals. Membership is required.

Lutheran Education Association (LEA)
7400 Augusta St., River Forest, IL 60305, 708-209-3343
www.lea.org • lea@lea.org

The LEA website contains a variety of resources, forums, and emailing lists for school educators and parish educators. Membership is required to access some of the resources and services.

Hearing Impaired

The Mill Neck Family of Organizations
Frost Mill Rd., Mill Neck, NY 11765, 800-264-0662
www.millneck.org • info@millneck.org

Mill Neck is a Recognized Service Organization of the LCMS dedicated to enhancing the quality of life for people who are deaf or have other communication needs. It does this by providing educational, vocational, and spiritual resources.

Blind and Visually Impaired

Lutheran Braille Workers, Inc.
P.O. Box 5000, 13471 California St., Yucaipa, CA 92399, 909-795-8977
www.lbwinc.org • lbw@lbwinc.org

Lutheran Braille Workers publishes, free of charge, biblical, Christ-centered literature in braille and large-print formats.

Recording for the Blind & Dyslexic
National Headquarters, 20 Roszel Rd., Princeton, NJ 08540
866-RFBD-585 (866-732-3585) • www.rfbd.org

RFB&D is the leading accessible audiobook library for the visually impaired and dyslexic.

Speech Disorders

American Speech-Language-Hearing Association (ASHA)
2200 Research Blvd., Rockville, MD 20850, 800-638-8255
www.asha.org • actioncenter@asha.org

The Stuttering Foundation
800-992-9392
www.stutteringhelp.org

Learning Disabilities and Attention Deficit Disorders

National Center for Learning Disabilities
www.ncld.org

The website includes an Educator Center and Topics by Age sections.

The Schwab Foundation for Learning
www.schwablearning.org

Funded by Charles Schwab, this well-established site assists individuals with special learning needs. It links directly to the special-needs page of Greatschools.net: Learning Disabilities, www.greatschools.net.

LD OnLine WETA Public Television
2775 S. Quincy St., Arlington, VA 22206
www.ldonline.org • ldonline@weta.org

LD Online contains a variety of resources and information concerning learning disabilities, learning differences, and attention deficit disorder. Their Q & A and Expert Advice sections are rich with information and ideas.

LD Resources
www.ldresources.org • rwanderman@gmail.com

Richard Wanderman is an educational consultant and an LD adult who gathers an array of articles, resources, topics, and links for individuals with learning disabilities and shares these at this site. The site has been upgraded to a blog, providing RSS feeds and the ability to comment.

The International Dyslexia Association
40 York Rd., 4th Floor, Baltimore, MD 21204, 410-296-0232
www.interdys.org

CHADD (Children and Adults with Attention Deficit/Hyperactivity Disorder)
8181 Professional Place, Suite 150, Landover, MD 20785
www.chadd.org

National Resource Center on AD/HD
800-233-4050

Attention Deficit Disorder Association (ADDA)
15000 Commerce Pkwy., Suite C, Mount Laurel, NJ 08054, 856-439-9099
www.add.org • adda@add.org

Tourette Syndrome

Tourette Syndrome Association, Inc. (TSA)
42-40 Bell Blvd., Suite 205, Bayside, NY 11361-2820, 718-224-2999
www.tsa-usa.org

Autism Spectrum, Asperger Syndrome, and Pervasive Developmental Disorders

The Gray Center for Social Learning and Understanding
4123 Embassy Dr. SE, Kentwood, MI 49546, 616-954-9747
www.thegraycenter.org • info@thegraycenter.org,

Autism Society of America (ASA)
7910 Woodmont Ave., Suite 300, Bethesda, MD 20814-3067, 800-3AUTISM (800-328-8476)
www.autism-society.org

O.A.S.I.S. (Online Asperger Syndrome Information and Support)
www.udel.edu/bkirby/asperger/ • bkirby@udel.edu

Barbara Kirby is the parent of a child with Asperger syndrome. Her website, hosted by the University of Delaware, and her book *The OASIS Guide to Asperger Syndrome* contain a wealth of information to assist children and adults with Asperger syndrome, autism, and cognitive differences in general.

Down Syndrome

National Down Syndrome Society (NDSS)
666 Broadway, 8th Floor, New York, NY 10012, Helpline 800-221-4602
www.ndss.org • info@ndss.org

Behavioral Disorder or Emotionally Impaired

Dakota Boys & Girls Ranch
P.O. Box 5007, Minot, ND 58702-5007, 800-593-3098
www.dakotaranch.org • info@dakotaranch.org

Dakota Boys & Girls Ranch is a Recognized Service Organization of the LCMS that offers a safe setting for troubled teens.

14

Special Celebrations

by Cheryl LaBelle

Take a moment and think about the special activities your family does for certain events. For example, some families have an annual tradition of buying a Christmas tree for their home. The whole family loads up into the car the day after Thanksgiving and drives out to the tree farm. The kids run around seeking out the perfect tree for Dad to cut down, and once the family gets it home, Mom makes popcorn and hot cocoa while the kids decorate the tree with ornaments that have been collected and passed down for years. It sounds like a lot of fun and might even give you a case of "warm fuzzies" if it is anything similar to what your family does. With every special celebration, we have set activities that provoke emotions, memories, and even teachable moments for our own children.

The Church is no different. In fact, we use a Church calendar to guide us in celebrating the full life of Christ from birth to death. Through these special days, we remember what Christ has done for us in the past as we look forward to the promise of heaven yet to come. We use colored vestments, paraments, and banners to represent various emotions and elements of each season of the Church Year, and we have selected readings and songs that enhance our worship experience. We celebrate biblical historical events such as Christmas, Easter, and Pentecost, and we incorporate other events that are meaningful to our own congregation and the Lutheran Church, such as Reformation, confirmation, and church anniversaries. As adults, we experience the Sunday worship service and walk away with the pastor's message, but we may not always understand the meaning behind why we do the things we do, unless someone teaches it to us. Confirmation is a perfect time to teach your youth the history of the Christian Church and how important and meaningful special celebrations really are. It is something you hope these young people will remember for years to come and even teach to their own children. This chapter gives examples of some special celebrations you can use with your confirmation students to teach them about our Christian past and present. Hopefully, it will inspire you to bring in even more ideas and opportunities.

Advent and the Twelve Days of Christmas

"On the first day of Christmas my true love gave to me . . ." Does that sound familiar? December shopping tends to leave us humming familiar tunes, and often they are more focused on Santa Claus and what the kids want than on the true Christmas account. Use this time with your confirmands to emphasize the significance of Jesus' birth. Help them to focus on the coming of our Savior. What would things be like if He hadn't come yet? For one thing, we would probably still be sacrificing animals and making burnt offerings in the temple. Take this time to look at how society focuses on Christmas: the music, the television specials, the ads, the parties, and the lack of Christ on His special day.

Santa Claus is based on a real person. Concordia Publishing House offers a great resource for teaching about the original St. Nick—*Saint Nicholas: The Real Story of the Christmas Legend* by Julie Stiegemeyer. Read the book to your students, even if they protest that they are too old. (Make some hot cocoa and cookies for them to snack on—that should quiet their complaints.) Challenge your kids to find out how St. Nicholas, a real pastor from Lycia, turned into the jolly fat man people celebrate today. Do a little research on the Internet and share some interesting facts. For example, did you know that Santa used to be portrayed as a short, elflike man dressed in green? It was actually Coca-Cola and its advertising department that created the image we are familiar with today. Do you know why we bring trees into our home and decorate them? It comes from a German pagan ritual of bringing a part of nature into the home for worship.

A little research into what we celebrate and why can amuse and amaze you. But more important, it offers a great example of how Satan uses his powers to distract us from the truth of God's Son and focus us on worldly things.

Getting back to the twelve days of Christmas—it's more than a song. In fact, it is a season in the Church Year that begins on December 26 and leads up to Epiphany, or the coming of the Magi. Often, we think these days lead up to Christmas, but it is more appropriate to celebrate them afterward with our parties and hymn sings. Surprise your youth and have a Christmas party the Sunday after Christmas. See how many parents come up to you and ask if it is a typo in the bulletin. During the party, you can ask the youth how many of them know all the words to "The Twelve Days of Christmas." Aside from the song sounding like a collection of odd gifts that would cost a ridiculous sum of money, it is thought to have been used in sixteenth-century England as a mnemonic device to teach the basics of Christianity and the catechism. Here is one interpretation of the symbolism behind each set of gifts:

- **My true love**—God the loving Father, who has given us many gifts
- **Partridge in a pear tree**—Jesus, God's Son
- **Two turtle doves**—Old and New Testaments
- **Three French hens**—three theological virtues: faith, hope, and love (1 Corinthians 13:13)

- **Four calling birds**—four Gospels: Matthew, Mark, Luke, and John
- **Five golden rings**—first five books of the Bible: Genesis, Exodus, Leviticus, Numbers, and Deuteronomy
- **Six geese a-laying**—six days of creation: Genesis 1
- **Seven swans a-swimming**—gifts of the Holy Spirit (Romans 12:6–8)
- **Eight maids a-milking**—Beatitudes (Matthew 5:3–10)
- **Nine ladies dancing**—fruit of the Holy Spirit (Galatians 5:22–23)
- **Ten lords a-leaping**—Ten Commandments (Exodus 20:1–17)
- **Eleven pipers piping**—faithful disciples (does not include Judas, who betrayed Jesus)
- **Twelve drummers drumming**—twelve major points of doctrine in the Apostles' Creed

The Seder

Among many Jewish festivals, the Seder is one that we as Christians can celebrate today with added meaning. The New Testament is a fulfillment of the Old Testament, and we often focus heavily on the Gospel without remembering the events of the past. Many of the festivals that the Jews celebrated were intended to remind them of what God had done for them years ago. As Christians, we can lay claim to that same history as God's chosen people, since Christ died for all nations. We can look at the people from early centuries and relate to them, recognize our own sinfulness, and rejoice in the reminders of how God has blessed and saved us from our sin and oppressors just as He did in the days of old.

One of the most well-known events from the Old Testament is that of Moses and the exodus from Egypt. Through miraculous events, Moses was hand-picked by God from the beginning of his life and then used for God's greater purpose to deliver His chosen people from their bondage. The tenth plague that befell the Egyptians was the death of the firstborn son among men and animals. The Jewish people were specifically instructed to take a year-old male lamb without defect, slaughter it, roast it, and eat it with bitter herbs and unleavened bread. They were to take some of the blood from the lamb and put it on the sides and tops of the doorframes of their homes. In these homes, God would not take life, but instead would pass over them. This is how we received the word *Passover*, and it became an annual festival for the Jews to celebrate and remember how God delivered them.

Seder, a Hebrew word for "order" or "procedure," is the dinner that takes place on the first night of the Passover celebration. It is a commemoration of the exodus and a popular Jewish tradition celebrated as a family in the home; everyone participates. This was considered the primary means of teaching children about the exodus. At the time of Christ, many families made the pilgrimage to Jerusalem, that their lambs could be sacrificed in the temple. We know that Jesus celebrated this festival as well. In fact, we read about it on Holy Thursday. Jesus entered Jerusalem for the Passover with His disciples. He requested an upper room in which to have an intimate Seder meal with them. This was also His Last Supper. Here He instituted Communion for His disciples and all Christians. The image that often comes to mind is Leonardo da Vinci's painting *The Last Supper*, which is a fairly accurate picture of the relaxing and reclining that would have taken place at such an event.

While the meal has evolved over time, the Seder contains many significant elements, including a lamb, unleavened bread, *moror* (bitter herbs), *haroseth*, wine, the reading of the *Haggadah*, or the retelling of the story as related in the Book of Exodus, and the singing of psalms. Two candles on the table are lit by a woman, because it will be a woman who brings the light into this world (it was Mary who gave birth to Jesus, our Savior).

The *Pesach*, or lamb, is necessary because it is what God instructed the Israelites to eat. They were to pick a male lamb without defect or broken bone. Then the blood was used to mark the doorframe. The lamb was roasted and eaten. By partaking in the Seder, Jews of today experience the same experience as their ancestors years ago. Today, we know that Jesus is our Paschal Lamb, who was without sin or broken bone. If you think of the design of blood on a doorframe, both the top and the sides, it creates an image of the cross—all of which foreshadows our Savior, who shed His blood on the cross. The lamb's blood saved the Jews that night, while Jesus' blood saves us from the death we deserve because of our sin. Each time we partake of Communion, we, too, remember Christ's death and resurrection by eating and drinking His body and blood, a command He gave in Luke 22:19 and that is repeated during the worship service in the Words of Institution.

Matzo, or unleavened bread, was used in the exodus because there was no time to leaven it with yeast. It is referred to as the "bread of affliction" because it was made of only water and flour. The Jews shared this bread together as a sign of unity. Unleavened bread must be pierced several times so that it does not create large air bubbles. This gives a beautiful representation of Christ, whose body was pierced multiple times for us. There is also an association of leavening with sin. Since the bread is unleavened, it also reminds us of Jesus' perfection and lack of sin. Three loaves of bread are used, the second of which is broken. Some Christians think of the three loaves as representing the Trinity—Father, Son, and Holy Spirit. When the middle matzo is broken, it represents the crucifixion of Jesus for our sins. A piece of bread designated as the *afikoman* is wrapped in a napkin and hidden for the children to seek out and find. For Christians, this symbolizes Jesus' burial in the tomb and resurrection from the dead.

The *Moror*, or bitter herbs (parsley), are dipped in salt and eaten with horseradish to remind the Jews of the bitterness of slavery and the tears shed under Egyptian rule. As Christians, we are reminded of the bitterness of our slavery to sin. However, just as God delivered the Jews from their bondage, Christ has released us from ours.

Haroseth, a mixture of chopped apples, nuts, cinnamon, and wine, represented the mortar used for the many building projects the Jews were forced to complete. In John 2:19–22, Jesus compares His body to the stone-and-mortar temple. Like the temple, His body was torn down; but unlike the temple, his body was raised to new life.

Wine at the Seder was originally drunk from a common bowl to express the unity of the people. Four glasses are drunk in the traditional Seder to represent the four statements from Exodus 6:6–7, in which God declares, "Say therefore to the people of Israel, 'I am the LORD, and *I will bring you out* from under the burdens of the Egyptians, and *I will deliver you* from slavery to them, and *I will redeem you* with an outstretched arm and with great acts of judgment. *I will take you to be My people*, and I will be your God, and you shall know that I am the LORD your God, who has brought you out from under the burdens of the Egyptians'" (emphasis added). During Jesus' Last

Supper with His disciples, He took the third cup of wine, also called the cup of blessing, and consecrated it.

The *Haggadah*, or retelling the story of the exodus, is one of the most important aspects of the Seder, because it fulfills God's command in Exodus 13:8–10: "You shall tell your son on that day, 'It is because of what the LORD did for me when I came out of Egypt.' And it shall be to you as a sign on your hand and as a memorial between your eyes, that the law of the LORD may be in your mouth. For with a strong hand the LORD has brought you out of Egypt. You shall therefore keep this statute at its appointed time from year to year." In this way, the children are taught about God's mighty acts and love for His people through the exodus.

The singing of psalms is the final aspect of the Seder, as is the singing of prayers of thanksgiving to God for His deliverance. Psalms 113–118 are appropriately titled the Egyptian *Hallel* and were sung throughout the meal.

Jesus is our Passover Lamb, and we as Christians can celebrate the Seder meal with new meaning. He is the perfect Lamb, who delivered us from our sin with His own blood. This is a great experiential teaching opportunity in which to include your confirmation class and their families or to experience as a congregational event led by the youth.

There are a variety of ways you can host such an event. If you have a small confirmation class, invite them to your house (or a house that is accommodating). Consider inviting families to participate as well; each family could bring one of the items. As leaders in the church, we encourage personal devotions as well as family devotions outside of Sunday morning worship. Bringing the Seder into the home is both traditional and a great way to build family spiritual growth.

If you want to host a larger congregational Seder, ask your youth and their parents to help with setting the tables and preparing the food. The event can be as lavish as you like, with a whole feast, or simply a sampling of the traditional foods. Advertise the event early so that you know how many to prepare for. If cost is an issue, sell tickets or ask for a door offering. Get your pastor involved in this as well. Not many adults are fully aware of the Seder. Perhaps your pastor would be willing to lead a sermon series through the Lenten season focusing on a different food or aspect of the Seder during each service. On Palm Sunday, host your Seder for the congregation and then experience the new and deeper understanding Holy Week and Easter have for your youth.

There are helpful websites where you can find an order of service for a pre-written Christian Seder. Messianic Jewish sites such as Apple of His Eye and Jews for Jesus can be helpful, as is the website for Congregation Chai v'Shalom: www.chaivshalom.com/Chai_vShalom/Resources.html. Your pastor may also have resources, or perhaps he would be willing to write his own for your use. Consider contacting some local churches or your District Office to see if any of them have led such an event. They might give you permission to use their service.

Pentecost

As Christians, we are living in the days after Pentecost and are awaiting Christ's return on the Last Day. God gave us the gift of the Holy Spirit on Pentecost to grow our faith and equip us to spread His Word. This is an important lesson to teach youth in a world where tolerance is preached and Christianity is frowned upon. We hold the truth in our hands through the Holy Bible; however, there are so many people whose eternity is condemnation because they do not know the truth and are filled with the lies that Satan spreads. Look at the story of Pentecost in the Bible (Acts 2).

After Jesus was arrested and crucified, the disciples ran and hid, afraid that they, too, would be punished. Upon Jesus' return, they were emboldened by their Savior and then equipped by the Holy Spirit with flames of fire and the ability to speak in tongues. Many people were brought to faith on Pentecost Day.

Often, we are hesitant to jump up and share our faith, but on Pentecost Sunday, or even on the Sundays after Pentecost, it would be appropriate to celebrate the gifts of the Spirit by encouraging our youth to think about their faith. It is easy to be afraid to talk about our faith because of the risk of being rejected; however, we must be bold in sharing this faith and realize that Christ, too, was rejected. He suffered for us, and as His chosen people we are chosen to suffer for the sake of Him (1 Peter). But we are not left alone in this task. God has equipped us with His Word and the Holy Spirit, who opens doors and gives us the words we need at the right time.

There are several ways we can give our students practice at sharing their faith. We have a set of three creeds, or "I believe" statements, that lay out our beliefs. Challenge your youth to write their own creed to instill ownership of their faith. Another idea is to take a day and break kids up into small groups, where they can practice role-playing. Assign some youth to be Christians and others to be nonbelievers. Give them experience at facing adversity within a controlled environment, and be ready to discuss the outcomes. Opening your classroom up to this teaching style might open your eyes to see what your kids' friends and environments are saying about God, religion, and the world.

Encourage your youth to pray out loud to build up their confidence and overcome their insecurities. God loves to hear us speak to Him, no matter what it is about, and He promises to hear our petitions. With cell phones and computer technology, our youth have plenty of experience carrying on conversations with others, so have them focus on speaking with God their Father and Jesus their personal Savior. Use the Lord's Prayer as a guide for the different kinds of petitions they can offer. Encourage them to work in groups and take requests from one another. Then have them pray out loud. If you are interested in having your youth bond and care for one another, this is a great way to achieve that. It can also bring about accountability and a closeness that we as Christians have through Christ's love.

Galatians 5:22–23 references the fruit of the Spirit: love, joy, peace, patience, kindness, goodness, faithfulness, gentleness, and self-control. All of these gifts enrich our Christian character. Incorporate this Scripture into a lesson, and challenge the youth to look at their personal lives. Ask them to give examples of how they live out these gifts or how their parents, friends, media, or other role models show these gifts in their character and behavior. Challenge them to find areas of their lives where they need to improve, and hold them accountable by following up with them at a set time.

A spiritual-gifts inventory is a wonderful tool to use with youth to help them find where their strengths are and areas where they would be good at serving the Lord. While your youth are young and still developing into the wonderful adults they will become, this is an interesting activity for them to learn more about themselves. It should be clear that the inventory is not a final, end-all statement about who they are, but a tool to help them discover who they are today. There are several inventories available from various publishing houses and websites. Some are highly detailed and might be better put to use after being shortened. Consult with your pastor to see what resources and thoughts he might have regarding this topic.

Finally, this is also a great time to talk about how God calls each of us. He has made us His children through Baptism and brought us to faith through the Holy Spirit. How else is He calling your youth to be disciples for Him? This would be a great time to discuss church work among your students. The Concordia University System offers a list of careers within the LCMS, such as director of Christian education, parish musician, deaconess, teacher, and pastor. For those youth who attend public schools, hearing about these options at church may be the only way they learn about the possibilities for their future.

The Reformation

The Reformation had a huge historical impact on Europe. It was the first time that someone challenged Catholicism in a public forum, was excommunicated from the Catholic Church, and survived to tell about it. Whereas most accused heretics were burned at the stake and used as an example to warn others not to oppose the Catholic Church, Martin Luther opened the door for Christians to read the Bible and interpret it for themselves. He emphasized that our salvation is through grace and not works, and he challenged the power of the pope himself. Luther wrote many books and hymns that we use regularly in the Lutheran Church today. However, his actions are spoken of beyond church walls. Public schools also teach of Luther as a historical figure and of the role he played in the Reformation, which began in Germany and spread throughout Europe.

Your confirmation class will have heard of Martin Luther in some setting or another, so use this time to teach your students a little more about him within the context of being a Lutheran. Emphasize that he was not only a great man but also one whom God used to help spread the truth of His Word. There are many approaches you can take, from reading out of a textbook to finding interesting facts your youth never knew. Your church library, Concordia Publishing House, and the Internet are all great resources for in-depth information.

Have a Marty Party! Find quotes from Martin Luther and other famous Martins or Luthers (Lex Luthor, Martin Luther King, etc.). See if your students can figure out who said what. Talk about how important it is to be able to read the Bible for yourself. Discuss how God used one man to stand up for the faith and how He prepared Luther for what was yet to come. Luther originally studied law but then left the university to become a monk when he was caught in a terrible thunderstorm. Luther was not trying to start his own denomination. Rather, he wanted to debate, and correct, the false teachings being spread by the Catholic Church. He began the process with the posting of the Ninety-Five Theses in Wittenberg, which led him and many other Christians down a life-changing path.

There are two great movies about Luther that are good to have your youth watch. *Martin Luther,* starring Niall Maginnis and distributed by Unicorn Video, is a black-and-white movie with historically accurate and valuable information. The more recent 2003 production *Luther,* starring Joseph Fiennes, gives an edgier and more entertaining story without as much historical information, but it does include events that are not in the first movie. Consider watching them with your students on a two year cycle. Make an evening out of it with popcorn and drinks. Consider using a "fill in the blank" worksheet to keep students focused along the way and to allow further discussion after you've watched the movie.

Public Examination

Most confirmation services begin with the Great Commission from Matthew 28:18b–20: "All authority in heaven and on earth has been given to Me. Go therefore and make disciples of all nations, baptizing them in the name of the Father and of the Son and of the Holy Spirit, teaching them to observe all that I have commanded you. And behold, I am with you always, to the end of the age."

Through confirmation instruction, we teach our youth from Luther's Small Catechism and other resources, hoping they take the information that is in their minds and connect it with their hearts to live out a faithful life, devoted to Christ and active as members of the church. There are those youth who sit and never ask questions, and you wonder if they really get anything at all. How do you determine that the youth are ready for the responsibilities of confirmation, ready to publicly confess their faith and what they believe?

The answer for some churches is a public examination that takes place the week or the night before the confirmation service. Some churches lead the public examination during the worship service, while others set aside an evening or Sunday School hour devoted solely to the questioning. Often, an elder, deacon, or other church leader approves the answers and announces if each youth is ready to be confirmed. Prior to the public examination, a list of questions has been compiled from what has been taught, and youth are expected to know the answers. Sometimes, the pastor might let the youth know which questions will be assigned to each of them; however, it is more common to expect the confirmands to know all of the answers and for the pastor to ask the youth at random.

Questions cover the teachings of Luther's Small Catechism: the Ten Commandments, the Apostles' Creed, the Lord's Prayer, Baptism, Confession, and Holy Communion, including explanations. Additional questions can be added based on other content that has been taught. Examples of these kinds of questions:

- What is the Bible?
- Who is the center and focus of all the Scriptures?
- What are the two main teachings of the Scriptures?
- What is the Second Commandment? What does it mean to curse? Is swearing always wrong? When is it permitted, and when is it forbidden?
- What are the two creeds we use most often in worship?
- What does the word *Christ* mean?
- Why did Jesus have to be true God? Why did He have to be true man?
- What is prayer? To whom alone should we pray?
- What benefits does Baptism give?
- What is Confession?
- What does the name *Jesus* mean?

- What is close Communion, and why do we practice it?

In addition to questioning, youth are often asked to write an essay that answers a specific question regarding their faith. These essays are read in front of the congregation at the time of public examination or during the confirmation service. They can also be published in the monthly newsletter, the weekly bulletin, or a special folder printed just for the confirmation service. Examples of essay topics:

- What does faith mean to me?
- Who is the Holy Spirit, and how has He helped me?
- Why is infant Baptism important?
- How can I be a witness among my peers?
- Why can I call Jesus my personal Savior?

Sponsorship, Gifts, and Beyond

Some parents and youth have the attitude that confirmation is a rite of passage, and once "graduated" from the program, there is no need to remain tied to the congregation. Throughout the confirmation process, youth are publicly announcing their faith in Christ and the teachings of the Bible, all of which provoke in us a response to live out our lives as active Christians, continuing our spiritual growth through church attendance and Bible study. One way to help that process and make the transition from confirmation student to confirmed youth is to begin a sponsorship program. People from the congregation volunteer to sponsor or "adopt" a confirmand throughout his or her training. During this time, the sponsor prays for the youth and sends cards of encouragement and affirmation. If you choose to make these persons secret sponsors, ask them to reveal themselves at a special event, perhaps public examination, the confirmation service, or another event set aside just for this occasion. If the sponsors are not secret, encourage them to be mentors to the youth and incorporate them into confirmation lessons as appropriate. Encourage a relationship to grow, and this will also create accountability beyond the confirmation program.

As confirmation is a celebration and milestone in and of itself, make the moment special with a gift for each student. There are many resources, especially personal devotion books, that encourage youth to continue their spiritual growth. Concordia Publishing House has a gift section that would be appropriate for this occasion. You can also make it more personal by creating a scrapbook of pictures, with the help of parents, that begins with the child's Baptism, leads up to confirmation, and has open pages remaining for the ongoing faith walk. Personal banners can be created with the youth's confirmation verse or other significant words, pictures, and decorations that are meaningful and even used as a part of the confirmation service.

My favorite gift to give is a picture frame with a parchment paper in it that has been personalized for each youth. Download a special font into your word processor, and use it to type the youth's first name. Below it, in another elegant font, add the youth's confirmation verse, followed by his or her birth date, Baptism date, and confirmation date. It has a professional look and can be hung on a wall or placed on a side table as a constant reminder to the person that he or she is a child of God confirmed in Christ. There are many gift ideas; however, I encourage you to be intentional with the gift, just as you have been intentional with the information you have taught throughout the program.

Get creative, and think about the impact you have made on these youth and where you desire to see them in their involvement in future youth activities. Encourage the senior high youth to support the confirmation students by asking them to be present at the public examination or confirmation service. Begin building relationships early on, and upon confirmation, create an opportunity for the next grade of youth to whisk away the newly confirmed for a special bonding activity. If you have a youth room with a wall mural or other significant item, ask the incoming youth to contribute something personal to it so that they are considered a part of the youth family. For example, one idea is to bring the newly confirmed eighth graders into the youth room, where they place their handprints on the wall. Throughout their four years in the senior high youth program, they write the big events in which they participate on their handprints, such as a servant event or National Youth Gathering. When they are seniors and heading off to college, place their footprints on the wall so that the room represents the many youth who have come and gone and are still a part of the Body of Christ. There are many ways to incorporate special celebrations into your confirmation program. While you are teaching a group of technological and multisensory individuals who are soaking up every new fad and focusing on the future, they also need to be taught about what was done for them in the past. Be intentional with the time you have with these young minds, and remember that you are planting seeds of faith that will last an eternity.

DCE Cheryl (Knollman) LaBelle works with youth, children, and families at St. Paul Lutheran Church in Columbus, Indiana.

15

Confirmation Retreats: Wanna Get Away?

by Leon Jameson

My Pastor and His Toothbrush

It was early. I unzipped my sleeping bag, and with a short hop, stumbled out of my upper bunk. Commence morning routine: rub my eyes, grab my toothbrush, and oh-so-stealthily land-mine waltz my way across a floor covered with backpacks, shoes, and Doritos bags on my way to the bathroom.

This was one of those sort of cold, austere retreat-center bathrooms connected to a large room shared by a group of ten eighth-grade boys. The room itself is really designed to encourage people not to linger. Even at fourteen, I appreciated a warm shower. And as tired as I was, I knew waking up before the others guaranteed hot water. (Funny, even today I wake up earlier than anyone on retreats to ensure a hot shower.)

I opened the door to the bathroom, and that's when I saw him. My pastor, brushing his teeth, wearing a pair of blue and orange sleep pants, a white muscle shirt, and fuzzy Garfield slippers. And I had a moment of what can only be called revelation—well, at least as much of a revelation that a fourteen-year-old boy can have. I stared at the man, thinking, *My pastor brushes his teeth?*

Funny. It wasn't until later that I thought about those Garfield slippers.

Like most adolescents, the only context in which I knew my pastor was that of organized church, where he wore a suit, led prayers, preached in a pulpit, and taught confirmation class. And he was good at it. I always felt comfortable with my pastor. He knew my name. But I can honestly say that encountering him brushing his teeth connected with me on a different level. Over the course of the weekend, not only did I see my pastor brush his teeth, but I also saw him in jeans. I tossed the football with him. I even tried to make him smile during a round of "Honey, If You Love Me." I had known my pastor all of my life. But it took an early morning sighting of him brushing his teeth to help me realize that I could have a relationship with my pastor.

Establishing relationships is part of the core foundation of a solid youth ministry program. Unfortunately, all too often, well-intentioned confirmation instructors focus so much on teaching the Commandments, rehearsing the memory work, and generating worship notes that requirements replace opportunities for relationships. Quality youth ministry operates from the essential foundation of Christ as He works in Word and Sacraments. And those are relational encounters. Ministry is relational. Our truest example of that is Jesus Himself.

After many years of confirmation instruction, the thing I remember most is not the three uses of the Law or the Means of Grace (and yes, I "know" those things, but we are talking about memories here); it was talking with my pastor as he brushed his teeth. And guess what? All of the necessary knowing became more intimate, lasting, and significant once I felt truly connected to the person who was mentoring and leading my spiritual formation.

This memory remains so strong in my own mind that I have made it a priority to incorporate a retreat in my ministry. I just wish I could find a pair of those Garfield slippers.

The Retreat

Note: There are models for confirmation instruction designed in a retreat format. This chapter focuses on the value of the retreat as an addition to a traditional classroom teaching model.

Relationship. Spiritual formation. Connection. These are worthwhile learning outcomes to strive for in religious instruction. Including a retreat in your planning is one way to achieve them.

Retreats provide you and your confirmands extended time to grow in relationship with one another and with God as students spend structured, intentional time away from all of the competing influences in their lives. On well-planned retreats, students focus on their relationship with God, engage in fellowship with other Christian kids and adults, and are nurtured in personal growth.

Youth ministry truly is all about relationships—the most central being each student's relationship with Jesus Christ. Retreats also provide unique opportunities for students to grow in relationship with others and with you. On these trips and overnights, your contact hours with youth are typically more than you might have over the course of an entire month. Your decision to include a retreat as part of your confirmation instruction is a significant educational and formational decision that will improve your entire program.

While there are compelling reasons to have a retreat, there's no one-size-fits-all template for every retreat. Retreats will vary in their length and makeup. Typically, the primary reason for a retreat is to complement a larger program of spiritual formation. By clarifying and prioritizing your goals, you can design an event that is best suited to your students and memorable as a milestone in their religious education. Most retreats include fellowship, opportunities for instruction and education outside of the traditional classroom, community building, rest, reflection, and renewal. Knowing your number one priority while keeping the other objectives in mind will focus your planning efforts, point you to the right facility, and streamline your program decisions.

Retreats offer intentional moments for connection between youth and adult members of your congregation and church/school staff. As you program, include opportunities to draw students and families together, work to create a sense of community, and don't shy away from nurturing community that enjoys laughter and fun. Community is God designed. As students connect through fun and fellowship, they become more comfortable sharing on deeper, more significant levels. Fun and faith are not antithetical.

Relationship. Spiritual formation. Connection. Keep these words in mind as you program your retreat with purpose.

You Gotta Have a Good Reason

Retreats don't just happen. A retreat is an educational tool that should be used as part of a larger educational strategy for religious education and faith formation. Sure, there are times when spur-of-the-moment events or unexpected chances create memorable experiences. But for the most part, retreats require a great deal of planning and preparation. Outstanding organization will impact the outcome of a retreat.

Here are a few things to remember when organizing an effective retreat.

Prayer

"The prayer of a righteous person has great power as it is working" (James 5:16). Our most powerful resource is communion with God through prayer. The results are often greater than we think possible. Some people see prayer as a last resort to be tried when all else fails. This is backward. Prayer comes first and is fundamental in the development of a confirmation retreat.

- Pray and ask the Lord to show you and your leaders the direction your retreat should take.
- Once initial preparations have been made, ask parents, the church staff, and the youth to begin praying for the retreat while it is still months away.
- Consider having a parent prayer team that supports the entire process through prayer.
- During the retreat itself, ask parents and the congregation to pray for you while you are away. Provide specific petitions that can be used.

Purpose

Before you begin plotting out the details of your retreat, clearly articulate its purpose. Have a vision for how this retreat will be a blessing to your students and to the larger congregation. Hold a brainstorming session with your confirmation leaders, a group of trusted parents, or the board of elders. Share your vision, and engage their enthusiasm and support for the program. Ask questions that will help to define the retreat's purpose and general structure.

Ask:

- What do we want to accomplish with this confirmation retreat?

- What do we want the participants to walk away with?
- Where are our kids spiritually?
- Is our purpose consistent with our confirmation program's mission/ministry objectives?
- How will we define "success" on this retreat?

Planning

Plan like Nehemiah. "And I told them of the hand of my God that had been upon me for good, and also of the words that the king had spoken to me. And they said, 'Let us rise up and build.' So they strengthened their hands for the good work" (Nehemiah 2:18).

Nehemiah had a vision. He shared it with enthusiasm and inspired Jerusalem's leaders to rebuild the broken walls of the city. People are deeply motivated by God's Word and want to be challenged to be part of programs that impact faith formation. When God plants an idea in your mind, share it with others. Trust the Holy Spirit to impress them with similar thoughts.

After defining the purpose, plan, plan, plan in advance. There are no shortcuts for this stage of a successful retreat, and you should begin eight to twelve months in advance. I find it helpful to set aside a day or two each year just to outline retreats for the following year. Keep a binder or digital file, and use these annual planning notes as you prepare for each retreat.

As your leadership team plans, ask these questions:

- How many students do we have room for at this retreat?
- What are the budgeted revenues and expenses?
- How many volunteer leaders will we need?
- What do we need to do to train the volunteers?
- What events will we include to make sure there is a proper balance of activities?
- Does the date compete with other school events?
- How often should we meet to continue our planning process?

Establishing these fences opens up the creativity of the team, and you can plan with purpose and efficiency. Meet regularly to ensure that the team members are progressing with their assigned responsibilities. Not only does careful planning produce a more meaningful retreat, but it also builds stronger relationships among volunteers and staff prior to the event.

On our staff, our three pastors, our junior high DCE, and I work together to answer these questions. Together, we develop a theme, designate responsibilities, recruit a leadership team, and set our timetable.

Choosing a Facility

After you determine your purpose and establish your plan, you need to select and contract a facility. Ideally, your facility will be a complement to your program goals.

Your facility is your home away from home, so it needs to be comfortable for you as well as for your students. If your group is miserable because it is twenty degrees and you are staying in cabins with no heat, you probably won't have much opportunity for the group to grow.

I have held retreats in a number of settings. Ideally, if you do a little research in your community and among your church membership, you will find several options to fit your budget and goals. Consider camp settings, retreat centers, campgrounds, hotels, farms, gymnasiums, YMCA buildings, another church, your church basement, a family cottage or cabin, a university, or a guesthouse. Remember that the one of the advantages of a retreat is taking students away from their everyday lives. Often, hotels make it difficult for students to unplug because of the ready access to television and the like. You don't need to backpack through the wilderness, but give good thought to being away from "the norm" as you focus your students on the primary goals for your event.

Camps, retreat centers, and hotels often book a year or more in advance and require a deposit to hold the space, so plan ahead. If you can't get in the camp you want, ask to be put on a waiting list in case room becomes available, and book it for the following year.

Once you narrow down the options, do a site inspection to make sure that the facility and staff will meet your group's needs.

Meeting Space

Consider your meeting-space needs as you plan your retreat. Appropriate meeting space is very important. Will you always meet as a large group, or do you need breakout rooms? If so, how many and when? These are answers that camps and retreat facilities will want to know.

Typically, the staff of the facility will want your exact schedule in advance (two weeks to one month) in case another group is sharing space with you. If you are in a camp setting, you usually have more flexibility with a twenty-four-hour reserve on your meeting space, meaning that you have it during the entire time you are on-site. If you have a similar schedule from a prior event, give it to your facility contact when you are negotiating a contract to indicate what type of space you used in the past as well as your program requirements.

You will need to determine your meeting-room setup and your planned use for the space. How many students do you want to fit comfortably in the room? Will they sit on chairs or the floor? Will you be doing group-building exercises or other activities that require more space? Do you have loud activities planned? Make sure you have space to do what you need to do, while also being courteous of other guests and observant of facility guidelines. Do you need chairs? If so, how many? A stage or platform? If so, what size? Skirted tables? If so, how many and where? Audiovisual equipment? You get the idea.

Finally, view your facility as an essential tool that will help you achieve your goals. The most important aspect of dealing with meeting space is to keep your contact at the selected facility informed and take time to build a good relationship with this person. Be clear and detail oriented, and include the contact in the vision for your event. These professionals want to help you meet your goals and will be very helpful if they know your hopes and plans for the event.

In our planning process, we designate one of our planners to be the direct contact for our group. That person is then responsible for the contract, housing, meeting space, meals, and payment.

Cost and Insurance

Although an accurate budget can be difficult to estimate, it is essential to a successful retreat. (A financially successful retreat will make the church treasurer happy.) A basic formula to use is to divide the total of all expenses by the lowest number of students who might attend the retreat. Regardless of your formula, be sure to figure in the following:

- Lodging and meals
- Transportation
- Program expenses

You will need to decide if you will include the cost of adult volunteers and the leadership team's lodging and meals in the cost per person or if your church will absorb these costs or if your adult leaders will cover all or a portion of these costs. Think ahead, and make arrangements so that money never becomes a deterrent for student participation. Often, a church budget may provide funds for the overall retreat or provide scholarship funds for students who need them.

Often, a church's liability policy will cover insurance for retreats, but verify this fact. If the policy does not cover retreats, work out a plan, even if it is just for the weekend.

Transportation

Depending on the size of your group and the distance you need to travel, transportation options vary greatly. You may want to recruit parents and leaders to drive your students to the retreat, or taking a school bus might be fun.

As with the facility, organizing your transportation needs well in advance will save you many hours of undue stress. Parents feel more confident and relaxed knowing their children are traveling in a safe, reliable vehicle. Be wise in this area, and never take safety for granted.

Food

Good food does not mean expensive food. Spaghetti is fine as long as it is not overcooked. Hot dogs and sloppy joes are great as long as they are not soggy. If the food is poor, the kids will never forget it.

Food should also accommodate the theme or purpose of retreat. If this is a confirmation retreat with six-hour work projects each day, you want hearty meals. Also consider what youth like. Liver and onions may not be the best choice for students—or for most adults, either!

Registration

From the moment students receive the first registration information, your retreat has begun. A well-done registration packet sets the stage for your retreat and shows parents that as a planning team you are prepared. Registration materials should be detailed for parents, but also offer a fun and inviting look for students that includes a sneak peek at the planned program.

Parents need to feel assured as they drop their children off for the retreat that you are organized and ready to take responsibility. Be sure to provide parents with information sheets that include the facility location, phone number, and emergency information.

Making Your Retreat Memorable

Memorable retreats make everyone feel comfortable; the settings are familiar and the challenges are kept to a minimum. Right? Wrong!

Memorable retreats usually make participants uncomfortable (at some point), offer different experiences, and provide choices to take on new challenges in a safe way. People learn best when their equilibrium is just a bit off. But this takes intentional, structured, educationally focused planning.

Be Prepared

Jesus taught that the wise builder made a careful inventory before he began building. That's a good lesson to keep in mind. Nothing tanks a retreat faster than arriving at the campsite without food or discovering that the bus driver was supposed to go north instead of south a hundred miles ago.

Take Time to Play

Plan for fun. Retreats are about learning and growing in the Lord. They also are times for building social skills and relationships while having fun with one another. And that includes you. Don't be a sideline watcher—get involved in the fun. When you are out throwing a Frisbee with a group of students, you may be amazed at the conversations that take place.

In addition to scheduled games and contests, allow "free choice" time for optional activities. Students need to have programmed "unprogrammed" time so that they can be better engaged throughout the event.

People—Program—Facility

Although a great deal has been shared on facility and program, people need to be first in the fundamental order of priorities for any retreat philosophy.

Some people might argue that facilities are most important. But fancy cabins with loads of amenities are no match for strong leadership and solid programming. Spend time equipping your leaders to lead and preparing your students to engage. Choose a location that is a match to your objectives, and focus on your goals for relationship, spiritual formation, and connection. Poor, even inadequate facilities can be compensated for if the program is age appropriate and the leadership is genuine.

Tension

Retreats are great places for addressing the fears of adolescents. Often when a student is faced with a different experience, positive tension can result. Remember, retreats are one tool to complement the larger educational model you are using for your students' religious education. Use them to their full advantage. You are out of the classroom, and that means you can create unique encounters to help students learn in new ways.

Channeling positive tension in creative ways lets students experience the satisfaction of accomplishing something that previously seemed impossible. Retreats that create opportunities to overcome present fears can increase confidence for the future.

At our confirmation retreat, we arrange with the camp for a series of low ropes challenge elements to be provided. These challenge elements, which are facilitated by trained staff members of the camp, are designed to provide groups with a variety of experiential learning situations. Challenge elements promote a healthy tension in the group that can launch young people into greater levels of learning and community.

The Unfamiliar

When a retreat is held in a new location, or when new circumstances are introduced, youth discover confidence and curiosity in exploring unseen territory. Confidence and curiosity are important traits for learners. As they experience the unfamiliar, students tap into a childlike enthusiasm as they try something for the first time. In familiar settings, youth too often get caught up in the bumps and bruises of being adolescents. On a retreat, these new experiences often make new memories. Because everyone is on new turf, a positive dependency on the group's leadership is often formed.

Encouragement

Even if one of your youth doesn't remember the theme of the retreat, the content of your talks, or the results of the games you played, one meaningful compliment or heart-to-heart may change his or her life forever. Like we've said, it's all about relationships.

Rest

It's fun to start building your program and planning your retreat schedule. But be careful not to over-program your kids. No surprises here, but recent brain research argues against keeping young people up all night. And it is clear (often on Sunday mornings for many confirmands) that fatigued minds will learn little and remember less. In my planning, I try to reach a balance. While fast-paced schedules can be important to the success of your retreat, adequate rest is crucial.

Program down time or, as some camps call it, "body on bunk." Designate the hour before dinner of the first full day of the retreat as quiet time. Designate this as a time where there is no talking. Encourage kids to sleep, go on a walk, pray, journal, or do something else that is relaxing.

On the second night of the retreat, schedule "Lights Out" one hour earlier than the evening before. By then, much of the excitement of arriving and being away from home will have lessened.

Post-Retreat

A retreat isn't over once you return home. Encourage parents and the rest of the congregation to see and support what happened on the retreat. We conclude our retreat with the parents joining us at the camp or retreat center for our closing worship service. This also provides plenty of drivers for the trip home.

It is also important to take time following the retreat to jot down some notes about your experience. What should change, what needs to be added, what should you keep, and so forth.

Leadership

No matter how sophisticated your program may be, the success or failure of a retreat is largely dependent on the qualities displayed by the retreat leadership team. Each of us has our own distinct styles of leadership, but there are a few things that improve everyone's ability to lead effective retreats.

Visionary

A great leader pictures the desired outcome and diligently works toward it. Establish your vision for the retreat. Whether it is just you, a group of volunteers, or three pastors and two DCEs, take time to establish your vision. What is the preferred future you are working toward? Make this vision challenging yet attainable. "Where there is no vision, the people perish" (Proverbs 29:18 KJV).

Our retreat vision for our confirmands is simple: to be able to articulate in word and action our love for Christ. Because the retreat is one component of our larger philosophy for confirmation education, we have decided to focus our retreats on relationships. Our goal is for our students first to grow in relationship with Jesus, and second to grow closer with their confirmation class and its leaders.

See the Potential

Much like Jesus, who saw the incredible potential in the bumbling, bragging Peter, we should strive to recognize the potential of our youth. Retreats provide opportunities for students to dwell in a community of encouragement and emotional safety. Work hard to nurture an atmosphere that propels students to achieve the outcomes you established.

I mentioned earlier that our group often participates in group challenge elements. These challenge elements have varied from large-group games to low rope challenges to high rope challenges. One of the common threads in each of these challenges has been the opportunity for the community to encourage one another.

Flexibility

Although you can't prepare for everything, it is important to prepare in advance to meet the unexpected with a sense of quiet expectation, trusting God for guidance and direction. Whether it is taking a wrong turn, leaving your teaching notes at home, or forgetting the guitar (I've done all three and more), God is sovereign and always creates wonderful gems out of these rough times.

Now, maybe you're wondering about that pastor from my childhood. Well, he's still in my life. Each Christmas, as I travel home with my wife and our daughter to visit family, I look forward to seeing him. Although he is retired now, I am always glad to shake his hand on a Sunday morning and to look into the wise eyes of a dear friend who has known me since I was a punk-nosed seventh grader. Yes, indeed. Pastor Grassinger knows me. And he still cares about my ministry, my family, and most significantly, about my faith in Jesus. I like to ponder the eternal significance of those Garfield slippers. Who would've thought?

Rev. Leon Jameson serves as pastor of youth and family at Hales Corners Lutheran Church in Hales Corners, Wisconsin.

16

Communion Instruction

by Bob Brantsch

What Luther Said

Get out your favorite, most used, and most loved edition of Luther's Small Catechism. What are the Six Chief Parts of Luther's catechism? Note that confirmation is not one of them. Now count all the pages in the catechism that cover the Sacrament of Holy Communion. In my catechism, that amounts to seventeen pages. Now count how many pages are devoted to confirmation. In my catechism, I count one page. Confirmation is not clearly identified as a practice of the Bible. At the time of Luther, confirmation was a sacrament of the Church. Luther did not believe confirmation to be a sacrament. Neither do we.

I am not saying that confirmation is not important, nor should it be minimized. But the Sacrament of Holy Communion is vital to our life of faith in the Church. Communion ought to be taught, celebrated in our churches, and lifted up as the power it gives to our lives. Communion not only gives us forgiveness of sins and strength for daily living, but it also binds us together with fellow believers. Why not offer this vital aspect of our faith to those already taking confirmation classes? Offering Communion before and during confirmation instruction provides all the benefits and blessings to our young people, as outlined by Luther in the catechism. Participating in Communion during the confirmation instruction process can greatly enhance the instruction about the Sacrament, the work of Christ, and the power of the Holy Spirit.

Practice

This chapter is not prescriptive about what you should do in your congregation. It is only descriptive of what we do in our congregation. Perhaps you can take a few ideas for use in your congregation and make them your own. Some of the best ideas I have learned from others. But I usually change ideas to make them unique to my situation.

Our congregation practices early Communion, beginning in fifth grade. Confirmation occurs in eighth grade. This may be something new to some congregations of The Lutheran Church—Missouri Synod. I've always hoped to serve a church that practices early Communion, but this is the first that has actually done so. Early Communion is a wonderful blessing in the life of our church and in the lives of the students who receive the Sacrament. According to the 1998 document *A Study of Youth Confirmation and First Communion in The Lutheran Church—Missouri Synod,* 20% of LCMS congregations practice early Communion.

One of the biggest fears with those who have not experienced early Communion is that the student will not attend confirmation instruction. That has not been this case with our congregation. Confirmation is held in very high regard by the members of our congregation. The educational process, commitment of time and energy, and the actual Rite of Confirmation have a long history in our church. Instead of lowering the expectations for confirmation, our practice raised the place of Communion as a crucial element in the spiritual development and formation in the lives of all people, especially young people.

Delaying participation in Communion until after confirmation may send a few mixed messages. First, attendance in Communion is not earned or dependent on what we do. It is solely Christ's meal, completely His gift. It has nothing do to with how good or how bad we are. We receive the Sacrament to receive forgiveness and strengthening of body and spirit. Another potentially negative message concerning the practice of Communion after confirmation is that we inadvertently raise confirmation to an almost sacramental level. Confirmation is not a sacrament, nor should it be a prerequisite for the Sacrament of Holy Communion. Confirmation is a rite of the Church whereby students confirm the vows spoken for them at their Baptism. Third, we may mistakenly convey that confirmation is somehow equal to Communion.

Instruction

We have found January and February to be a better time of year to focus on First Communion instruction. Our congregation, like many congregations, is quite busy in the fall with Rally Sunday, classes, and other programs beginning. These are followed closely by a Reformation celebration, a confirmation retreat, Advent and Christmas preparations, and much more. In March and April, we have our Lenten focus and a second confirmation retreat. In May, we have the Rite of Confirmation, Mother's Day, Memorial Day, and Pentecost. In June, we have Vacation Bible School. We carefully plan early Communion instruction in January and February to celebrate First Communion toward the end of February.

There is much value to conducting early Communion instruction during Lent and then celebrating First Communion on Palm Sunday, Holy Thursday, at the Easter Vigil, during the Easter season, or at Pentecost. Also, there is historical practice of the Church to receive new members and conduct Baptisms at the Easter Vigil. Years ago, we celebrated First Communion at our Easter Vigil celebration, but we found that to be a busy time of year as well. Conducting First Communion instruction in February gives families, the congregation, and church staff an exciting event in the life of the church when the church calendar is not quite so busy.

We approach first Communion as an individual and family decision. Students' first Communion instruction in our congregation takes shape in two ways. After Christmas, our fifth-grade Sunday School classes take a break from their normal Growing in Christ Sunday School lessons. For eight weeks, our fifth graders explore the This Is the Feast Communion curriculum from Concordia Publishing House. This curriculum includes a teacher guide, which our lay teacher uses. While the curriculum targets older elementary ages, it could easily be adapted to younger readers. Toward the end of the eight-week course, our pastor attends one of the Sunday morning classes with the fifth graders, addressing their questions. Hosting this instruction on Sunday mornings with a lay teacher provides a solid background. This system of instruction provides an additional adult to cover the basic principles of Communion while teaching the power and blessing that Communion will be for these young people.

Communion Retreat

The other portion of Communion instruction involves a half-day retreat at our church. Our first Communion retreat is held every year, usually in February. The day lasts from 10:00 a.m. to 4:00 p.m., and we provide lunch and a variety of learning experiences. We also require that at least one parent attend the day with each child. If parents cannot attend with their child or attend all day, we encourage them to attend next year. We want families to know this is a personal decision and readiness on part of the student and family is important. At our retreat, we usually have sixth, seventh, and eighth graders whose families do not feel their child is ready for first Communion at fifth grade. I have found that some families that delay first Communion for their children base the decision more on tradition than on readiness. Regardless, we leave that decision up to each family.

The key with such a long day of instruction is being sensitive to the age of the students. Each student learns differently and has a different capacity for staying focused on the content. I have found no one curriculum or program that is helpful for our half-day retreat experience. So I decided on our learning goals and objectives and then developed the lessons myself. Some worksheets from our retreat are included at the end of this chapter.

Content

The content of our first Communion retreat focuses only on Communion. We don't get too much into other aspects of Luther's catechism because that is the purpose of confirmation instruction. We don't cover much on Baptism but remain focused on Communion. We don't want children and their families coming away from the day with thoughts other than Communion.

The first hour of the day, both student and parent work through a forty-question worksheet that explores the background of Communion as it is connected to Passover. The worksheet is not a static activity. We have the kids go to different learning stations. They make metal chains to symbolize the slavery of the Israelites in Egypt. They paint a doorframe with red paint to symbolize painting the doorframes with blood from the Passover lamb. They sample matzo bread. They look on a calendar to see when Holy Thursday, Good Friday, and Easter are celebrated this year. The majority of their time is spent looking up Scripture verses pertaining to Passover and Communion.

The next activity is what I call musical drawings. We play Communion music or music that refers to Jesus as the Lamb. As we play the songs, we display the words on a screen or on handouts. While the song is playing, we ask students and parents to draw, using crayons, markers, or colored pencils, what they hear. We then have volunteers share what they drew and what they heard from the song. A few years ago, I played a Latino arrangement of the Hymn of Praise "This Is the Feast" from the 1995 LCMS Youth Gathering in San Antonio, Texas. One picture drawn was of Jesus at the altar giving us His body and blood while wearing a sombrero. It provided a wonderful opportunity to explain that Jesus and His body and blood are for all people.

One significant retreat activity involves a worksheet comparing the three primary Christian viewpoints concerning Holy Communion. I believe it is important to discuss this in an open, unifying way without breaking the Eighth Commandment. We look up various passages in the Bible and demonstrate how our Lutheran understanding of the real presence is clearly based on the words of Scripture. One of the best images of this one-day retreat for me is watching parents explore and discover the truths about Holy Communion with their child.

Time with Pastor

The final session at the church is spent with the pastor. He takes the children to the altar area and shows them the various elements of Holy Communion. The students are allowed to taste the unconsecrated bread and wine. Pastor teaches the students about our wine, bread, and Communionware, as well as how it's cared for and where it is stored. Since we use a common cup, intinction cup, and individual cups, our pastor covers our various procedures for receiving the blood of Christ as well.

Making a Memory

The final activity of the day is conducted off-site at a local pottery studio. Students and their parents paint their own ceramic chalice. The chalices are prepared in advance but have not been decorated (glazed) or fired. I encourage students to use colors that have Christian meanings associated with them as well as religious symbols related to Communion. Students may also write on their chalices "Communion Class" or "The Blood of Christ" or another appropriate Communion phrase. (See the list of suggested chalice phrases in the sidebar.) We provide one chalice per family, so parents guide and help the children paint. After painting, the chalices are fired and must remain in the kiln for a few days. On the Sunday after first Communion is celebrated, we place the completed chalices on our altar. The congregation can see these chalices before and after services and when they come to Communion.

Chalice Phrases

IHS—Latin abbreviation for Jesus the Savior

INRI—Latin abbreviation for Jesus of Nazareth, King of the Jews

"This is My blood." Matthew 26:28

"This cup is the new covenant in My blood." 1 Corinthians 11:25

"Christ, our Passover lamb, has been sacrificed." 1 Corinthians 5:7

"The blood of Jesus His Son cleanses us from all sin." 1 John 1:7

The blood of Christ shed for you.

The blood of Christ shed for ________.

The Lord's Table

The Lord's Supper

The Sacrament of the Altar

Holy Communion

First Communion Class

First Communion Sunday

During Communion distribution on First Communion Sunday, I read from the lectern the names of each new communicant and invite the child and his or her families and friends to come forward to receive Holy Communion. If you do this at your church, make sure you talk to the pastor and music director so they know you are going to talk during the distribution hymns. It may seem like talking over the singing of hymns during distribution would be confusing. But it works, and people like hearing the names of the students and seeing their families and friends come forward to support them and receive Communion with them. We also publish the names of the new communicants in our church bulletin and newsletter.

Early Communion may be a new and difficult change for some congregations steeped in tradition. But if you would like to change your existing confirmation program to include early Communion, it will be a blessing to your congregation and the lives of those who participate. To make such a change, develop a special task force or committee to look into this practice. Involve your pastor, elders, confirmation teachers, and those who work in Christian education. Do research and educate your members about the differences between Communion and confirmation.

May the Lord bless you and all you do as you teach, educate, and nurture the lives of young people and their families!

To Him be the glory!

DCE Bob Brantsch oversees adult education, small groups, confirmation, and First Communion for Gloria Dei Lutheran Church in Hudson, Ohio.

What Is Communion?

According to **1 Corinthians 10:16**, when we eat the bread, what do we receive?

According to **1 Corinthians 10:16**, when we drink the cup of wine, what do we receive?

According to **1 Corinthians 10:17**, what does Communion do for us?

According to **1 Corinthians 11:26**, what does our participation in Communion do?

According to **1 Corinthians 11:27**, what attitude should we have about Communion?

According to **1 Corinthians 11:28–29**, what should we do before coming to Communion?

According to the following verses, what are the various names for Communion?

1 Corinthians 10:16
1 Corinthians 10:21
1 Corinthians 11:20
Acts 2:42

Where Does Communion Come From?

Passover

1. Read **Exodus 1:1**. Where did Jacob and his twelve sons live? ____________________

2. Read **Exodus 1:7**. What happened to the Israelites? ____________________

____

3. Read **Exodus 1:8**. Who did not know about Joseph and the Israelites?

____

4. Read **Exodus 1:9–14**. What did the new king do to the Israelites? ____________________

____

5. Read **Exodus 12:3–5**. What kind of sacrifice did God want the people to make?

____

6. Read **Exodus 12:7**. What were the Israelites to do with the blood?

____

7. Read **Exodus 12:12–13**. What did the blood mean?

____

8. Read **Exodus 12:12**. Who was to die in Egypt on the night of Passover?

____

9. Read **Exodus 12:31–36**. What did Pharaoh demand of the Israelites that night?

____

10. Read **Exodus 12:11–13**. What is the name of the festival that remembers these events?

____

11. Why is it called this? ______________________________________

12. The sacrifice was to be a __________ or _________ without _________. **(Exodus 12:5–6)**

Holy Communion

13. Jesus is described as a _________ without __________ or ___________. **(1 Peter 1:19)**

14. God commanded them to eat ______________ without ______________. **(Exodus 12:8)**

15. Jesus commanded His disciples to eat His __________ and _________ His __________. **(Matthew 26:26–27)**

16. It was the ___________________ that saved the people. **(Exodus 12:13)**

17. It is the ____________________ of Jesus that cleanses us from every sin. **(1 John 1:7)**

18. They were not to ____________ any of the ___________ of the sacrifice. **(Exodus 12:46)**

19. The soldiers did not break any of Jesus' ______________________. **(John 19:31–36)**

20. God told them to celebrate the Passover to ____________________ for the generations to come. (**Exodus 12:14**)

21. Jesus told His disciples, "Do this in ____________________________ of Me." (**Luke 22:19**)

22. Read **John 1:29**. John the Baptist said that Jesus is the ______________________ of God,

    who takes away the __________________ of the world!

23. Read **1 Corinthians 5:7**. Jesus is called our "_________________ ___________________."

24. Look up **Matthew 26:18–19**. Jesus began the Lord's Supper while He was eating the

    __________________________________ with His disciples.

25. Holy Week is the last week in the life of Jesus before His suffering, death, and resurrection. Identify these important days during Holy Week.

    a. Jesus came into Jerusalem on a donkey with people welcoming Him as their King.

    _________________________ _____________________.

    b. Holy Communion was given by Jesus on this day. ______________ _________________.

    c. Jesus suffered and died on the cross for the sins of the whole world.

    _________________ ____________________

    d. Jesus rose from the dead. ______________ _______________

True/False

26. All the bones of the Passover sacrifice had to be broken.	True	False
27. Jesus had none of His bones broken when He died.	True	False
28. We call Jesus our Passover Lamb.	True	False
29. The Passover sacrifice had to have one defect to represent the devil.	True	False
30. Jesus was perfect like the Passover lamb.	True	False
31. The wine in Communion is Christ's blood.	True	False
32. The bread in Communion represents Jesus' body.	True	False
33. One reason to take Communion is to remember Jesus.	True	False
34. We call Jesus the Lamb of God.	True	False
35. Communion gives us forgiveness of sins.	True	False
36. Another name for Communion is the Sacrament of the Altar.	True	False
37. Make up your own True/False statement.		
______________________________	True	False

17

Nontraditional Students

by Terry Dittmer

It Will Never Again Be like It Once Was, No Matter How Good It Once Was

If you are reading this chapter, there is a strong likelihood that confirmation for you is something you know to be a kind of rite of passage for thirteen- or fourteen-year-old youth in which they publicly confess their faith before their congregation and express their desire to fully be members of the church. They have gone through a period of instruction and examination and most likely, in a public worship service, they have been "confirmed" in the Lutheran faith. It is very likely that this is your own story.

There is a sense that this is the way we always have done confirmation (unless you were a rare adult convert) and that it is a good way to do it. And there is a sense among many that these things should not change. Indeed, confirmation for many is a tradition that must be maintained. It is curious, too, how many traditions are taken to be gospel truths. These things range from wearing white gowns, undergoing some kind of public examination (inquisition?), being pinned with red carnation corsages, kneeling before the altar, receiving the laying on of hands, holding the ceremony on Palm Sunday, and hosting a grand banquet/celebration for the confirmand. But, for the record, while these things may be good ideas, none of these things are prescribed in the Bible, the Lutheran Confessions, or any church handbook as requirements for confirmation.

All that being said, there is nothing wrong with these traditions. Many of us really love these traditions and many other local customs. Many of us work to preserve these traditions and bring new generations into an appreciation for them. But, it is not likely that any of these will be preserved forever, particularly in today's climate of religious diversity and neutrality. And thus the subtitle: "It will never again be like it once was, no matter how good it once was."

These are times where many people choose to ignore traditions or simply don't know them. When I was growing up, a significant part of the confirmation process was the celebration at home after the ceremony at church. It was a time for family and friends to gather for a meal and to congratulate the confirmand for his or her achievement. And don't forget the gifts. The confirmands dressed up. Nice white dresses for the girls. Coat and tie and leather shoes (yes, leather shoes) for the guys. An age of innocence, perhaps. These days, those white robes probably cover casual pants or jeans, a polo shirt, or the latest junior high fashions for the girls. And forget the banquet. Maybe lunch at a restaurant for the family. But it's not like it used to be for many confirmands. Confirmation is something to be endured, and then it's over.

We live in an age of spiritual diversity, where anybody can be spiritual and most religious systems (e.g., Lutheranism) have lost their value for a lot of people. Families are less committed to one faith community or congregation and are more open to exploring options. Young people may be fully engaged in their own church but would never presume to challenge their friends about their faith, their beliefs, or their church membership. While the National Study of Youth and Religion in 2005 (NSYR) notes that Lutheran families have Lutheran kids (and Catholic families have Catholic kids and Hindu families have Hindu kids), there is little encouragement in Lutheran churches (or in most denominations) to share the Lutheran faith outside Lutheran circles. The NSYR also notes that Lutherans are among church bodies that retain 86% of the youth they confirm through high school. That is a very encouraging statistic. But there isn't much of an effort to confirm youth who are not already a part of the church community. What is anyone doing to reach unchurched and marginally churched young people?

As young people grow through high school and into young adulthood, they become less tradition and confession bound, more open to other faith expressions, and more critical of the church they grew up in. Especially as they move into their twenties and thirties, the organized church often becomes the target of both their challenges and disregard.

In his book *They Like Jesus but Not the Church*, Dan Kimball notes that today's young adults are often very leery of the church. Youth and young adults often perceive organized mainline churches as having these traits:

- **An organization with a political agenda**
- **Judgmental and negative**
- **Dominated by men and oppressive of women**
- **Homophobic**
- **Arrogantly claiming all other religions to be wrong**
- **Full of fundamentalists who take the whole Bible literally**

Now, nobody is arguing that these young adults are right. Nor are we saying that we should surrender to their biases. But these perceptions are keeping many youth and young adults out of church communities. And it's not about not loving Jesus. Many times these young people like—and even love—Jesus very much. They consider Jesus to be a dear friend. But they see no value in belonging to any kind of church community. Unfortunately, this prejudice can be passed on to any church community regardless of whether it is true or not. Perception is for many their reality.

Lest the reader think these thoughts belong to one man, they seem to be confirmed by an increasing number of people who study faith, the faithful, and life. In his book *unChristian*, David Kinnaman lists the words and phrases people use to describe religious faith. They are very similar to Kimball's:

- **Anti-homosexual**
- **Judgmental**
- **Hypocritical** (saying one thing, doing another)
- **Old-fashioned**
- **Too involved in politics**
- **Out of touch with reality**
- **Insensitive to others**
- **Boring**
- **Not accepting of other faiths**
- **Confusing**

Another new movement seems to be a trend toward people involved in discipleship but disdaining membership. These days, we find people engaged in a lifelong spiritual journey that may involve elements from any number of religious systems, some of them designed by the journeyers themselves. They may love Jesus and consider Him their Savior and follow Him their whole life but never commit to one church community and never become a member of anything.

These individuals may also engage in multiple faith communities and be quite active in any number of them. They may go to one church for the music (and they may like the organist at one church and the praise band at another), to another church because of the sermons, to yet another church for the youth program, to a different church for the Bible study small groups, and to a certain social ministry organization because they like the way it helps people. They have a relationship with a number of communities but are not tied to any one. They may also practice yoga, engage in an interfaith dialogue with Muslims and Jews, and channel with the spirits of the departed. It is a pick-and-choose world people live in, a spiritual smorgasbord. You can sing Christian spirituals, celebrate Kwanzaa, light a menorah, meditate under an apple tree, and walk a prayer labyrinth. Weird as it sounds, there are many who consider themselves devoutly spiritual in these kinds of ways and equally confirmed in their not being religious. But they may also strongly consider themselves to be followers of Christ.

So, what place does confirmation play in this new world? As much as I hate to say it, those white robes and the laying on of hands aren't going to make much difference to an awful lot of people. When we talk about confirmation in the twenty-first century, much of it may be accomplished in very nontraditional ways. And while the nurturing of faith and spiritual formation will always be its goal, actual "confirmation" may never happen. We may find in a few years that we have all kinds of "disciples" and relatively few "members," per se. And what does that mean in the long term? What does the new confirmation look like?

First, we Lutherans probably have one of the best resources to help people grapple with the faith. Luther's Small Catechism is a masterful resource for people who are often just looking for answers and somebody to be up front with them. Got a question about the faith? Check the catechism. An especially helpful version also includes an explanation of the Six Chief Parts with Scripture references—the version most older Lutherans used in confirmation class. Want to know how Jesus is both divine and human? Check the questions on the Second Article of the Apostles' Creed. It's a practical, user-friendly, "frequently asked questions" resource about God and faith, hope and salvation. We don't want to lose the catechism. It's a great spiritual handbook for those seeking to know about God.

Second, we who are already members of the Church need to know what we believe, why we believe it, and then share it. It's one thing for me to say I believe that Jesus is my Lord and Savior. But how do I answer when a young adult asks me why I believe that? or what that statement means? We need to be prepared to give an answer for "the hope that is in you," as St. Peter challenges us in 1 Peter 3:15. This, then, in turn, means that our own faith development and spiritual nurture is a lifelong process and not something that is over when we "get confirmed." The catechism needs to be a lifelong resource for everyone who believes—it's that good.

Third, we need to meet youth and young adults where they are. Got a parking lot at your church? Put in a basketball court and make it available to the community for pickup games. (Please, no fences and padlocks.) Then hang out at the court and talk to the guys (and gals) shooting hoops. Make sure the youth in your youth group know that they can invite their friends to your youth activities. Open your youth programs to those not connected to a church. Be a friendly place, a welcoming place, a place without rules for membership.

Dan Kimball suggests in his book that you get out of the office and into the coffee shop. He tells how he takes his laptop to the local Starbucks and "sets up shop" to work on his next sermon or Bible study. A key to doing this is establishing a relationship with the people who frequent the shop. It doesn't begin with the question "Can I tell you about Jesus?" or "If you were to die tonight . . ." It's a process of building relationships with people and, over several meetings, getting to know them and they you—and then letting the conversation go where it will. When things turn spiritual, God has given you an opportunity. Will you ever confirm someone you meet in a coffee shop? Only God knows.

Fourth, set up opportunities for dialogue and conversation. Give people the opportunity to share what's on their heart without judging what they say or how they say it. In many cases, it's probably a good idea not to go one-on-one with another person. Couch what you say in terms of what you believe and why rather than condemning someone to eternal perdition because he or she doesn't believe the same as you. It's important that people know why something is important to you and that you are their friend. Will you ever confirm someone you have spent a lot of time talking with? Only God knows.

Fifth, remember technology. Young adults are into online. Facebook, Instagram, blogs, forums, discussion groups, Twitter. They take up the latest technology without hesitation. (There's even a Twitter site where viewers are challenged to write their confession of faith in less than 140 characters, which is an interesting challenge when considering how many books have been written just about Lutheran theology.) Use technology to your advantage. Establish online conversations. Questions online can be raised with some sense of anonymity. These technologies can result in some spirited conversation about spiritual things. Will you ever confirm someone online? Only God knows.

Another way to use technology is online instruction, one-on-one. Young people who are not able to participate in a class may be able to join online and complete lessons and tests electronically. This can be helpful for young people without a local or nearby church community or for those who are out of the country (e.g., children of deployed military) or whose families will not help them get to church.

Can you be comfortable with new paradigms for confirming the faith? Perhaps only God knows. There are, of course, all kinds of ramifications for Word and Sacrament ministry. What about Baptism? How do you handle Communion? What if one of your online "believers" comes to your church and wants to receive the Lord's Supper but has not been formally confirmed? What is your best pastoral practice under the circumstances? In some ways, it might sound a little messy. Make that *very* messy. But those are most likely the realities of a new age. Those are the opportunities God gives us in the twenty-first century. Like we said at the beginning, it will never again be like it once was, no matter how good it once was.

Rev. Dr. Terry Dittmer is now retired after many years of service to the Office of National Mission—Youth Ministry of The Lutheran Church—Missouri Synod.

18

Confirmed? Now What?

by Jeffrey Meinz

Here's Your Card

As a freshman in high school, I was told that I would be taking a "Hunter's Safety" class. I explained to the registrar that I had no intentions of hunting. At that time, I couldn't think of one reason why I would ever own a gun.

The registrar went on to explain that the one-credit course was a requirement for every freshman boy who would graduate from Farmington High School in southern Missouri. Seriously? *Every* boy? What would the girls be doing at this time? Canning tomatoes?

Coach Howard would be the instructor for "Hunter's Safety." Coach Howard was as wide as he was tall (mostly muscle). An entire wall in the weight room was dedicated to Coach Howard's various trophies from football, wrestling, and weight lifting. Apparently, Coach Howard was also an avid hunter. Coach Howard explained that since we lived in a small, rural town, and since many of our fathers and grandfathers were hunters, we would learn to become hunters also.

I raised my hand. "What if I don't want to hunt?" I asked.

"Do you like to eat meat?"

"Yes."

"Then you'll learn how to hunt," was Coach Howard's quick reply.

"I like beef, Coach Howard. Am I going to learn how to hunt for beef? I also like chicken. What kind of gun will I need to hunt chicken, Coach Howard?"

The class of forty-seven freshman boys laughed. Coach Howard did not. He cut me off before I could explain that I also like tuna. Coach immediately instructed me to give up my prime real estate, front-row seat on the bench press, and move to the back of the weight room, next to the dumbbells. Ha, Coach, I get it . . . I'm next to the *dumb*bells.

For the next hour, we watched a video of camouflaged men tiptoeing through the trees in search of an antlered animal. I learned that there is a point system in hunting, much like in football. Some deer are worth ten points, while some are worth only eight or six.

After watching the "blaze-orange fashion show," we were told by Coach Howard that we would be taking a test. If we passed the test, we would be given a plastic card for our wallets, apparently allowing us to shoot anything with four legs.

Believe it or not, I passed the test! It wasn't very difficult. I probably could have passed it without watching the video.

Question 31: True or False—You should never aim a loaded gun at another hunter.

I said true.

Four to six weeks later, I got my "Hunter's Safety" card in the mail. I explained to my mom that I needed to buy a gun.

"Why?"

"Because I can shoot things now," I explained.

Fast-forward twenty years. A hunter in the congregation where I serve was explaining to me that he can fill his freezer full of meat for the cost of one bullet. Well, that seemed interesting to me. Personally, I'm trying to feed six mouths, and the thought of stretching our grocery budget by avoiding the cost of meat intrigued me.

"You took a hunter's safety course, didn't you?"

"Of course, I took the course," I quipped.

"Have you ever been hunting?"

"No."

"Ever shoot anything?"

"No."

"Do you own a gun?"

"Nope."

"Take the class again." My hunter friend turned and walked away along with my vision of a freezer full of venison.

Take the class again? Honestly, it makes sense. I know I wouldn't want to go hunting with a thirty-five-year-old church worker who has never fired a gun.

Confirmation is much like a hunter's safety course. You take the class, take the test, and then accidentally take your "card" to the curb on trash day. Statistics tell us that depending on the congregation, somewhere between 40 and 60% of students walk away from the church after confirmation.

Why, then, did these young people go through confirmation? Some were forced. Many chose to confirm because it was the "thing" to do in eighth grade. Some, however, genuinely desire to confirm their faith begun at their Baptism. These students honestly plan to remain faithful to the commitments they made on Confirmation Sunday.

Abide

Abide. This is the word we must consider as we talk about the "Now What?" after confirmation.

Jesus has something to say about abiding in John 15. In fact, He uses the word ten times in verses 1–10 (emphasis added):

> **I am the true vine, and My Father is the vinedresser. Every branch in Me that does not bear fruit He takes away, and every branch that does bear fruit He prunes, that it may bear more fruit. Already you are clean because of the word that I have spoken to you. ABIDE in Me, and I in you. As the branch cannot bear fruit by itself, unless it ABIDES in the vine, neither can you, unless you ABIDE in Me. I am the vine; you are the branches. Whoever ABIDES in Me and I in him, he it is that bears much fruit, for apart from Me you can do nothing. If anyone does not ABIDE in Me he is thrown away like a branch and withers; and the branches are gathered, thrown into the fire, and burned. If you ABIDE in Me, and My words ABIDE in you, ask whatever you wish, and it will be done for you. By this My Father is glorified, that you bear much fruit and so prove to be My disciples. As the Father has loved Me, so have I loved you. ABIDE in My love. If you keep My commandments, you will ABIDE in My love, just as I have kept my Father's commandments and ABIDE in His love.**

Some might ask, "What does it look like to abide?" The Greek word for *abide* is *meno* ("to continue," "to endure," "to be present," and "to remain"). Abiding is easier to see than we might think.

A friend of mine wakes up nearly every morning at 4:00 a.m. and jogs for at least an hour. He's inspiring; inspiring enough that I, too, have spent several mornings in a row rolling out of bed and into my running shoes. My friend is lean and in shape. So am I, when I remain faithful to working out. But days turn into weeks and weeks turn into months and I begin telling myself the lies.

"I'll sleep in today. I deserve a day off. I'll run farther tomorrow."

Unfortunately, days turn into weeks and weeks turn into months and I notice that my pants are beginning to feel snug again. Let's be honest, sometimes they are barely buttonable. I notice that playing football in the backyard with my kids is harder than it was a few months ago. I notice that the trash can is filled with more candy wrappers than banana or orange peels. Eventually, I must acknowledge that I have not remained faithful to exercise or healthy eating.

It is easy to tell the difference between the runner who endures the marathon and the runner who succumbs to the desire to quit.

It is easy to tell the difference between the spouse who is present in the marriage and the spouse who puts more effort into work or sports or cooking or cars or . . .

It is easy to spot those people who continue on a consistent workout schedule and those who celebrate the comforts of their mattress morning after morning.

Yes, it is quite easy to understand what it means to abide.

What, then, does it look like to abide in Jesus, especially after confirmation?

We begin by looking at the vine. In John 15, Jesus explains that He is the true vine. In the Old Testament, Israel was described as the vine/vineyard (Psalm 80:8–11; Isaiah 5:1–7). A quick glance at the history of Israel proves that Israel was anything but a perfect vine.

Does the golden calf ring a bell?

Israel wavered between being God's thriving vine and being a withering one. Israel knew the nourishment of being connected to God, their deliverer. They also experienced, firsthand, the cold chasm of distance when they voluntarily left the presence of God. They went from watered to dry. They went from the green of growth to a withering brown. They sagged. They drooped. God longed for a lasting relationship with His chosen people, the people whom He had delivered out of slavery. Israel longed for convenience and comfort.

Jesus, by contrast, is the constant vine, the true vine. Jesus is the vine that never falters or fails. Hebrews 13:8 says it this way: "Jesus Christ is the same yesterday and today and forever." Abiding understands that we are connected to a perfect vine, Jesus. We, as Christians, never need worry about the status or security of the true vine, Jesus Christ.

Now that we've established Jesus as our vine, we ask, "What does this mean for us and for those who confirm their faith—the branches?"

We falter, wither, and fail, just like Israel. Yet, as believers in Jesus as Savior, we are never cut off. What follows is a healthy, seven-ingredient recipe for abiding in Jesus after confirmation (according to John 15: 5–12).

Bearing Fruit

"Whoever abides in Me and I in him, he it is that bears much fruit, for apart from Me you can do nothing." John 15:5

We know that Ephesians 2:8–9 clearly states that we are saved by grace. That's good news, literally! Yet verse 10 tells us one way to share that good news—good works. Those good works can be found in the fruit of the Spirit in Galatians 5:22–23. The fruit Jesus encourages us to bear while remaining on the vine are love, joy, peace, patience, kindness, goodness, faithfulness, gentleness, and self-control.

What fertilizer does your congregation or youth ministry provide for fruit-growing efforts? What programs provide an opportunity to practice peace and patience? Consider plugging youth who have confirmed their faith in Jesus Christ into service opportunities such as volunteering at soup kitchens, homeless shelters, or servant events. Living out faith through service to others helps keep good fruit growing on the branch.

Knowing the Word

"If you abide in Me, and My words abide in you . . ." John 15:7a

It would be easy to say that since your congregation offers Sunday School for youth, you have this one covered. Not so fast. Let's consider our vine-and-branch analogy again. Do you think that a healthy branch simply pulls up to the true vine for nourishment once a week? No way! The branch needs to remain connected to the vine day-by-day, hour-after-hour. Try eating for one hour once a week, and you'll know what I'm talking about. Yet we treat our need for biblical nourishment the same way.

Practical ways to help those people who have confirmed their faith might include sending daily Bible verses via a text message or e-mail, offering Midweek classes or small-group studies, making daily devotions or Bible readings programs available. I know a congregation that purchases small pocket Bibles for every person who confirms his or her faith in Jesus. They encourage their confirmands to keep that Bible in their backpack or locker for a quick reading of God's Word. I've heard more than one story about a guy or gal who grabbed that little Bible on the way to study hall or even the bathroom.

Prayer

". . . ask whatever you wish, and it will be done for you." John 15:7b

It's tempting to think that since you open and close each youth ministry meeting in a one-minute prayer, you've got this one covered. If the youth you serve believe that prayer is nothing more than the slices of white bread on the ends of your meeting meat, you've got a problem on your hands. So what does vital prayer look like in a post-confirmation youth ministry? I was recently on vacation with my wife. After "finger walking" through the yellow pages, we settled on a nearby Lutheran Church to visit. Members of the congregation quickly greeted us in the parking lot and welcomed us into the church building. We met several locals and were politely ushered to our seat. The Christ-centered worship began with some energetic singing. Suddenly, one after the other, the teens in the congregation made their way to the altar area of the church. They quietly stood and continued singing. As guests, we wondered what we were witnessing. A few moments later, individual members of the congregation stood and walked toward a youth. After ten seconds of whispering with one another, they knelt together and prayed! How cool! When the members would return to their seats, the youth remained, patiently waiting for the next member in need of prayer. Clearly, this was an example of youth who were experiencing fruit that will last.

Consider a youth ministry prayer chain to pray for the needs of those in your church and beyond. Or simply consider getting a small group of youth to gather prior to or after a worship service to pray quietly together somewhere in the sanctuary or youth room.

Being a Disciple in Action

"So prove to be My disciples." John 15:8b

The root of being a disciple of something or someone simply means to be a follower, pupil, or student of. This might be the most difficult task for those people in our congregations who have recently confirmed their faith. We've previously discussed what it means to study God's Word in youth ministry, but in this section we talk about applying it to our daily walk. As I often say in the youth ministry where I serve, "If you aren't here trying to figure out how to apply any of this stuff you're learning to your Monday-through-Saturday life, then just go hang out in the nursery." One purpose of studying God's Word is to ask, "How will God use this truth to change the way I live this week?" Here are some ways to encourage confirmed people in your congregation to be disciples of Jesus: At the beginning of Sunday School, ask students what they learned last week and tell a story about how it applied to their life. Send a midweek e-mail or text encouraging students to live out their faith. Consider asking youth how they could apply that day's teaching for the next week.

Obedience

"If you keep My commandments, you will abide in My love, just as I have kept My Father's commandments and abide in His love." John 15:10

I recently put a chart on the dry-erase board in our youth room. I wrote the numbers 1–10 in the left column and asked the senior high youth to fill in, from memory, the corresponding Commandments from Exodus 20 in the right column. After five minutes of their bumbling and fumbling, I taught for the next fifty-five minutes a review of the Ten Commandments. Somewhere in our minds, many of us have decided that since our kids learned this stuff in the early grades and reviewed it in confirmation class, we shouldn't need to revisit the Commandments.

However, a study of obedience is far more than consistently reviewing the Ten Commandments. God's Word is full of basic instructions He gives us to guide our lives today. We have to be careful in balancing God's desire for our obedience with His free gift of grace. Because of our sin, we will fail to be obedient more often than we will succeed. At the same time, God assures us of His free forgiveness for the times that we fail.

Experiencing Joy

"These things I have spoken to you, that My joy may be in you, and that your joy may be full." John 15:11

Luke 10 discusses the joy of the seventy-two whom Jesus sent into the towns to gather in the harvest: "The seventy-two returned with joy, saying, 'Lord, even the demons are subject to us in Your name!'" (v. 17). Were the seventy-two filled with joy because they could manipulate and control many demons? Partially. But mainly, the seventy-two were full of joy because they were given the opportunity to be effective servants for Christ.

Does your youth ministry experience that same joy? After the initial fear, do the youth you serve find joy in serving the homeless or the hungry? Do they enjoy the annual trip to a nursing home, listening to story after story about the "way things used to be"? Would your youth consider serving for the afternoon by sorting clothes at a thrift store to be joyful? or spending part of a weekend helping an elderly woman clean up her neglected yard? Would they enjoy a weeklong mission trip leading Vacation Bible School in a foreign country? Would they feel joy in crossing state lines to repair homes for those less fortunate? Ask anyone who includes these ingredients in their post-confirmation youth ministry program, and you'll see the joy in their eyes as they share stories from the heart.

Loving One Another

"This is My commandment, that you love one another as I have loved you. Greater love has no one than this, that someone lay down his life for his friends." John 15:12–13

The message of the cross is one that is told Sunday after Sunday. I once heard a presenter explain that he tells the Gospel message every time he's in front of a crowd because he never knows who is or isn't a believer in Jesus Christ. Many churches focus on the journey of Jesus to the cross once a year, at Lent and Easter. However, this true story about Christ's laying down His life is so important that we must never lose the awe and wonder of Jesus' love for us, sinners. Romans 5:8 explains it this way: "But God shows His love for us in that while we were still sinners, Christ died for us."

An effective youth ministry celebrates and continually focuses on the death and resurrection of Jesus Christ, our Savior and Friend. The sacrificial death and resurrection of Jesus Christ, and the calling and strengthening of the Holy Spirit, allow us to remain faithful to Him after confirmation until He calls us to our eternal glory in heaven.

A Lifelong Commitment

I still haven't been hunting in my thirty-five years. I've never worn an orange vest or felt the kick of a freshly fired gun. So far, I've never felt the need.

I have, however, felt the intense need to remain faithful to the commitment I made as a fourteen-year-old boy in a small rural community in southern Missouri.

Hymnals come and hymnals go. But for the last several decades, the commitment outlined in the Rite or Service of Confirmation has stayed the same. Even though my eighth-grade mind didn't understand all of the "behooveth" and "beseech Thee" verbiage, I did understand my pledge to God and to the Church.

I know God made a covenant with me at my Baptism.

I do, by the power of the Holy Spirit, renounce the devil and all his works and all his ways.

I do believe in God the Father; in Jesus, His only Son; and in the Holy Spirit.

I do believe the Bible to be the true and inspired Word of God.

I do intend to remain steadfast in this confession, even unto death.

Finally, I do by the grace of God, intend to conform my life to be in line with the teachings of the divine Word and to walk in faith and truth even unto death.

That was the commitment I made on May 10, 1987. That is the commitment I still make today.

Rev. Jeffrey Meinz works with youth and family ministries for Holy Cross Lutheran Church in Colorado Springs, Colorado.